Substance Abuse Counselor Vocabulary Workbook

By Lewis Morris

Copyright © Network4Learning, Inc. 2019.

www.insiderswords.com/substance

ISBN-13: 978-1694290670

Copyright © 2019, Network4Learning, inc.
All rights reserved. No part of this publication may be reproduced, distributed, or transmitted in any form or by any means, including photocopying, recording, or other electronic or mechanical methods, without the prior written permission of the publisher, except in the case of brief quotations embodied in critical reviews and certain other noncommercial uses permitted by copyright law. For permission requests, write to the publisher, addressed
"Attention: Permissions Coordinator," at the address below.

Network4Learning, inc.
109 E 17th St STE 63
Cheyenne, WY 82001-4584

www.InsidersWords.com

We hope you find this vocabulary workbook helpful with your studies. If you do, please consider leaving a brief review at this link:
http://www.amazon.com/review/create-review?&asin=1694290670

Table of Contents

Introduction	5
Crossword Puzzles	24
Multiple Choice	74
Matching	100
Word Search	136

What is "Insider Language"?

Recent research has confirmed what we have known for decades: The strongest students and leaders in industry have a mastered an Insider Language in their subject and field. This Insider language is made up of the technical terms and vocabulary necessary to communicate effectively in classes or the workplace. For those who master it, learning is easier, faster, and much more enjoyable.

Most students who are surveyed report that the greatest challenge to any course of study is learning the vocabulary. When we examine typical college courses, we discover that there is, on average, 250 Insider Terms a student must learn over the course of a semester. Further, most exams rely heavily on this set of words for assessment purposes. The structure of multiple choice exams lends itself perfectly to the testing of this Insider Language. Students who can differentiate between Insider Language terms can handle challenging exam questions with ease and confidence.

From recent research on learning and vocabulary we have learned:

- Your knowledge of any subject is contained in the content-specific words you know. The more of these terms that you know, the easier it is to understand and recall important information; the easier it will be to communicate your ideas to peers, professors, supervisors, and co-workers. The stronger your content-area vocabulary is, the higher your scores will be on your exams and written assignments.

- Students who develop a strong Insider Language perform better on tests, learn faster, retain more information, and express greater satisfaction in learning.

- Familiarizing yourself with subject-area vocabulary before formal study (pre-learning) is the most effective way to learn this language and reap the most benefit.

- The vocabulary on standardized exams come directly from the stated objectives of the test-makers. This means that the vocabulary found on standardized exams is predictable. Our books focus on this vocabulary.

- Most multiple-choice exams are glorified vocabulary quizzes. Think about the format of a multiple-choice question. The question stem is a definition of a term and the choices (known as distractors) are 4 or 5 similar words. Your task is to differentiate between the meanings of those terms and choose the correct word.

- It takes a person several exposures to a new word to be able to use it with confidence in conversation or in writing. You need to process these words several different ways to make them part of your long-term memory.

The goals of this book are:
- To give you an "Insider Language" for your subject.
- Pre-teach the most important words before you set out on a traditional course of review or study.
- Teach you the most important words in your subject area.
- Teach you strategies for learning subject-area words on your own.
- Boost your confidence in your ability to master this language and support you in your study.
- Reduce the stress of studying and provide you with fun activities that work.

How it works:

The secret to mastering Insider Language is through repetition and exposure. We have eleven steps for you to follow:

1. Read the word and definition in the glossary out loud. "See it, Say it"
2. Identify the part of speech the word belongs to such as noun, verb, adverb, or adjective. This will help you group the word and identify similar words.
3. Place the word in context by using it in a sentence. Write this sentence down and read it aloud.
4. Use "Chunking" to group the words. Make a diagram or word cloud using these groups.
5. Make connections to the words by creating analogies.
6. Create mnemonics that help you recognize patterns and orders of words by substituting the words for more memorable items or actions.
7. Examine the morphology of the word, that is, identify the root, prefix, and suffix that make up the word. Identify similar and related words.
8. Complete word games and puzzles such as crosswords and word searches.
9. Complete matching questions that require you to differentiate between related words.
10. Complete Multiple-choice questions containing the words.
11. Create a visual metaphor or "memory cartoon" to make a mental picture of the word and related processes.

By completing this word study process, you will be exposed to the terminology in various ways that will activate your memory and create a lasting understanding of this language.

The strategies in this book are designed to make you an independent expert at learning insider language. These strategies include:

- Verbalizing the word by reading it and its definition aloud ("See It, Say It"). This allows you to make visual, auditory, and speech connections with its meaning.

- Identifying the type of word (Noun, verb, adverb, and adjective). Making this distinction helps you understand how to visualize the word. It helps you "chunk" the words into groups, and gives you clues on how to use the word.

- Place the word in context by using it in a sentence. Write this sentence down and read it aloud. This will give you an example of how the word is used.

- "Chunking". By breaking down the word list into groups of closely related words, you will learn them better and be able to remember them faster. Once you have group the terms, you can then make word clouds using a free online service. These word clouds provide visual cues to remembering the words and their meanings.

- Analogies. By creating analogies for essential words, you will be making connections that you can see on paper. These connections can trigger your memory and activate your ability to use the word in your writing as you begin to use them. Many of these analogies also use visual cues. In a sense, you can make a mental picture from the analogy.

- Mnemonics. A device such as a pattern of letters, ideas, or associations that assists in remembering something. A mnemonic is especially useful for remembering the order of a set of words or the order of a process.

- Morphology. The study of word roots, prefixes, and suffixes. By examining the structure of the words, you will gain insight into other words that are closely related, and learn how to best use the word.

- Visual metaphors. This is the most sophisticated and entertaining strategy for learning vocabulary. Create a "memory cartoon" using one or more of the vocabulary terms. This activity triggers the visual part of your memory and makes fast, permanent, imprints of the word on your memory. By combining the terms in your visual metaphor, you can "chunk" the entire set of vocabulary terms into several visual metaphors and benefit from the brain's tendency to group these terms.

The activities in this book are designed to imprint the words and their meanings in your memory in different ways. By completing each activity, you will gain the necessary exposures to the word to make it a permanent part of your vocabulary. Each activity uses a different part of your memory. The result is that you will be comfortable using these words and be able to tell the difference between closely related words. The activities include:

A. Crossword Puzzles and Word Searches- These are proven to increase test scores and improve comprehension. Students frequently report that they are fun and engaging, while requiring them to analyze the structure and meaning of the words.

B. Matching- This activity is effective because it forces you to differentiate between many closely related terms.

C. Multiple Choice- This classic question format lends itself to vocabulary study perfectly. Most exams are in this format because they are simple to make, easy to score, and are a reliable type of assessment. (Perfect for the Vocabulary Master!) One strategy to use with multiple choice questions that enhance their effectiveness is to cover the answer choices while you read the question. After reading the question, see if you can answer it before looking at the choices. Then look at the choices to see if you match one of them.

Conducting a thorough "word study" of your insider language will take time and effort, but the rewards will be well worth it. By following this guide and completing the exercises thoughtfully, you will become a stronger, more effective, and satisfied student. Best of luck on your mastery of this Insider Language!

Insider Language Strategies

"See It, Say It!" Reading your Insider Language set aloud

"It is better to fail in originality than to succeed in imitation."
-Herman Melville

Reading aloud is the foundation for the development of an Insider Language. It is the single most important thing you can do for vocabulary acquisition. Done correctly, it engages the visual, auditory, and speech centers of the brain and hastens its storage in your long-term memory.

Reading aloud demonstrates the relationship between the printed word and its meaning.

You can read aloud on a higher level than you can initially understand, so reading aloud makes complex ideas more accessible and exposes you to vocabulary and patterns that are not part of your typical speech. Reading aloud helps you understand the complicated text better and makes more challenging text easier to grasp and understand. Reading aloud helps you to develop the "habits of mind" the strongest students use.

Reading aloud will make connections to concepts in the reading that requires you to relate the new vocabulary to things you already know. Go to the glossary at the end of this book and for each word complete the five steps outlined below:

1. Read the word and its definition aloud. Focus on the sound of the word and how it looks on the paper.
2. Read the word aloud again try to say three or four similar words; this will help you build connections to closely related words.
3. Read the word aloud a third time. Try to make a connection to something you have read or heard.
4. Visualize the concept described in the term. Paint a mental picture of the word in use.
5. Try to think of the opposite of the word. Discovering a close antonym will help you place this word in context.

Create a sentence using the word in its proper context

"OPPORTUNITIES DON'T HAPPEN. YOU CREATE THEM." –CHRIS GROSSER

Context means the circumstances that form the setting for an event, statement, or idea, and which it can be fully understood and assessed. Synonyms for context include conditions, factors, situation, background, and setting.

Place the word in context by using it in a sentence. Write this sentence down and read it aloud. By creating sentences, you are practicing using the word correctly. If you strive to make these sentences interesting and creative, they will become more memorable and effective in activating your long-term memory.

Identify the Parts of Speech

"SUCCESS IS NOT FINAL; FAILURE IS NOT FATAL: IT IS THE COURAGE TO CONTINUE THAT COUNTS." –WINSTON S. CHURCHILL

Read through each term in the glossary and make a note of what part of speech each term is. Studying and identifying parts of speech shows us how the words relate to each other. It also helps you create a visualization of each term. Below are brief descriptions of the parts of speech for you to use as a guide.

VERB: A word denoting action, occurrence, or existence. Examples: walk, hop, whisper, sweat, dribbles, feels, sleeps, drink, smile, are, is, was, has.

NOUN: A word that names a person, place, thing, idea, animal, quality, or action. Nouns are the subject of the sentence. Examples: dog, Tom, Florida, CD, pasta, hate, tiger.

ADJECTIVE: A word that modifies, qualifies, or describes nouns and pronouns. Generally, adjectives appear immediately before the words they modify. Examples: smart girl, gifted teacher, old car, red door.

ADVERB: A word that modifies verbs, adjectives and other adverbs. An "ly" ending almost always changes an adjective to an adverb. Examples: ran swiftly, worked slowly, and drifted aimlessly. Many adverbs do not end in "ly." However, all adverbs identify when, where, how, how far, how much, etc. Examples: run hot, lived hard, moved right, study smart.

Chunking

"YOUR POSITIVE ACTION COMBINED WITH POSITIVE THINKING RESULTS IN SUCCESS." SHIV KHERA

Chunking is when you take a set of words and break it down into groups based on a common relationship. Research has shown that our brains learn by chunking information. By grouping your terms, you will be able to recall large sets of these words easily. To help make your chunking go easily use an online word cloud generator to make a set of word clouds representing your chunks.

1. Study the glossary and decide how you want to chunk the set of words. You can group by part of speech, topic, letter of the alphabet, word length, etc. Try to find an easy way to group each term.
2. Once you have your different groups, visit www.wordclouds.com to create a custom word cloud for each group. Print each one of these clouds and post it in a prominent place to serve as constant visual aids for your learning.

Analogies

"CHOOSE THE POSITIVE. YOU HAVE CHOICE, YOU ARE MASTER OF YOUR ATTITUDE, CHOOSE THE POSITIVE, THE CONSTRUCTIVE. OPTIMISM IS A FAITH THAT LEADS TO SUCCESS."– BRUCE LEE

An analogy is a comparison in which an idea or a thing is compared to another thing that is quite different from it. Analogies aim at explaining an idea by comparing it to something that is familiar. Metaphors and similes are tools used to create analogies.

Analogies are useful for learning vocabulary because they require you to analyze a word (or words), and then transfer that analysis to another word. This transfer reinforces the understanding of all the words.

As you analyze the relationships between the analogies you are creating, you will begin to understand the complex relationships between the seemingly unrelated words.

  A   is to   B   as   C   is to   D

This can be written using colons in place of the terms "is to" and "as."

  A:B::C:D

The two items on the left (items A & B) describe a relationship and are separated by a single colon. The two items on the right (items C & D) are shown on the right and are also separated by a colon. Together, both sides are then separated by two colons in the middle, as shown here: Tall: Short :: Skinny: Fat. The relationship used in this analogy is the antonym.

How to create an analogy

Start with the basic formula for an analogy:

____ : ____ :: ____ : ____

Next, we will examine a simple synonym analogy:

<u>automobile</u> : <u>car</u> :: <u>box</u> : <u>crate</u>

The key to figuring out a set of word analogies is determining the relationship between the paired set of words.

Here is a list of the most common types of Analogies and examples

Synonym	Scream : Yell :: Push : Shove
Antonym	Rich : Poor :: Empty : Full
Cause is to Effect	Prosperity : Happiness :: Success : Joy
A Part is to its Whole	Toe : Foot :: Piece : Set
An Object to its Function	Car : Travel :: Read : Learn
A Item is to its Category	Tabby : House Cat :: Doberman : Dog
Word is a symptom of the other	Pain : Fracture :: Wheezing : Allergy
An object and it's description	Glass : Brittle :: Lead : Dense
The word is lacking the second word	Amputee : Limb :: Deaf : Hearing
The first word Hinders the second word	Shackles : Movement :: Stagger : Walk
The first word helps the action of the second	Knife : Bread :: Screwdriver : Screw
This word is made up of the second word	Sweater : Wool :: Jeans : Denim
A word and it's definition	Cede : Break Away :: Abolish : To get rid of

Using words from the glossary, make a set of analogies using each one. As a bonus, use more than one glossary term in a single analogy.

_____ : _____ :: _____ : _____

Name the relationship between the words in your analogy:_____

_____ : _____ :: _____ : _____

Name the relationship between the words in your analogy:_____

_____ : _____ :: _____ : _____

Name the relationship between the words in your analogy:_____

Mnemonics

> "IT ISN'T THE MOUNTAINS AHEAD TO CLIMB THAT WEAR YOU OUT; IT'S THE PEBBLE IN YOUR SHOE."   –MUHAMMAD ALI

A mnemonic is a learning technique that helps you retain and remember information. Mnemonics are one of the best learning methods for remembering lists or processes in order. Mnemonics make the material more meaningful by adding associations and creating patterns. Interestingly, mnemonics may work better when they utilize absurd, startling, or shocking examples and references. Mnemonics help organize the information so that you can easily retrieve it later. By giving you associations and cues, mnemonics allow you to form a mental structure ordering a list or process to help you remember it better. This mental structure allows you to create a structure of association between items that may not appear to have any relationship. Mnemonics typically use references that are easy to visualize and thus easier to remember. Through visualization of vivid images and references, the information is much easier to imprint into long-term memory. The power of making mnemonics lies in converting dull, inert and uninspiring information into something vibrant and memorable.

How to make simple and effective mnemonics
Some of the best mnemonics help us remember simple rules or lists in order.

Step 1. Take a list of terms you are trying to remember in order. For example, we will use the scientific method:

observation, question, hypothesis, methods, results, and conclusion.

Next, we will replace each word on the list with a new word that starts with the same letter. These new words will together form a vivid sentence that is easy to remember:

Objectionable Queens Haunted Macho Rednecks Creatively.

As silly as the above sentence seems, it is easy to remember, and now we can call on this sentence to remind us of the order of the scientific method.

Visit http://www.mnemonicgenerator.com/ and try typing in a list of words. It is fun to see the mnemonics that it makes and shows how easy it is to make great mnemonics to help your studying.

Using vivid words in your mnemonics allows you to see the sentence you are making. Words that are gross, scary, or name interesting animals are helpful. Profanity is also useful because the shock value can trigger memory. The following are lists of vivid words to use in your mnemonics:

Gross words
Moist, Gurgle, Phlegm, Fetus, Curd, Smear, Squirt, Chunky, Orifice, Maggots, Viscous, Queasy, Bulbous, Pustule, Putrid, Fester, Secrete, Munch, Vomit, Ooze, Dripping, Roaches, Mucus, Stink, Stank, Stunk, Slurp, Pus, Lick, Salty, Tongue, Fart, Flatulence, Hemorrhoid.

Interesting Animals
Aardvark, Baboon, Chicken, Chinchilla, Duck, Dragonfly, Emu, Electric Eel, Frog, Flamingo, Gecko, Hedgehog, Hyena, Iguana, Jackal, Jaguar, Leopard, Lynx, Minnow, Manatee, Mongoose, Neanderthal, Newt, Octopus, Oyster, Pelican, Penguin, Platypus, Quail, Racoon, Rattlesnake, Rhinoceros, Scorpion, Seahorse, Toucan, Turkey, Vulture, Weasel, Woodpecker, Yak, Zebra.

Superhero Words
Diabolical, Activate, Boom, Clutch, Dastardly, Dynamic, Dynamite, Shazam, Kaboom, Zip, Zap, Zoom, Zany, Crushing, Smashing, Exploding, Ripping, Tearing.

Scary Words
Apparition, Bat, Chill, Demon, Eerie, Fangs, Genie, Hell, Lantern, Macabre, Nightmare, Owl, Ogre, Phantasm, Repulsive, Scarecrow, Tarantula, Undead, Vampire, Wraith, Zombie.

There are several types of mnemonics that can help your memory.

1. Images
Visual mnemonics are a type of mnemonic that works by associating an image with characters or objects whose name sounds like the item that must be memorized. This is one of the easiest ways to create effective mnemonics. An example would be to use the shape of numbers to help memorize a long list of them. Numbers can be memorized by their shapes, so that: 0 -looks like an egg; 1 -a pencil, or a candle; 2 -a snake; 3 -an ear; 4 -a sailboat; 5 -a key; 6 -a comet; 7 -a knee; 8 -a snowman; 9 -a comma.

Another type of visual mnemonic is the word-length mnemonic in which the number of letters in each word corresponds to a digit. This simple mnemonic gives pi to seven decimal places:

3.141582 becomes "How I wish I could calculate pi."

Of course, you could use this type of mnemonic to create a longer sentence showing the digits of an important number. Some people have used this type of mnemonic to memorize thousands of digits.

Using the hands is also an important tool for creating visual objects. Making the hands into specific shapes can help us remember the pattern of things or the order of a list of things.

2. Rhyming
Rhyming mnemonics are quick ways to make things memorable. A classic example is a mnemonic for the number of days in each month:
"30 days hath September, April, June, and November.
All the rest have 31
Except February, my dear son.
It has 28, and that is fine
But in Leap Year it has 29."

Another example of a rhyming mnemonic is a common spelling rule:
"I before e except after c
or when sounding like a
in neighbor and weigh."

Use **rhymer.com** to get large lists of rhyming words.

3. Homonym
A homonym is one of a group of words that share the same pronunciation but have different meanings, whether spelled the same or not.

Try saying what you're attempting to remember out loud or very quickly, and see if anything leaps out. If you know other languages, using similar-sounding words from those can be effective.

You could also browse this list of homonyms at http://www.cooper.com/alan/homonym_list.html.

4. Onomatopoeia
An Onomatopeia is a word that phonetically imitates, resembles or suggests the source of the sound that it describes. Are there any noises made by the thing you're trying to memorize? Is it often associated with some other sound? Failing that, just make up a noise that seems to fit.

Achoo, ahem, baa, bam, bark, beep, beep beep, belch, bleat, boo, boo hoo, boom, burp, buzz, chirp, click clack, crash, croak, crunch, cuckoo, dash, drip, ding dong, eek, fizz, flit, flutter, gasp, grrr, ha ha, hee hee, hiccup, hiss, hissing, honk, icky, itchy, jiggly, jangle, knock knock, lush, la la la, mash, meow, moan, murmur, neigh, oink, ouch, plop, pow, quack, quick, rapping, rattle, ribbit, roar, rumble, rustle, scratch, sizzle, skittering, snap crackle pop, splash, splish splash, spurt, swish, swoosh, tap, tapping, tick tock, tinkle, tweet, ugh, vroom, wham, whinny, whip, whooping, woof.

5. Acronyms

An acronym is a word or name formed as an abbreviation from the initial components of a word, such as NATO, which stands for North Atlantic Treaty Organization. If you're trying to memorize something involving letters, this is often a good bet. A lot of famous mnemonics are acronyms, such as ROYGBIV which stands for the order of colors in the light spectrum (Red, Orange, Yellow, Green, Blue, Indigo, and Violet).

A great acronym generator to try is: www.all-acronyms.com.

A different spin on an acronym is a backronym. A **backronym** is a specially constructed phrase that is supposed to be the source of a word that is an acronym. A backronym is constructed by creating a new phrase to fit an already existing word, name, or acronym.

The word is a combination of *backward* and *acronym*, and has been defined as a "reverse acronym." For example, the United States Department of Justice assigns to their Amber Alert program the meaning "**A**merica's **M**issing: **B**roadcast **E**mergency **R**esponse." The process can go either way to make good mnemonics.

Visit: https://arthurdick.com/projects/backronym/ to try out a simple backronym generator.

6. Anagrams

An anagram is a direct word switch or word play, the result of rearranging the letters of a word or phrase to produce a new word or phrase, using all the original letters exactly once; for example, the word anagram can be rearranged into nag-a-ram.

Try re-arranging letters or components and see if anything memorable emerges. Visit http://www.nameacronym.net/ to use a simple anagram generator.

One particularly memorable form of anagram is the spoonerism, where you swap the initial syllables or letters of words to make new phrases. These are usually humorous, and this makes them easier to remember. Here are some examples:

"Is it kisstomary to cuss the bride?" (as opposed to "customary to kiss")
"The Lord is a shoving leopard." (instead of "a loving shepherd")
"A blushing crow." ("crushing blow")
"A well-boiled icicle" ("well-oiled bicycle")
"You were fighting a liar in the quadrangle." ("lighting a fire")
"Is the bean dizzy?" (as opposed to "is the dean busy?")

7. Stories

Make up quick stories or incidents involving the material you want to memorize. For larger chunks of information, the stories can get more elaborate. Structured stories are particularly good for remembering lists or other sequenced information. Have a look at https://en.wikipedia.org/wiki/Method_of_loci for a more advanced memory sequencing technique.

Visual Metaphors

"LIMITS, LIKE FEAR, IS OFTEN AN ILLUSION." –MICHAEL JORDAN

What is a Metaphor?

A metaphor is a figure of speech that refers to one thing by mentioning another thing. Metaphors provide clarity and identify hidden similarities between two seemingly unrelated ideas. A visual metaphor is an image that creates a link between different ideas.

Visual metaphors help us use our understanding of the world to learn new concepts, skills, and ideas. Visual metaphors help us relate new material to what we already know. Visual metaphors must be clear and simple enough to spark a connection and understanding. Visual metaphors should use familiar things to help you be less fearful of new, complex, or challenging topics. Metaphors trigger a sense of familiarity so that you are more accepting of the new idea. Metaphors work best when you associate a familiar, easy to understand idea with a challenging, obscure, or abstract concept.

How to make a visual metaphor

1. Brainstorm using the words of the concept. Use different fonts, colors, or shapes to represent parts of the concept.

2. Merge these images together

3. Show the process using arrows, accents, etc.

4. Think about the story line your metaphor projects.

Examples of visual metaphors:

A skeleton used to show a framework of something.

A cloud showing an outline.

A bodybuilder whose muscles represent supporting ideas and details.

A sandwich where the meat, tomato, and lettuce represent supporting ideas.

A recipe card to show a process.

Your metaphor should be accurate. It should be complex enough to convey meaning, but simple and clear enough to be easily understood.

Morphology
"SCIENCE IS THE CAPTAIN, AND PRACTICE THE SOLDIERS." LEONARDO DA VINCI

Morphology is the study of the origin, roots, suffixes, and prefixes of the words. Understanding the meaning of prefixes, suffixes, and roots make it easier to decode the meaning of new vocabulary. Having the ability to decode using morphology increases text comprehension when initially reading as well.

The capability of identifying meaningful parts of words (morphemes), including prefixes, suffixes, and roots can be helpful. Identifying morphemes improves decoding accuracy and fluency. Reading speed improves when you can decode larger chunks of text quickly. When you can recognize morphemes in words, you will be better able to make sense of new words in context. Below are charts containing the most common prefixes, suffixes, and root words. Use them to help you decode your vocabulary terms.

Prefixes

Prefix	Meaning	Example words and meanings	
a, ab, abs	away from	absent	not to be present, to give up an office or throne.
		abdicate	
ad, a, ac, af, ag, an, ar, at, as	to, toward	Advance	To move forward
		advantage	To have the upper hand
anti	against	Antidote	To repair poisoning
		antisocial	refers to someone who's not social
		antibiotic	
bi, bis	two	bicycle	two-wheeled cycle
		binary	two number system
		biweekly	every two weeks
circum, cir	around	circumnavigate	Travel around the world
		circle	a figure that goes all around
com, con, co, col	with, together	Complete	To finish
		Complement	To go along with
de	away from, down, the opposite of	depart	to go away from
		detour	to go out of your way
dis, dif, di	apart	dislike	not to like
		dishonest	not honest
		distant	away
En-, em-	Cause to	Entrance	the way in.
epi	upon, on top of	epitaph	writing upon a tombstone
		epilogue	speech at the end, on top of the rest
		epidemic	
equ, equi	equal	equalize	to make equal
		equitable	fair, equal
ex, e, ef	out, from	exit	to go out
		eject	to throw out
		exhale	to breathe out
Fore-	Before	Forewarned	To have prior warning

Prefix	Meaning	Example Words and Meanings	
in, il, ir, im, en	in, into	Infield Imbibe	The inner playing field to take part in
in, il, ig, ir, im	not	inactive ignorant irreversible irritate	not active not knowing not reversible to put into discomfort
inter	between, among	international interact	among nations to mix with
mal, male	bad, ill, wrong	malpractice malfunction	bad practice fail to function, bad function
Mid	Middle	Amidships	In the middle of a ship
mis	wrong, badly	misnomer	The wrong name
mono	one, alone, single	monocle	one lensed glasses
non	not, the reverse of	nonprofit	not making a profit
ob	in front, against, in front of, in the way of	Obsolete	No longer needed
omni	everywhere, all	omnipresent omnipotent	always present, everywhere all powerful
Over	On top	Overdose	Take too much medication
Pre	Before	Preview	Happens before a show.
per	through	Permeable pervasive	to pass through, all encompassing
poly	many	Polygamy polygon	many spouses figure with many sides
post	after	postpone postmortem	to do after after death
pre	before, earlier than	Predict Preview	To know before To view before release
pro	forward, going ahead of, supporting	proceed pro-war promote	to go forward supporting the war to raise or move forward
re	again, back	retell recall reverse	to tell again to call back to go back
se	apart	secede seclude	to withdraw, become apart to stay apart from others
Semi	Half	Semipermeable	Half-permeable

Prefix	Meaning	Example Words and Meanings	
Sub	under, less than	Submarine	under water
super	over, above, greater	superstar superimpose	a start greater than her stars to put over something else
trans	across	transcontinental transverse	across the continent to lie or go across
un, uni	one	unidirectional unanimous unilateral	having one direction sharing one view having one side
un	not	uninterested unhelpful unethical	not interested not helpful not ethical

Roots

Root	Meaning	Example words & meanings	
act, ag	to do, to act	Agent Activity	One who acts as a representative Action
Aqua	Water	Aquamarine	The color of water
Aud	To hear	Auditorium	A place to hear music
apert	open	Aperture	An opening
bas	low	Basement Basement	Something that is low, at the bottom A room that is low
Bio	Living thing	Biological	Living matter
cap, capt, cip, cept, ceive	to take, to hold, to seize	Captive Receive Capable Recipient	One who is held To take Able to take hold of things One who takes hold or receives
ced, cede, ceed, cess	to go, to give in	Precede Access Proceed	To go before Means of going to To go forward
Cogn	Know	Cognitive	Ability to think
cred, credit	to believe	Credible Incredible Credit	Believable Not believable Belief, trust
curr, curs, cours	to run	Current Precursory Recourse	Now in progress, running Running (going) before To run for aid
Cycle	Circle	Lifecycle	The circle of life
dic, dict	to say	Dictionary Indict	A book explaining words (sayings)

Root	Meaning	Examples and meanings	
duc, duct	to lead	Induce Conduct Aqueduct	To lead to action To lead or guide Pipe that leads water somewhere
equ	equal, even	Equality Equanimity	Equal in social, political rights Evenness of mind, tranquility
fac, fact, fic, fect, fy	to make, to do	Facile Fiction Factory Affect	Easy to do Something that is made up Place that makes things To make a change in
fer, ferr	to carry, bring	Defer Referral	To carry away Bring a source for help/information
Gen	Birth	Generate	To create something
graph	write	Monograph Graphite	A writing on a particular subject A form of carbon used for writing
Loc	Place	Location	A place
Mater	Mother	Maternity	Expecting birth
Mem	Recall	Memory	The recall experiences
mit, mis	to send	Admit Missile	To send in Something sent through the air
Nat	Born	Native	Born in a place
par	equal	Parity Disparate	Equality No equal, not alike
Ped	Foot	Podiatrist	Foot doctor
Photo	Light	Photograph	A picture
plic	to fold, to bend, to turn	Complicate Implicate	To fold (mix) together To fold in, to involve
pon, pos, posit, pose	to place	Component Transpose Compose Deposit	A part placed together with others A place across To put many parts into place To place for safekeeping
scrib, script	to write	Describe Transcript Subscription	To write about or tell about A written copy A written signature or document
sequ, secu	to follow	Sequence	In following order

Root	Meaning	Examples and Meanings	
Sign	Mark	Signal	to alert somebody
spec, spect, spic	to appear, to look, to see	Specimen Aspect	An example to look at One way to see something
sta, stat, sist, stit, sisto	to stand, or make stand Stable, steady	Constant Status Stable Desist	Standing with Social standing Steady (standing) To stand away from
Struct	To build	Construction	To build a thing
tact	to touch	Contact Tactile	To touch together To be able to be touched
ten, tent, tain	to hold	Tenable Retentive Maintain	Able to be held, holding Holding To keep or hold up
tend, tens, tent	to stretch	Extend Tension	To stretch or draw out Stretched
Therm	Temperature	Thermometer	Detects temperature
tract	to draw	Attract Contract	To draw together An agreement drawn up
ven, vent	to come	Convene Advent	To come together A coming
Vis	See	Invisible	Cannot be seen
ver, vert, vers	to turn	Avert Revert Reverse	To turn away To turn back To turn around

Crossword Puzzles

1. Using the Across and Down clues, write the correct words in the numbered grid below.

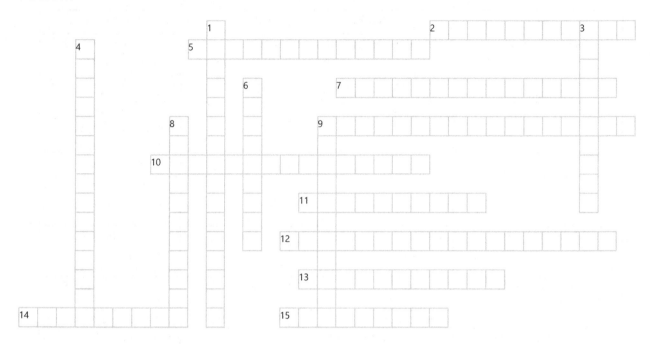

ACROSS

2. When two disorders or illnesses occur in the same person.
5. A psychological disorder characterized by the elevation or lowering of a person's mood, such as depression or bipolar disorder.
7. A conceptual framework that classifies clients in four basic groups based on relative symptom severity, rather than by diagnosis.
9. Systems that organize statewide services.
10. A drug that distorts perception, thought, and feeling. This term is typically used to refer to drugs with hallucinogenic effects.
11. Symptoms that can occur after long-term use of a drug is reduced or stopped.
12. Therapy groups in which recovery skills for co-occurring disorders are discussed.
13. An area of the brain crucial for learning and memory.
14. An inflammation of the liver, with accompanying liver cell damage and risk of death.
15. Delusional or disordered thinking detached from reality; symptoms often include hallucinations.

DOWN

1. The use of emotional, psychological, sexual, or physical force by one family member or intimate partner to control another.
3. Taken through the nose.
4. A disorder in which the individual refuses to maintain a normal body weight, is afraid of gaining weight, and exhibits a significant disturbance in the perception of body shape.
6. Short-term care provided in intensive care units, brief hospital stays, and emergency rooms for those who are severely intoxicated or dangerously ill.
8. Factors that increase the likelihood of beginning substance use, of regular and harmful use, and of other behavioral health problems associated with use.
9. A measure or estimate of a person's likelihood of committing suicide. A high-risk behavior associated with cod, especially (although not limited to) serious mood disorders.

A. Hippocampus
B. Hepatitis
C. Withdrawal
D. Suicidality
E. Acute Care
F. Single State Agency
G. Intranasal
H. Psychosis
I. Comorbidity
J. Mood Disorders
K. Psychedelic Drug
L. Anorexia Nervosa
M. Risk Factors
N. Quadrants of Care
O. Domestic Violence
P. Dual Recovery Groups

2. Using the Across and Down clues, write the correct words in the numbered grid below.

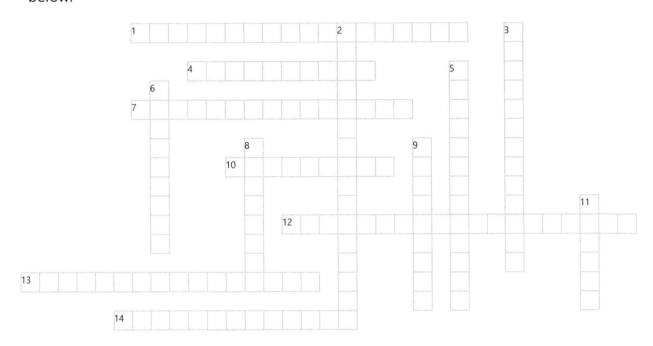

ACROSS

1. Drugs that have an effect on the function of the brain and that are often used to treat psychiatric disorders.
4. Pertaining to a person's ability to carry out tasks.
7. A state of confusion accompanied by trembling and vivid hallucinations.
10. A long-acting opioid agonist medication used for the treatment of opioid addiction and pain.
12. The receptor in the brain that recognizes and binds cannabinoids that are produced in the brain or outside the body.
13. The front part of the brain responsible for reasoning, planning, problem solving, and other higher cognitive functions.
14. People who abuse substances are at a higher risk for engaging in behaviors that are high risk and illegal.

DOWN

2. The way a drug acts on the body.
3. A broad group of drugs that cause distortions of sensory perception. The prototype hallucinogen is lysergic acid diethylamide (LSD).
5. The simultaneous provision of material and training to persons from more than one discipline.
6. An inflammation of the liver, with accompanying liver cell damage and risk of death.
8. A molecule located on the surface of a cell that recognizes specific chemicals and transmits the chemical message into the cell.
9. The use of strategies that soothe and distract the client who is experiencing intense pain or other strong emotions, helping the client anchor in the present and in reality.
11. A negative association attached to some activity or condition. A cause of shame or embarrassment.

A. Prefrontal Cortex
B. Psychotherapeutics
C. Receptor
D. Stigma
E. Delirium Tremens
F. Legal Problems
G. Cannabinoid Receptor
H. Functional
I. Methadone
J. Grounding
K. Cross Training
L. Hallucinogens
M. Pharmacodynamics
N. Hepatitis

3. Using the Across and Down clues, write the correct words in the numbered grid below.

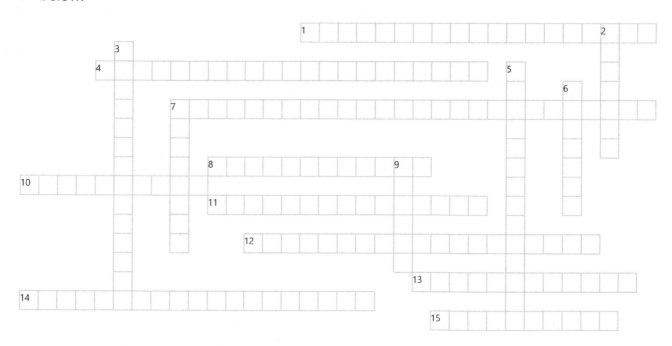

ACROSS

1. Biopsychosocial or other treatment that is adapted to suit the special cultural beliefs, practices, and needs of a client.
4. A drug used to treat psychosis, especially schizophrenia.
7. A therapeutic approach that seeks to modify negative or self-defeating thoughts and behavior.
8. Initial learning and the acquisition of skills necessary for everyday life.
10. Pertaining to a person's ability to carry out tasks.
11. An area of the brain that is part of the basal ganglia and includes the nucleus accumbens.
12. A battery-operated device that people use to inhale an aerosol, which typically contains nicotine, flavorings, and other chemicals.
13. Involving a person's psychological well-being, as well as housing, employment, family, and other social aspects of life circumstances.
14. The capacity and willingness of a clinician or other service provider to be open to working with issues of culture and diversity.
15. Taken through the nose.

DOWN

2. Slang term for methylenedioxymethamphetamine, a member of the amphetamine family. At lower doses, MDMA causes distortions of emotional perceptions.
3. A mental condition marked primarily by disorganization of personality, mind, and emotions that seriously impairs the psychological or behavioral functioning of the individual.
5. An illness whose essential feature is binge eating and inappropriate compensatory methods to prevent weight gain.
6. In drug addiction, relapse is the return to drug use after an attempt to stop.
7. Another name for the marijuana plant, cannabis sativa.
9. A type of depressant drug that diminishes pain and central nervous system activity.

A. Opioid
B. Culturally Competent
C. Neuroleptic Medication
D. Cultural Sensitivity
E. Intranasal
F. Ecstasy
G. Psychosocial
H. Habilitation
I. Cognitive Behavioral Therapy
J. Bulimia Nervosa
K. Cannabis
L. Functional
M. Mental Disorder
N. Relapse
O. Ventral Striatum
P. Electronic Cigarette

4. Using the Across and Down clues, write the correct words in the numbered grid below.

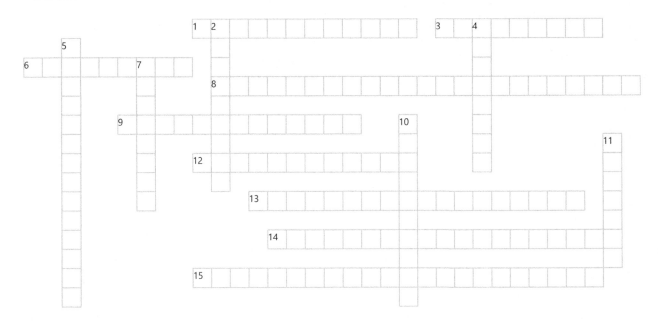

ACROSS

1. A brain circuit that includes the ventral tegmental area, the nucleus accumbens, and the prefrontal cortex.
3. A clinician's judgment or estimate of how well a disorder will respond to treatment.
6. A neurotransmitter involved in a broad range of effects on perception, movement, and emotions. Serotonin and its receptors are the targets of most hallucinogens.
8. Specific treatment strategies in which interventions for two or more disorders are combined in a single session or interaction, or in a series of interactions or multiple sessions.
9. A psychological disorder characterized by the elevation or lowering of a person's mood, such as depression or bipolar disorder.
12. Initial learning and the acquisition of skills necessary for everyday life.
13. Keeping clients involved in treatment activities and receiving required services.
14. Occurs when the nature of the client's disabilities requires more specific information and more complex and targeted intervention.
15. A treatment program that actively combines substance abuse and mental health interventions to treat disorders, related problems, and the whole person more effectively.

DOWN

2. Relying on observation or experience rather than theoretical principles or theory.
4. An overdose occurs when a person uses enough of a drug to produce a life-threatening reaction or death.
5. Driving a vehicle while impaired due to the intoxicating effects of recent drug use.
7. An opioid antagonist medication approved by the FDA to reverse an opioid overdose.
10. Pertaining to a person's ability to carry out tasks.
11. A powerful, often overwhelming desire to use drugs.

A. Reward System
D. Formal Collaboration
G. Habilitation
J. Empirical
M. Functional
B. Serotonin
E. Integrated Interventions
H. Mood Disorders
K. Treatment Retention
N. Drugged Driving
C. Overdose
F. Fully Integrated Program
I. Prognosis
L. Craving
O. Naloxone

5. Using the Across and Down clues, write the correct words in the numbered grid below.

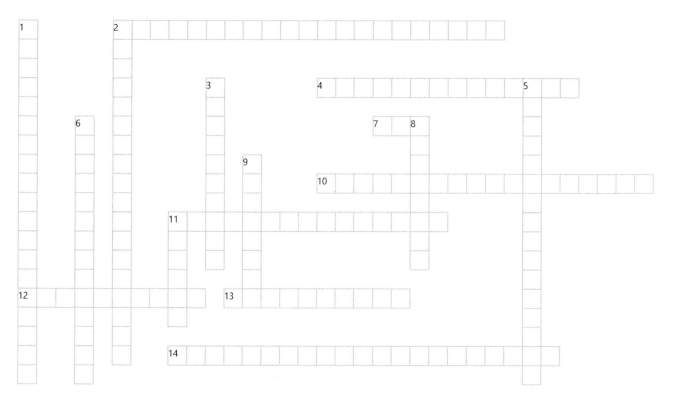

ACROSS

2. A class of substance-related disorders that includes both substance abuse and substance dependence.
4. A mental condition marked primarily by disorganization of personality, mind, and emotions that seriously impairs the psychological or behavioral functioning of the individual.
7. Delta-9-tetrahydrocannabinol; the main mind-altering ingredient in marijuana.
10. Therapy groups in which recovery skills for co-occurring disorders are discussed.
11. An area of the brain that is part of the basal ganglia and includes the nucleus accumbens.
12. Able to spread by an agent such as a virus or bacterium.
13. A condition that can occur with the regular use of illicit or some prescription drugs, even if taken as prescribed.
14. Of or pertaining to programs that have a higher than average level of integration of substance abuse and mental health treatment services.

DOWN

1. The capacity and willingness of a clinician or other service provider to be open to working with issues of culture and diversity.
2. No one set of treatment interventions constitutes integrated treatment.
3. Not using drugs or alcohol.
5. Having been diagnosed with two disorders, for example a substance use disorder and a mental health disorder.
6. A type of CNS depressant sometimes prescribed to relieve anxiety, panic, or acute stress reactions. Some benzodiazepines are prescribed short-term to promote sleep.
8. Slang term for tactile hallucinations that feel like bugs crawling on or under the skin.
9. An overdose occurs when a person uses enough of a drug to produce a life-threatening reaction or death.
11. Brand name for benzodiazepine diazepam.

A. Substance Use Disorders
D. Dual Diagnosis Enhanced
G. Valium
J. Abstinence
M. Dependence
P. THC

B. Overdose
E. Infectious
H. Dually Disordered
K. Cultural Sensitivity
N. Ventral Striatum

C. Coke Bugs
F. Mental Disorder
I. Benzodiazepine
L. Dual Recovery Groups
O. Service Integration

6. Using the Across and Down clues, write the correct words in the numbered grid below.

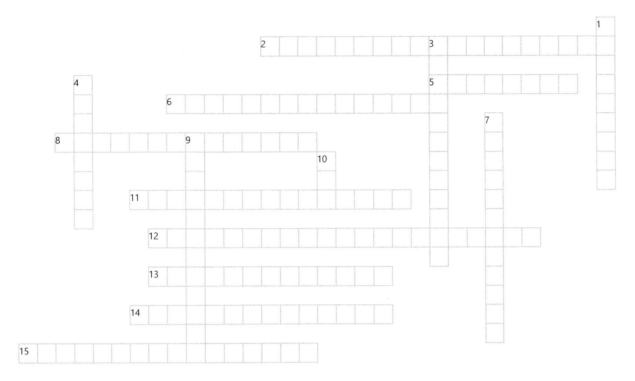

ACROSS

2. A battery-operated device that people use to inhale an aerosol, which typically contains nicotine, flavorings, and other chemicals.
5. An opioid antagonist medication approved by the FDA to reverse an opioid overdose.
6. A state of confusion accompanied by trembling and vivid hallucinations.
8. Sensations, sounds and
11. Treatment using medications.
12. A class of substance-related disorders that includes both substance abuse and substance dependence.
13. The simultaneous provision of material and training to persons from more than one discipline.
14. A process in which the body rids itself of a drug, or its metabolites.
15. The way a drug acts on the body.

DOWN

1. A neurotransmitter involved in a broad range of effects on perception, movement, and emotions. Serotonin and its receptors are the targets of most hallucinogens.
3. In the context of treatment programs, consultation is a traditional type of informal relationship among treatment providers, such as a referral or a request for exchanging information.
4. A brain chemical, classified as a neurotransmitter, found in regions of the brain that regulate movement, emotion, motivation, and reinforcement of rewarding behavior.
7. Encompasses the specific treatment strategies, therapies, or techniques that are used to treat one or more disorders.
9. The study of the anatomy, function, and diseases of the brain and nervous system.
10. Slang term for Smoke able methamphetamine.

A. Pharmacotherapy
D. Dopamine
G. Naloxone
J. Hallucinations
M. Intervention

B. Electronic Cigarette
E. Cross Training
H. Pharmacodynamics
K. Detoxification
N. Consultation

C. Neurobiology
F. Delirium Tremens
I. Substance Use Disorders
L. Ice
O. Serotonin

7. Using the Across and Down clues, write the correct words in the numbered grid below.

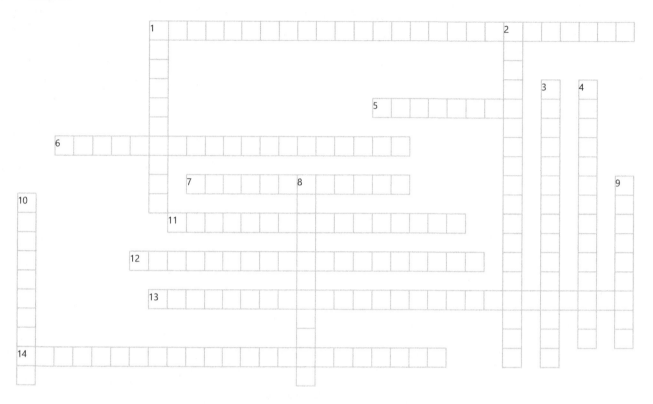

ACROSS

1. A therapeutic approach that seeks to modify negative or self-defeating thoughts and behavior.
5. A period of amnesia or memory loss, typically caused by chronic, high-dose substance abuse.
6. The feelings, reactions, biases, and images from the past that the clinician may project onto the client with cod.
7. Involving a person's psychological well-being, as well as housing, employment, family, and other social aspects of life circumstances.
11. Having been diagnosed with two disorders, for example a substance use disorder and a mental health disorder.
12. The receptor in the brain that recognizes and binds cannabinoids that are produced in the brain or outside the body.
13. Synthetic substances similar to the male hormone testosterone.
14. Practices or actions through which an individual shows that he or she regards other cultures as inferior to the dominant culture.

DOWN

1. An ability, capacity, skill, or set of skills.
2. Keeping clients involved in treatment activities and receiving required services.
3. An illness whose essential feature is excessive anxiety and worry.
4. A process in which the body rids itself of a drug, or its metabolites.
8. A measure or estimate of a person's likelihood of committing suicide. A high-risk behavior associated with cod, especially (although not limited to) serious mood disorders.
9. Delusional or disordered thinking detached from reality; symptoms often include hallucinations.
10. A group of medications that reduce pain.

A. Anxiety Disorder
B. Psychosocial
C. Blackout
D. Cultural Destructiveness
E. Countertransference
F. Competency
G. Dually Disordered
H. Cannabinoid Receptor
I. Psychosis
J. Treatment Retention
K. Analgesics
L. Anabolic Androgenic Steroids
M. Detoxification
N. Cognitive Behavioral Therapy
O. Suicidality

8. Using the Across and Down clues, write the correct words in the numbered grid below.

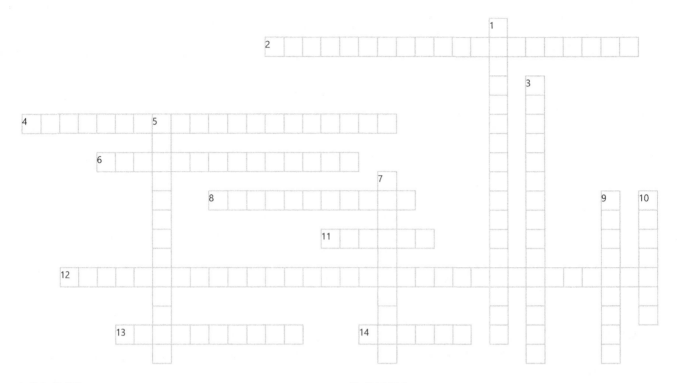

ACROSS

2. The system consisting of the heart and blood vessels. It delivers nutrients and oxygen to all cells in the body.
4. A medical illness caused by disordered use of a substance or substances.
6. A process in which the body rids itself of a drug, or its metabolites.
8. A stimulant drug that acts on the central nervous system (CNS).
11. A unique type of cell found in the brain and throughout the body that specializes in the transmission and processing of information.
12. Community-based initiatives that link treatment providers, researchers, and policymakers in order to build a strong foundation to effect action.
13. Pertaining to a person's ability to carry out tasks.
14. Inhaling the aerosol or vapor from an electronic cigarette, e-vaporizer, or other device.

DOWN

1. A brief alcoholism screening tool.
3. An illness whose essential feature is excessive anxiety and worry.
5. The simultaneous provision of material and training to persons from more than one discipline.
7. Taken through the nose.
9. Relating to the act or process of thinking, understanding, learning, and remembering.
10. Slang term for drugs that exert a depressant effect on the central nervous system. In general, downers are sedative-hypnotic drugs, such as benzodiazepines and barbiturates.

A. Functional
C. Downers
E. Cognition
G. Anxiety Disorder
I. Intranasal
K. Substance Use Disorder
M. Detoxification

B. Practice Improvement Collaborative
D. Vaping
F. Cross Training
H. Neuron
J. Cage Questionnaire
L. Cardiovascular System
N. Amphetamine

9. Using the Across and Down clues, write the correct words in the numbered grid below.

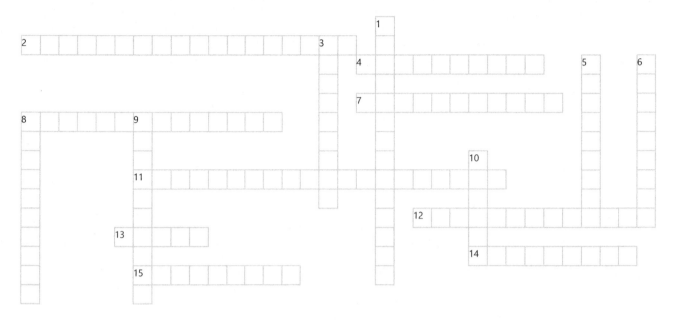

ACROSS

2. The capacity of a service provider to understand and work effectively in accordance with the cultural beliefs and practices of persons from a given ethnic
4. Able to spread by an agent such as a virus or bacterium.
7. A component of the marijuana plant without mind-altering effects that is being studied for possible medical uses.
8. A clearing of toxins from the body.
11. The system consisting of the nerves in the brain and spinal cord.
12. People who abuse substances are at a higher risk for engaging in behaviors that are high risk and illegal.
13. A place or a setting for some activity.
14. An older diagnostic term that defined use that is unsafe, use that leads a person to fail to fulfill responsibilities or gets them in legal trouble.
15. A chronic, relapsing disorder characterized by compulsive (or difficult to control) drug seeking and use despite harmful consequences, as well as long-lasting changes in the brain.

DOWN

1. A mental condition marked primarily by disorganization of personality, mind, and emotions that seriously impairs the psychological or behavioral functioning of the individual.
3. Pertaining to the mind's capacity to understand concepts and ideas.
5. Relying on observation or experience rather than theoretical principles or theory.
6. Delusional or disordered thinking detached from reality; symptoms often include hallucinations.
8. A condition that can occur with the regular use of illicit or some prescription drugs, even if taken as prescribed.
9. Pertaining to a person's ability to carry out tasks.
10. Pleasurable feelings that reinforce behavior and encourage repetition.

A. Psychosis
B. Addiction
C. Cultural Competence
D. Legal Problems
E. Central Nervous System
F. Reward
G. Functional
H. Drug Abuse
I. Dependence
J. Infectious
K. Cognitive
L. Empirical
M. Detoxification
N. Cannabidiol
O. Mental Disorder
P. Locus

10. Using the Across and Down clues, write the correct words in the numbered grid below.

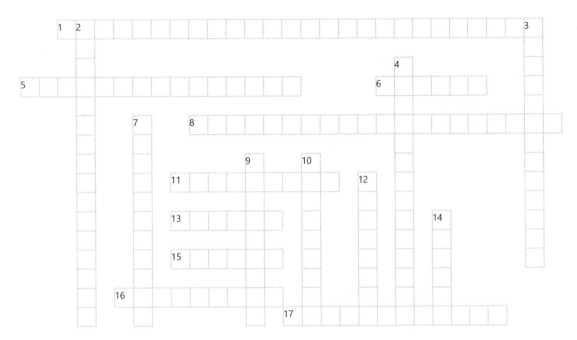

ACROSS

1. Synthetic substances similar to the male hormone testosterone.
5. A disorder in which the individual refuses to maintain a normal body weight, is afraid of gaining weight, and exhibits a significant disturbance in the perception of body shape.
6. Brand name for benzodiazepine diazepam.
8. The system consisting of the heart and blood vessels. It delivers nutrients and oxygen to all cells in the body.
11. Short-term care provided in intensive care units, brief hospital stays, and emergency rooms for those who are severely intoxicated or dangerously ill.
13. A unique type of cell found in the brain and throughout the body that specializes in the transmission and processing of information.
15. An involuntary and rhythmic movement in the muscles, most often in the hands, feet, jaw, tongue, or head.
16. A mental disorder that is characterized by distinct distortions of a person's mental capacity, ability to recognize reality, and relationships to others.
17. A brain circuit that includes the ventral tegmental area, the nucleus accumbens, and the prefrontal cortex.

DOWN

2. A chemical compound that acts as a messenger to carry signals from one nerve cell to another.
3. A sign of depressant intoxication. When people consume significant amounts of sedative-hypnotics and opioids, their speech may become garbled, mumbled, and slow.
4. Sensations, sounds and
7. A collection of pus formed as a result of bacterial infection.
9. A neurotransmitter involved in a broad range of effects on perception, movement, and emotions. Serotonin and its receptors are the targets of most hallucinogens.
10. An older diagnostic term that defined use that is unsafe, use that leads a person to fail to fulfill responsibilities or gets them in legal trouble.
12. An illness or a disruption of some mental or physical process.
14. Slang term used to describe drugs that have a stimulating effect on the central nervous system. Examples include cocaine, caffeine, and amphetamines.

A. Drug Abuse
D. Cardiovascular System
G. Serotonin
J. Valium
M. Reward System
P. Tremor

B. Neurotransmitter
E. Slurred Speech
H. Anorexia Nervosa
K. Anabolic Androgenic Steroids
N. Psychosis
Q. Neuron

C. Disorder
F. Skin Abscess
I. Hallucinations
L. Uppers
O. Acute Care

11. Using the Across and Down clues, write the correct words in the numbered grid below.

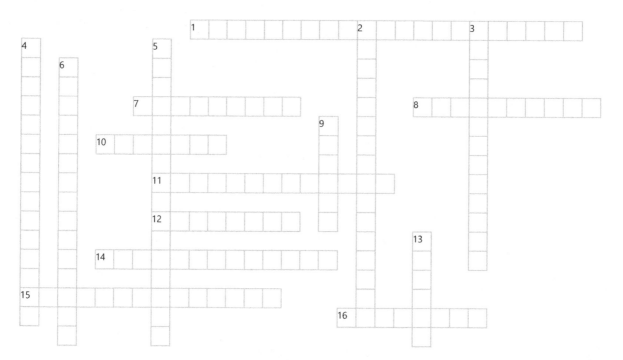

ACROSS

1. A drug used to treat psychosis, especially schizophrenia.
7. An older diagnostic term that defined use that is unsafe, use that leads a person to fail to fulfill responsibilities or gets them in legal trouble.
8. A client's commitment to and maintenance of treatment in all of its forms. A successful engagement program helps clients view the treatment facility as an important resource.
10. A breakdown or setback in a person's attempt to change or modify any particular behavior.
11. A broad group of drugs that cause distortions of sensory perception. The prototype hallucinogen is lysergic acid diethylamide (LSD).
12. Poisonous nature; poisonous quality.
14. People who abuse substances are at a higher risk for engaging in behaviors that are high risk and illegal.
15. A neurotransmitter that affects heart rate, blood pressure, stress, and attention.
16. A process for facilitating client

DOWN

2. The act of administering drugs by injection. Blood-borne viruses, like HIV and hepatitis, can be transmitted via shared needles or other drug injection equipment.
3. The action of working with someone to produce or create something.
4. A state of confusion accompanied by trembling and vivid hallucinations.
5. Approaches that actively seek out persons in a community who may have substance use disorders and engage them in substance abuse treatment.
6. A treatment program that has the capacity to provide integrated substance abuse and mental health treatment for clients with COD.
9. A negative association attached to some activity or condition. A cause of shame or embarrassment.
13. Slang term used to describe drugs that have a stimulating effect on the central nervous system. Examples include cocaine, caffeine, and amphetamines.

A. Stigma
B. Engagement
C. Toxicity
D. Delirium Tremens
E. Uppers
F. Norepinephrine
G. Outreach Strategy
H. Relapse
I. Neuroleptic Medication
J. Legal Problems
K. Hallucinogens
L. Injection Drug Use
M. Advanced Program
N. Collaboration
O. Drug Abuse
P. Referral

12. Using the Across and Down clues, write the correct words in the numbered grid below.

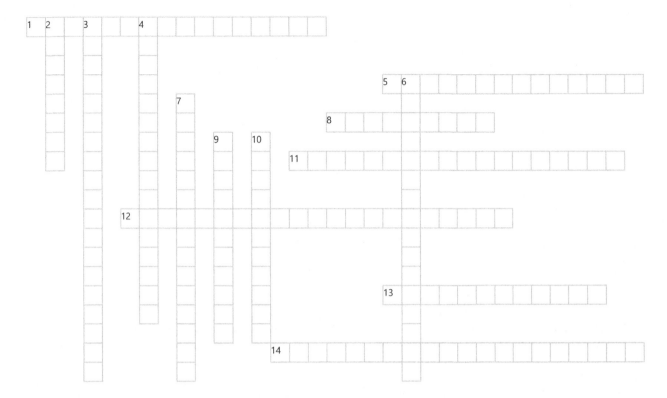

ACROSS

1. The front part of the brain responsible for reasoning, planning, problem solving, and other higher cognitive functions.
5. A neurotransmitter that affects heart rate, blood pressure, stress, and attention.
8. An inflammation of the liver, with accompanying liver cell damage and risk of death.
11. Keeping clients involved in treatment activities and receiving required services.
12. Of or pertaining to programs that have a higher than average level of integration of substance abuse and mental health treatment services.
13. A treatment program with the capacity to provide treatment for one disorder, but that also screens for other disorders and is able to access necessary consultations.
14. An illness whose essential feature is persistent and recurrent maladaptive gambling behavior that disrupts personal, family, or vocational pursuits.

DOWN

2. A process for facilitating client
3. Occurs when the nature of the client's disabilities requires more specific information and more complex and targeted intervention.
4. A brain region in the ventral striatum involved in motivation and reward.
6. Approaches that actively seek out persons in a community who may have substance use disorders and engage them in substance abuse treatment.
7. An area of the brain that is part of the basal ganglia and includes the nucleus accumbens.
9. A type of CNS depressant sometimes prescribed to promote relaxation and sleep, but more commonly used in surgical procedures and to treat seizure disorders.
10. Relationships among mental health and substance abuse providers in which both fields are moved into a single treatment setting and treatment regimen.

A. Ventral Striatum
D. Barbiturate
G. Nucleus Accumbens
J. Hepatitis
M. Treatment Retention

B. Integration
E. Referral
H. Norepinephrine
K. Prefrontal Cortex
N. Outreach Strategy

C. Basic Program
F. Formal Collaboration
I. Dual Diagnosis Enhanced
L. Pathological Gambling

13. Using the Across and Down clues, write the correct words in the numbered grid below.

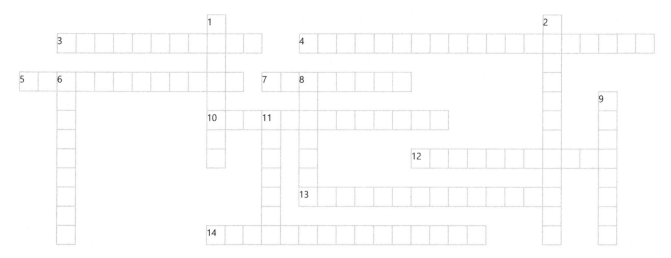

ACROSS

3. A tendency to act without foresight or regard for consequences and to prioritize immediate rewards over long-term goals.
4. A treatment program that focuses primarily on one disorder without substantial modification to its usual treatment.
5. Initial learning and the acquisition of skills necessary for everyday life.
7. A process of change through which people with substance use disorders improve their health and wellness, live self-directed lives, and strive to reach their full potential.
10. Pupils that have become temporarily enlarged.
12. A type of CNS depressant sometimes prescribed to promote relaxation and sleep, but more commonly used in surgical procedures and to treat seizure disorders.
13. A process in which the body rids itself of a drug, or its metabolites.
14. An area of the brain that is part of the basal ganglia and includes the nucleus accumbens.

DOWN

1. An illness or a disruption of some mental or physical process.
2. The feelings, reactions, biases, and images from the past that the client with cod may project onto the clinician.
6. A group of brain structures that process sensory information and control basic functions needed for survival such as breathing, heart rate, blood pressure, and arousal.
8. Legally forced or compelled.
9. A brand name amphetamine for treating ADHD.
11. A chemical substance that binds to and activates certain receptors on cells, causing a biological response.

A. Impulsivity
B. Habilitation
C. Ventral Striatum
D. Brainstem
E. Agonist
F. Adderall
G. Disorder
H. Recovery
I. Barbiturate
J. Transference
K. Dilated Pupils
L. Detoxification
M. Coerced
N. Intermediate Program

14. Using the Across and Down clues, write the correct words in the numbered grid below.

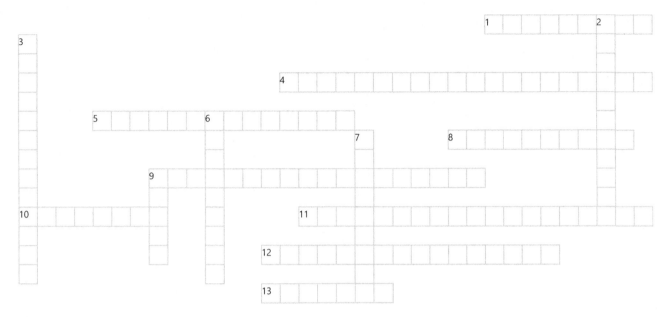

ACROSS

1. A chronic, relapsing disorder characterized by compulsive (or difficult to control) drug seeking and use despite harmful consequences, as well as long-lasting changes in the brain.
4. Refers to co-occurring substance use (abuse or dependence) and mental disorders.
5. The gray matter that covers the surface of the cerebral hemispheres, whose functions include sensory processing and motor control along with language, reasoning, and decision-making.
8. Symptoms that can occur after long-term use of a drug is reduced or stopped.
9. The capacity of a service provider to understand and work effectively in accordance with the cultural beliefs and practices of persons from a given ethnic
10. Extreme and unreasonable distrust of others.
11. The highest level of cultural capacity, which implies an ability to perceive the nuances of a culture in depth and a willingness to work to advance in proficiency through leadership.
12. A chemical compound that acts as a messenger to carry signals from one nerve cell to another.
13. In drug addiction, relapse is the return to drug use after an attempt to stop.

DOWN

2. Relationships among mental health and substance abuse providers in which both fields are moved into a single treatment setting and treatment regimen.
3. Pupils that have become temporarily enlarged.
6. A restless inability to keep still.
7. An inflammation of the liver, with accompanying liver cell damage and risk of death.
9. Cocaine that has been chemically modified so that it will become a gas vapor when heated at relatively low temperatures.

A. Agitation
B. Hepatitis
C. Paranoia
D. Relapse
E. Withdrawal
F. Co Occurring Disorders
G. Integration
H. Cerebral Cortex
I. Cultural Proficiency
J. Cultural Competence
K. Crack
L. Addiction
M. Neurotransmitter
N. Dilated Pupils

15. Using the Across and Down clues, write the correct words in the numbered grid below.

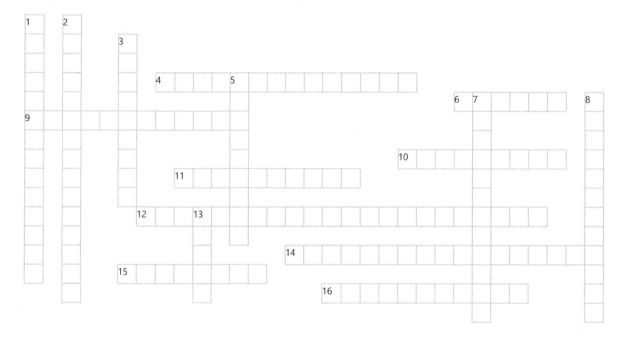

ACROSS

4. An approach to recovery from substance use disorders that emphasizes personal responsibility, self-management, and clients' helping one another.
6. Slang term used to describe drugs that have a stimulating effect on the central nervous system. Examples include cocaine, caffeine, and amphetamines.
9. Mentally and physically in harmony with and connected to the culture in which one lives.
10. Physical dependence on a substance of abuse. Inability to cease use of a substance without experiencing withdrawal symptoms.
11. A long-acting opioid antagonist medication that prevents receptors from being activated by other opioids. Naltrexone is used to treat alcohol and opioid use disorders.
12. A drug that has an effect on the mind and sometimes affects behavior as well.
14. A brief alcoholism screening tool.
15. Poisonous nature; poisonous quality.
16. A measure or estimate of a person's likelihood of committing suicide. A high-risk behavior associated with cod, especially (although not limited to) serious mood disorders.

DOWN

1. A maladaptive pattern of substance use manifested by recurrent and significant adverse consequences related to the repeated use of substances.
2. A treatment program that has the capacity to provide integrated substance abuse and mental health treatment for clients with COD.
3. An inflammation of the liver, with accompanying liver cell damage and risk of death.
5. A chronic, relapsing disorder characterized by compulsive (or difficult to control) drug seeking and use despite harmful consequences, as well as long-lasting changes in the brain.
7. Mind-altering.
8. The feelings, reactions, biases, and images from the past that the client with cod may project onto the clinician.
13. Cocaine that has been chemically modified so that it will become a gas vapor when heated at relatively low temperatures.

A. Uppers
B. Crack
C. Addiction
D. Psychotropic Medication
E. Substance Abuse
F. Toxicity
G. Mutual Self Help
H. Cage Questionnaire
I. Hepatitis
J. Suicidality
K. Transference
L. Psychotropic
M. Acculturated
N. Naltrexone
O. Addiction
P. Advanced Program

16. Using the Across and Down clues, write the correct words in the numbered grid below.

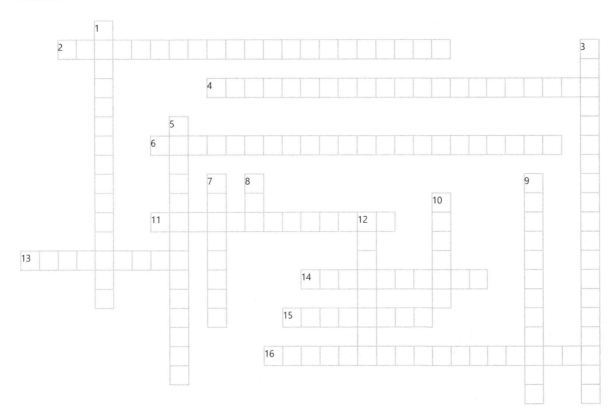

ACROSS

2. A drug used to treat psychosis, especially schizophrenia.
4. Pertaining to medications used to treat mental illnesses.
6. A treatment program that actively combines substance abuse and mental health interventions to treat disorders, related problems, and the whole person more effectively.
11. A sign of depressant intoxication. When people consume significant amounts of sedative-hypnotics and opioids, their speech may become garbled, mumbled, and slow.
13. An older diagnostic term that defined use that is unsafe, use that leads a person to fail to fulfill responsibilities or gets them in legal trouble.
14. Able to spread by an agent such as a virus or bacterium.
15. An illness or a disruption of some mental or physical process.
16. Keeping clients involved in treatment activities and receiving required services.

DOWN

1. A conceptual framework that classifies clients in four basic groups based on relative symptom severity, rather than by diagnosis.
3. The highest level of cultural capacity, which implies an ability to perceive the nuances of a culture in depth and a willingness to work to advance in proficiency through leadership.
5. An approach to recovery from substance use disorders that emphasizes personal responsibility, self-management, and clients' helping one another.
7. Extreme and unreasonable distrust of others.
8. Slang term for Smoke able methamphetamine.
9. Mentally and physically in harmony with and connected to the culture in which one lives.
10. An involuntary and rhythmic movement in the muscles, most often in the hands, feet, jaw, tongue, or head.
12. The upper part of the brain consisting of the left and right hemispheres.

A. Mutual Self Help
B. Ice
C. Treatment Retention
D. Drug Abuse
E. Tremor
F. Psychopharmacological
G. Disorder
H. Neuroleptic Medication
I. Fully Integrated Program
J. Cultural Proficiency
K. Cerebrum
L. Quadrants of Care
M. Infectious
N. Paranoia
O. Acculturated
P. Slurred Speech

17. Using the Across and Down clues, write the correct words in the numbered grid below.

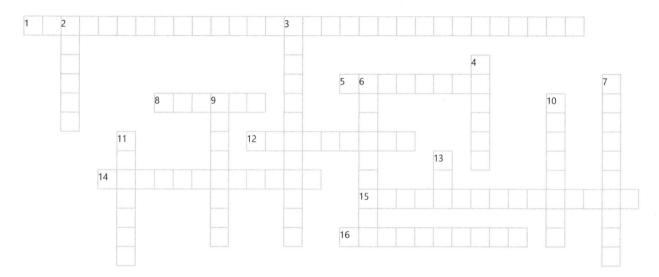

ACROSS

1. A counseling approach that uses motivational interviewing techniques to help individuals resolve any uncertainties they have about stopping their substance use.
5. Extreme and unreasonable distrust of others.
8. Pleasurable feelings that reinforce behavior and encourage repetition.
12. A group of brain structures that process sensory information and control basic functions needed for survival such as breathing, heart rate, blood pressure, and arousal.
14. A treatment program with the capacity to provide treatment for one disorder, but that also screens for other disorders and is able to access necessary consultations.
15. An illness whose essential feature is excessive anxiety and worry.
16. A part of the brain that helps regulate posture, balance, and coordination. It is also involved in the processes of emotion, motivation, memory, and thought.

DOWN

2. Violent mental or physical harm to a person, damage to an organ, etc.
3. A part of the brain that controls many bodily functions, including eating, drinking, body temperature regulation, and the release of many hormones.
4. Inhaling the aerosol or vapor from an electronic cigarette, e-vaporizer, or other device.
6. Short-term care provided in intensive care units, brief hospital stays, and emergency rooms for those who are severely intoxicated or dangerously ill.
7. Not using drugs or alcohol.
9. A brand name amphetamine for treating ADHD.
10. An opioid antagonist medication approved by the FDA to reverse an opioid overdose.
11. A powerful, often overwhelming desire to use drugs.
13. Slang term for Smoke able methamphetamine.

A. Abstinence
B. Vaping
C. Ice
D. Adderall
E. Basic Program
F. Brainstem
G. Craving
H. Naloxone
I. Paranoia
J. Anxiety Disorder
K. Trauma
L. Cerebellum
M. Motivational Enhancement Therapy
N. Hypothalamus
O. Reward
P. Acute Care

18. Using the Across and Down clues, write the correct words in the numbered grid below.

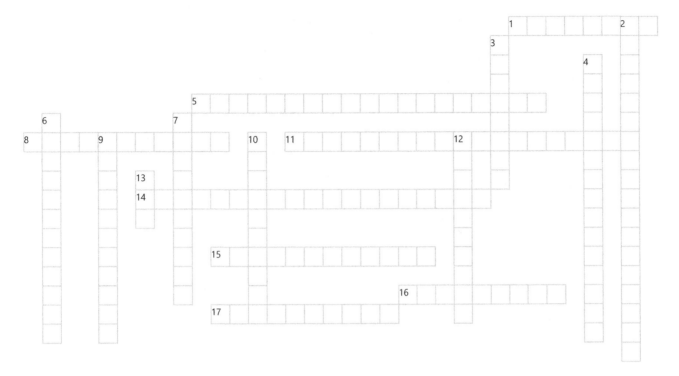

ACROSS

1. Poisonous nature; poisonous quality.
5. Any mechanism by which treatment interventions for co-occurring disorders are combined within the context of a primary treatment relationship or service setting.
8. A type of CNS depressant sometimes prescribed to promote relaxation and sleep, but more commonly used in surgical procedures and to treat seizure disorders.
11. A type of relationship between client and clinician in which both are working cooperatively toward the same goals, with mutual respect and understanding.
14. The right and left halves of the brain.
15. Interconnected brain structures that process feelings, emotions, and motivations. It is also important for learning and memory.
16. The use of strategies that soothe and distract the client who is experiencing intense pain or other strong emotions, helping the client anchor in the present and in reality.
17. Symptoms that can occur after long-term use of a drug is reduced or stopped.

DOWN

2. Keeping clients involved in treatment activities and receiving required services.
3. A brand name amphetamine for treating ADHD.
4. A treatment program that has the capacity to provide integrated substance abuse and mental health treatment for clients with COD.
6. Chemicals that bind to cannabinoid receptors in the brain.
7. A long-acting opioid antagonist medication that prevents receptors from being activated by other opioids. Naltrexone is used to treat alcohol and opioid use disorders.
9. A tendency to act without foresight or regard for consequences and to prioritize immediate rewards over long-term goals.
10. A client's commitment to and maintenance of treatment in all of its forms. A successful engagement program helps clients view the treatment facility as an important resource.
12. Able to spread by an agent such as a virus or bacterium.
13. Slang term for Smoke able methamphetamine.

A. Integrated Treatment
D. Treatment Retention
G. Engagement
J. Adderall
M. Infectious
P. Cerebral Hemispheres

B. Grounding
E. Therapeutic Alliance
H. Barbiturate
K. Naltrexone
N. Withdrawal
Q. Impulsivity

C. Toxicity
F. Cannabinoids
I. Advanced Program
L. Limbic System
O. Ice

19. Using the Across and Down clues, write the correct words in the numbered grid below.

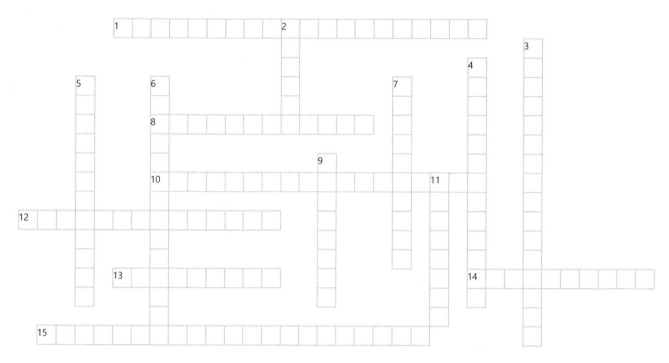

ACROSS

1. Rigid, inflexible, and maladaptive behavior patterns of sufficient severity to cause internal distress or significant impairment in functioning.
8. The feelings, reactions, biases, and images from the past that the client with cod may project onto the clinician.
10. Connections between substance abuse treatment and mental health systems that allow collaboration. Necessary because these are the primary care systems for persons with cod.
12. A clearing of toxins from the body.
13. A long-acting opioid agonist medication used for the treatment of opioid addiction and pain.
14. Able to spread by an agent such as a virus or bacterium.
15. A class of substance-related disorders that includes both substance abuse and substance dependence.

DOWN

2. An involuntary and rhythmic movement in the muscles, most often in the hands, feet, jaw, tongue, or head.
3. The use of emotional, psychological, sexual, or physical force by one family member or intimate partner to control another.
4. A broad term that describes objects used during the chemical preparation or use of drugs. These include syringes, syringe needles, roach clips, and marijuana or crack pipes.
5. Involving a person's psychological well-being, as well as housing, employment, family, and other social aspects of life circumstances.
6. A process in which the body rids itself of a drug, or its metabolites.
7. Not using drugs or alcohol.
9. A process of change through which people with substance use disorders improve their health and wellness, live self-directed lives, and strive to reach their full potential.
11. A brand name amphetamine for treating ADHD.

A. Detoxification
D. Paraphernalia
G. Personality Disorders
J. Tremor
M. Adderall
B. Substance Use Disorders
E. Transference
H. Detoxification
K. Intersystem Linkage
N. Infectious
C. Methadone
F. Recovery
I. Abstinence
L. Psychosocial
O. Domestic Violence

20. Using the Across and Down clues, write the correct words in the numbered grid below.

ACROSS

3. An organized array of services and interventions with a primary focus on treating mental health disorders, whether providing acute stabilization or ongoing treatment.
7. The upper part of the brain consisting of the left and right hemispheres.
8. Not using substances of abuse at any time.
9. A type of delusion, or false idea, that is unchanged by reasoned argument or proof to the contrary.
10. A type of CNS depressant sometimes prescribed to promote relaxation and sleep, but more commonly used in surgical procedures and to treat seizure disorders.
12. The gray matter that covers the surface of the cerebral hemispheres, whose functions include sensory processing and motor control along with language, reasoning, and decision-making.
13. Emphasizes shared decision making with the client as essential to the client's engagement process.
14. Relying on observation or experience rather than theoretical principles or theory.

DOWN

1. Pertaining to the mind's capacity to understand concepts and ideas.
2. Having a specific effect on the brain.
4. Care that supports a client's progress, monitors his or her condition, and can respond to a return to substance use or a return of symptoms of mental disorder.
5. Initial learning and the acquisition of skills necessary for everyday life.
6. A part of the brain that helps regulate posture, balance, and coordination. It is also involved in the processes of emotion, motivation, memory, and thought.
11. A process for facilitating client

A. Cerebral Cortex
C. Assertive Community Treatment
E. Cerebellum
G. Barbiturate
I. Continuing Care
K. Abstinent
M. Paranoia

B. Habilitation
D. Mental Health Program
F. Cerebrum
H. Cognitive
J. Empirical
L. Referral
N. Psychoactive

21. Using the Across and Down clues, write the correct words in the numbered grid below.

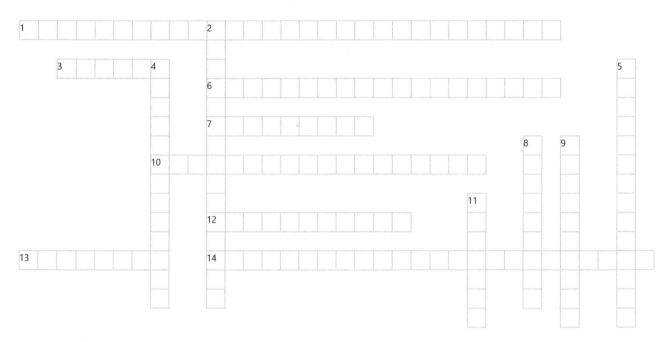

ACROSS

1. An illness whose features are a pervasive disregard for and violation of the rights of others and an inability to form meaningful interpersonal relationships.
3. Brand name for benzodiazepine diazepam.
6. The feelings, reactions, biases, and images from the past that the clinician may project onto the client with cod.
7. Relying on observation or experience rather than theoretical principles or theory.
10. Connections between substance abuse treatment and mental health systems that allow collaboration. Necessary because these are the primary care systems for persons with cod.
12. When two disorders or illnesses occur in the same person.
13. An opioid antagonist medication approved by the FDA to reverse an opioid overdose.
14. A variety of interventions designed to teach individuals who are trying to maintain health behavior changes how to anticipate and cope with the problem of relapse.

DOWN

2. A drug that distorts perception, thought, and feeling. This term is typically used to refer to drugs with hallucinogenic effects.
4. A psychological disorder characterized by the elevation or lowering of a person's mood, such as depression or bipolar disorder.
5. A type of CNS depressant sometimes prescribed to relieve anxiety, panic, or acute stress reactions. Some benzodiazepines are prescribed short-term to promote sleep.
8. A group of brain structures that process sensory information and control basic functions needed for survival such as breathing, heart rate, blood pressure, and arousal.
9. A drug that causes insensitivity to pain and is used for surgeries and other medical procedures.
11. Illegal or forbidden by law.

A. Valium
B. Naloxone
C. Intersystem Linkage
D. Anesthetic
E. Antisocial Personality Disorder
F. Benzodiazepine
G. Illicit
H. Psychedelic Drug
I. Countertransference
J. Relapse Prevention Therapy
K. Brainstem
L. Empirical
M. Comorbidity
N. Mood Disorders

22. Using the Across and Down clues, write the correct words in the numbered grid below.

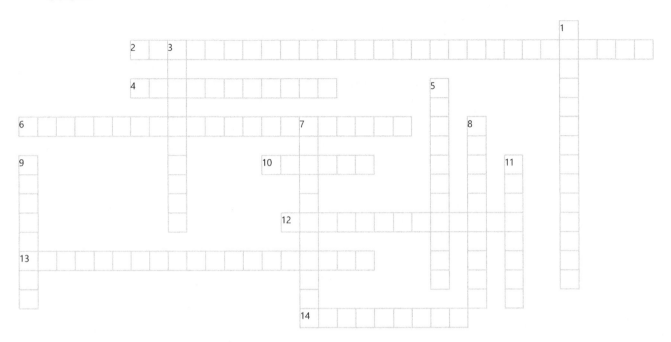

ACROSS

2. A therapeutic community whose approach to treatment adapts the principles and methods of the therapeutic community to the circumstances of the cod client.
4. A stimulant drug that acts on the central nervous system (CNS).
6. Of or pertaining to programs that have a higher than average level of integration of substance abuse and mental health treatment services.
10. Inhaling the aerosol or vapor from an electronic cigarette, e-vaporizer, or other device.
12. A type of psychosis where persons are subject to hallucinations occurring in the absence of insight into their pathological nature.
13. Any mechanism by which treatment interventions for co-occurring disorders are combined within the context of a primary treatment relationship or service setting.
14. A formal process of testing to determine whether a client warrants further attention at the current time for a particular disorder.

DOWN

1. An illness whose essential feature is binge eating and inappropriate compensatory methods to prevent weight gain.
3. A condition that can occur with the regular use of illicit or some prescription drugs, even if taken as prescribed.
5. A type of CNS depressant sometimes prescribed to promote relaxation and sleep, but more commonly used in surgical procedures and to treat seizure disorders.
7. An area of the brain crucial for learning and memory.
8. Slang term for the early stages of depressant-induced sleep.
9. Poisonous nature; poisonous quality.
11. A type of delusion, or false idea, that is unchanged by reasoned argument or proof to the contrary.

A. Integrated Treatment
C. Vaping
E. Toxicity
G. Dual Diagnosis Enhanced
I. Hippocampus
K. Amphetamine
M. Schizophrenia

B. Modified Therapeutic Community
D. Dependence
F. Paranoia
H. Screening
J. Nodding Out
L. Barbiturate
N. Bulimia Nervosa

23. Using the Across and Down clues, write the correct words in the numbered grid below.

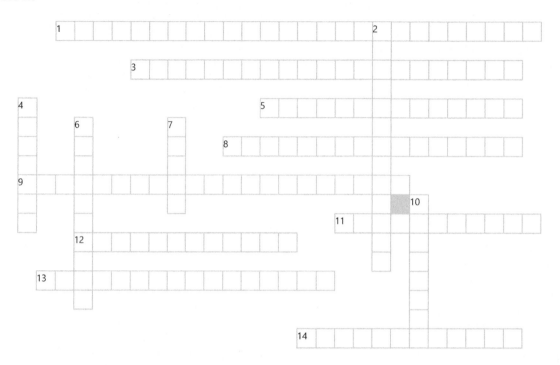

ACROSS

1. Synthetic substances similar to the male hormone testosterone.
3. A treatment approach based on providing incentives to support positive behavior change.
5. A class of drugs that include sedatives, tranquilizers, and hypnotics.
8. A chemical compound that acts as a messenger to carry signals from one nerve cell to another.
9. Pertaining to medications used to treat mental illnesses.
11. A collection of pus formed as a result of bacterial infection.
12. An entity that provides mental health services in two or three service settings and is not classified as a psychiatric or general hospital or as a residential treatment center.
13. The way a drug acts on the body.
14. Having a specific effect on the brain.

DOWN

2. A form of interpersonal exchange in which individuals present to each other their observations of, and reactions to, behaviors and attitudes that are matters of concern.
4. In drug addiction, relapse is the return to drug use after an attempt to stop.
6. Pertaining to a person's ability to carry out tasks.
7. Brand name for benzodiazepine alprazolam.
10. A type of delusion, or false idea, that is unchanged by reasoned argument or proof to the contrary.

A. Organization
D. Functional
G. Psychopharmacological
J. Confrontation
M. Anabolic Androgenic Steroids

B. CNS Depressants
E. Pharmacodynamics
H. Contingency Management
K. Paranoia
N. Skin Abscess

C. Neurotransmitter
F. Relapse
I. Psychoactive
L. Xanax

24. Using the Across and Down clues, write the correct words in the numbered grid below.

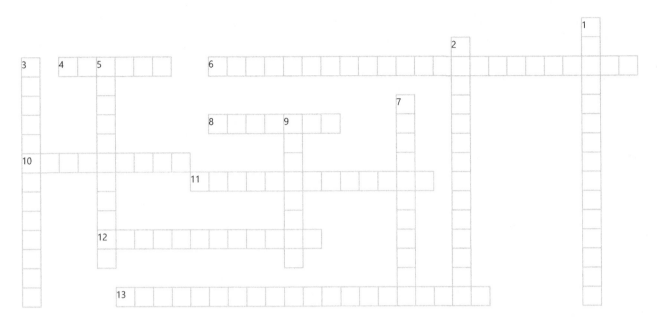

ACROSS

4. Violent mental or physical harm to a person, damage to an organ, etc.
6. Specific treatment strategies in which interventions for two or more disorders are combined in a single session or interaction, or in a series of interactions or multiple sessions.
8. In the context of substance abuse treatment, disability, or inability to function fully.
10. Substance abuse treatment is an organized array of services and interventions with a primary focus on treating substance abuse disorders.
11. Pupils that have become temporarily enlarged.
12. The study of the anatomy, function, and diseases of the brain and nervous system.
13. The system consisting of the heart and blood vessels. It delivers nutrients and oxygen to all cells in the body.

DOWN

1. A disorder in which the individual refuses to maintain a normal body weight, is afraid of gaining weight, and exhibits a significant disturbance in the perception of body shape.
2. A type of CNS depressant sometimes prescribed to relieve anxiety, panic, or acute stress reactions. Some benzodiazepines are prescribed short-term to promote sleep.
3. The simultaneous provision of material and training to persons from more than one discipline.
5. A stimulant drug that acts on the central nervous system (CNS).
7. A tendency to act without foresight or regard for consequences and to prioritize immediate rewards over long-term goals.
9. Slang term for tactile hallucinations that feel like bugs crawling on or under the skin.

A. Dilated Pupils
D. Integrated Interventions
G. Amphetamine
J. Cross Training
M. Deficit

B. Benzodiazepine
E. Neurobiology
H. Anorexia Nervosa
K. Cardiovascular System

C. Coke Bugs
F. Impulsivity
I. Treatment
L. Trauma

25. Using the Across and Down clues, write the correct words in the numbered grid below.

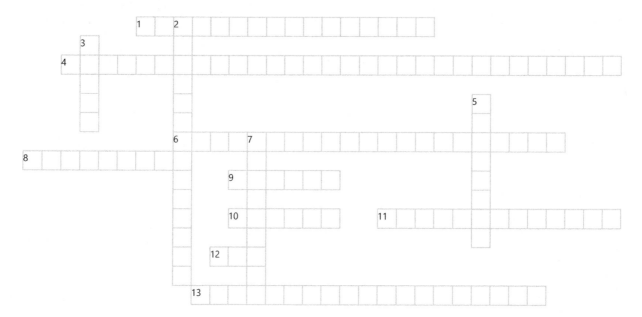

ACROSS

1. The use of emotional, psychological, sexual, or physical force by one family member or intimate partner to control another.
4. A counseling approach that uses motivational interviewing techniques to help individuals resolve any uncertainties they have about stopping their substance use.
6. A class of substance-related disorders that includes both substance abuse and substance dependence.
8. Pertaining to the mind's capacity to understand concepts and ideas.
9. A unique type of cell found in the brain and throughout the body that specializes in the transmission and processing of information.
10. A negative association attached to some activity or condition. A cause of shame or embarrassment.
11. A psychological disorder characterized by the elevation or lowering of a person's mood, such as depression or bipolar disorder.
12. Slang term for Smoke able methamphetamine.
13. The capacity and willingness of a clinician or other service provider to be open to working with issues of culture and diversity.

DOWN

2. An approach to recovery from substance use disorders that emphasizes personal responsibility, self-management, and clients' helping one another.
3. A place or a setting for some activity.
5. Extreme and unreasonable distrust of others.
7. Substance abuse treatment is an organized array of services and interventions with a primary focus on treating substance abuse disorders.

A. Mutual Self Help
C. Neuron
E. Locus
G. Ice
I. Paranoia
K. Treatment
M. Substance Use Disorders

B. Domestic Violence
D. Mood Disorders
F. Cultural Sensitivity
H. Cognitive
J. Stigma
L. Motivational Enhancement Therapy

1. Using the Across and Down clues, write the correct words in the numbered grid below.

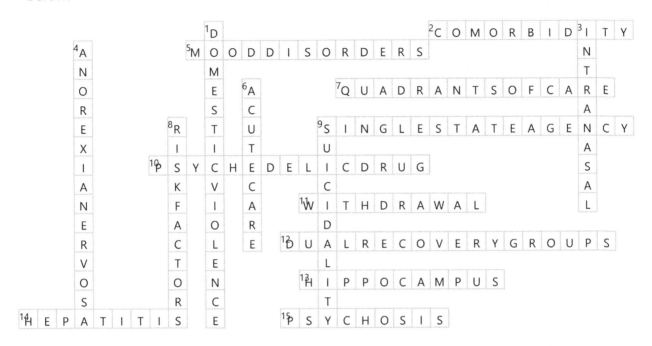

ACROSS

2. When two disorders or illnesses occur in the same person.
5. A psychological disorder characterized by the elevation or lowering of a person's mood, such as depression or bipolar disorder.
7. A conceptual framework that classifies clients in four basic groups based on relative symptom severity, rather than by diagnosis.
9. Systems that organize statewide services.
10. A drug that distorts perception, thought, and feeling. This term is typically used to refer to drugs with hallucinogenic effects.
11. Symptoms that can occur after long-term use of a drug is reduced or stopped.
12. Therapy groups in which recovery skills for co-occurring disorders are discussed.
13. An area of the brain crucial for learning and memory.
14. An inflammation of the liver, with accompanying liver cell damage and risk of death.
15. Delusional or disordered thinking detached from reality; symptoms often include hallucinations.

DOWN

1. The use of emotional, psychological, sexual, or physical force by one family member or intimate partner to control another.
3. Taken through the nose.
4. A disorder in which the individual refuses to maintain a normal body weight, is afraid of gaining weight, and exhibits a significant disturbance in the perception of body shape.
6. Short-term care provided in intensive care units, brief hospital stays, and emergency rooms for those who are severely intoxicated or dangerously ill.
8. Factors that increase the likelihood of beginning substance use, of regular and harmful use, and of other behavioral health problems associated with use.
9. A measure or estimate of a person's likelihood of committing suicide. A high-risk behavior associated with cod, especially (although not limited to) serious mood disorders.

A. Hippocampus
D. Suicidality
G. Intranasal
J. Mood Disorders
M. Risk Factors
P. Dual Recovery Groups

B. Hepatitis
E. Acute Care
H. Psychosis
K. Psychedelic Drug
N. Quadrants of Care

C. Withdrawal
F. Single State Agency
I. Comorbidity
L. Anorexia Nervosa
O. Domestic Violence

2. Using the Across and Down clues, write the correct words in the numbered grid below.

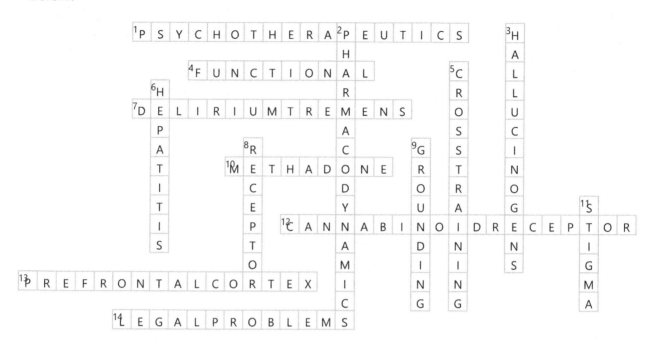

ACROSS

1. Drugs that have an effect on the function of the brain and that are often used to treat psychiatric disorders.
4. Pertaining to a person's ability to carry out tasks.
7. A state of confusion accompanied by trembling and vivid hallucinations.
10. A long-acting opioid agonist medication used for the treatment of opioid addiction and pain.
12. The receptor in the brain that recognizes and binds cannabinoids that are produced in the brain or outside the body.
13. The front part of the brain responsible for reasoning, planning, problem solving, and other higher cognitive functions.
14. People who abuse substances are at a higher risk for engaging in behaviors that are high risk and illegal.

DOWN

2. The way a drug acts on the body.
3. A broad group of drugs that cause distortions of sensory perception. The prototype hallucinogen is lysergic acid diethylamide (LSD).
5. The simultaneous provision of material and training to persons from more than one discipline.
6. An inflammation of the liver, with accompanying liver cell damage and risk of death.
8. A molecule located on the surface of a cell that recognizes specific chemicals and transmits the chemical message into the cell.
9. The use of strategies that soothe and distract the client who is experiencing intense pain or other strong emotions, helping the client anchor in the present and in reality.
11. A negative association attached to some activity or condition. A cause of shame or embarrassment.

A. Prefrontal Cortex
B. Psychotherapeutics
C. Receptor
D. Stigma
E. Delirium Tremens
F. Legal Problems
G. Cannabinoid Receptor
H. Functional
I. Methadone
J. Grounding
K. Cross Training
L. Hallucinogens
M. Pharmacodynamics
N. Hepatitis

3. Using the Across and Down clues, write the correct words in the numbered grid below.

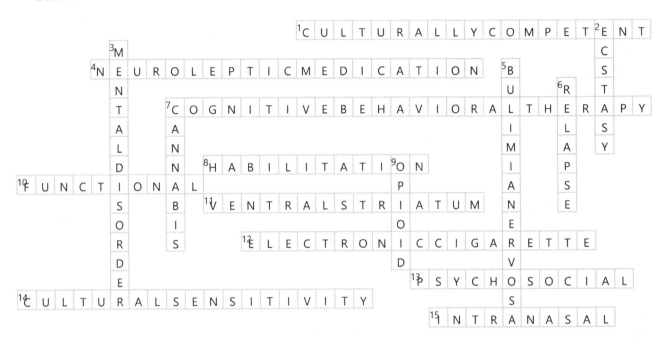

ACROSS

1. Biopsychosocial or other treatment that is adapted to suit the special cultural beliefs, practices, and needs of a client.
4. A drug used to treat psychosis, especially schizophrenia.
7. A therapeutic approach that seeks to modify negative or self-defeating thoughts and behavior.
8. Initial learning and the acquisition of skills necessary for everyday life.
10. Pertaining to a person's ability to carry out tasks.
11. An area of the brain that is part of the basal ganglia and includes the nucleus accumbens.
12. A battery-operated device that people use to inhale an aerosol, which typically contains nicotine, flavorings, and other chemicals.
13. Involving a person's psychological well-being, as well as housing, employment, family, and other social aspects of life circumstances.
14. The capacity and willingness of a clinician or other service provider to be open to working with issues of culture and diversity.
15. Taken through the nose.

DOWN

2. Slang term for methylenedioxymethamphetamine, a member of the amphetamine family. At lower doses, MDMA causes distortions of emotional perceptions.
3. A mental condition marked primarily by disorganization of personality, mind, and emotions that seriously impairs the psychological or behavioral functioning of the individual.
5. An illness whose essential feature is binge eating and inappropriate compensatory methods to prevent weight gain.
6. In drug addiction, relapse is the return to drug use after an attempt to stop.
7. Another name for the marijuana plant, cannabis sativa.
9. A type of depressant drug that diminishes pain and central nervous system activity.

A. Opioid
D. Cultural Sensitivity
G. Psychosocial
J. Bulimia Nervosa
M. Mental Disorder
P. Electronic Cigarette

B. Culturally Competent
E. Intranasal
H. Habilitation
K. Cannabis
N. Relapse

C. Neuroleptic Medication
F. Ecstasy
I. Cognitive Behavioral Therapy
L. Functional
O. Ventral Striatum

4. Using the Across and Down clues, write the correct words in the numbered grid below.

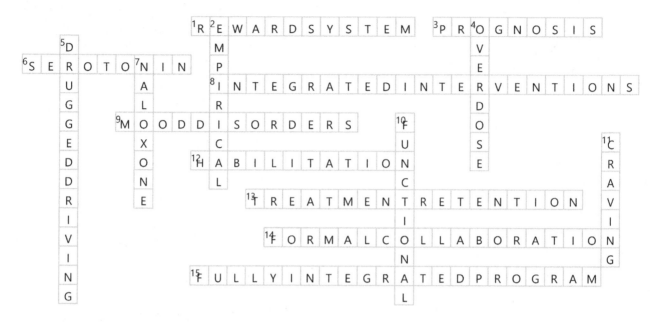

ACROSS

1. A brain circuit that includes the ventral tegmental area, the nucleus accumbens, and the prefrontal cortex.
3. A clinician's judgment or estimate of how well a disorder will respond to treatment.
6. A neurotransmitter involved in a broad range of effects on perception, movement, and emotions. Serotonin and its receptors are the targets of most hallucinogens.
8. Specific treatment strategies in which interventions for two or more disorders are combined in a single session or interaction, or in a series of interactions or multiple sessions.
9. A psychological disorder characterized by the elevation or lowering of a person's mood, such as depression or bipolar disorder.
12. Initial learning and the acquisition of skills necessary for everyday life.
13. Keeping clients involved in treatment activities and receiving required services.
14. Occurs when the nature of the client's disabilities requires more specific information and more complex and targeted intervention.
15. A treatment program that actively combines substance abuse and mental health interventions to treat disorders, related problems, and the whole person more effectively.

DOWN

2. Relying on observation or experience rather than theoretical principles or theory.
4. An overdose occurs when a person uses enough of a drug to produce a life-threatening reaction or death.
5. Driving a vehicle while impaired due to the intoxicating effects of recent drug use.
7. An opioid antagonist medication approved by the FDA to reverse an opioid overdose.
10. Pertaining to a person's ability to carry out tasks.
11. A powerful, often overwhelming desire to use drugs.

A. Reward System
B. Serotonin
C. Overdose
D. Formal Collaboration
E. Integrated Interventions
F. Fully Integrated Program
G. Habilitation
H. Mood Disorders
I. Prognosis
J. Empirical
K. Treatment Retention
L. Craving
M. Functional
N. Drugged Driving
O. Naloxone

5. Using the Across and Down clues, write the correct words in the numbered grid below.

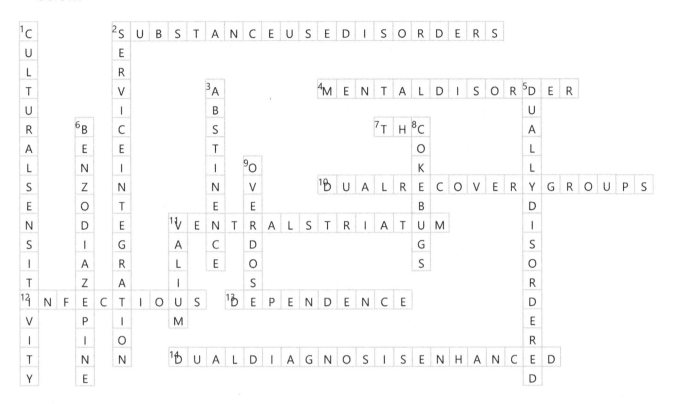

ACROSS

2. A class of substance-related disorders that includes both substance abuse and substance dependence.
4. A mental condition marked primarily by disorganization of personality, mind, and emotions that seriously impairs the psychological or behavioral functioning of the individual.
7. Delta-9-tetrahydrocannabinol; the main mind-altering ingredient in marijuana.
10. Therapy groups in which recovery skills for co-occurring disorders are discussed.
11. An area of the brain that is part of the basal ganglia and includes the nucleus accumbens.
12. Able to spread by an agent such as a virus or bacterium.
13. A condition that can occur with the regular use of illicit or some prescription drugs, even if taken as prescribed.
14. Of or pertaining to programs that have a higher than average level of integration of substance abuse and mental health treatment services.

DOWN

1. The capacity and willingness of a clinician or other service provider to be open to working with issues of culture and diversity.
2. No one set of treatment interventions constitutes integrated treatment.
3. Not using drugs or alcohol.
5. Having been diagnosed with two disorders, for example a substance use disorder and a mental health disorder.
6. A type of CNS depressant sometimes prescribed to relieve anxiety, panic, or acute stress reactions. Some benzodiazepines are prescribed short-term to promote sleep.
8. Slang term for tactile hallucinations that feel like bugs crawling on or under the skin.
9. An overdose occurs when a person uses enough of a drug to produce a life-threatening reaction or death.
11. Brand name for benzodiazepine diazepam.

A. Substance Use Disorders
D. Dual Diagnosis Enhanced
G. Valium
J. Abstinence
M. Dependence
P. THC

B. Overdose
E. Infectious
H. Dually Disordered
K. Cultural Sensitivity
N. Ventral Striatum

C. Coke Bugs
F. Mental Disorder
I. Benzodiazepine
L. Dual Recovery Groups
O. Service Integration

6. Using the Across and Down clues, write the correct words in the numbered grid below.

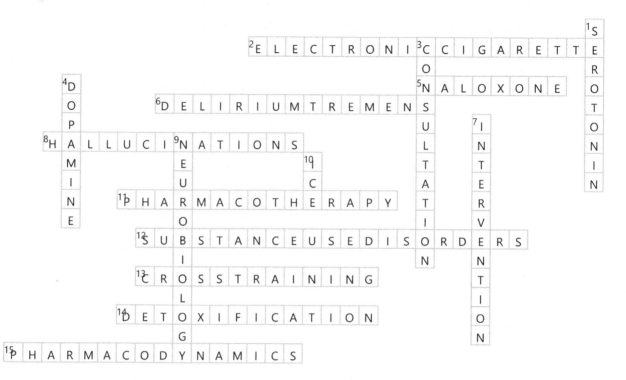

ACROSS

2. A battery-operated device that people use to inhale an aerosol, which typically contains nicotine, flavorings, and other chemicals.
5. An opioid antagonist medication approved by the FDA to reverse an opioid overdose.
6. A state of confusion accompanied by trembling and vivid hallucinations.
8. Sensations, sounds and
11. Treatment using medications.
12. A class of substance-related disorders that includes both substance abuse and substance dependence.
13. The simultaneous provision of material and training to persons from more than one discipline.
14. A process in which the body rids itself of a drug, or its metabolites.
15. The way a drug acts on the body.

DOWN

1. A neurotransmitter involved in a broad range of effects on perception, movement, and emotions. Serotonin and its receptors are the targets of most hallucinogens.
3. In the context of treatment programs, consultation is a traditional type of informal relationship among treatment providers, such as a referral or a request for exchanging information.
4. A brain chemical, classified as a neurotransmitter, found in regions of the brain that regulate movement, emotion, motivation, and reinforcement of rewarding behavior.
7. Encompasses the specific treatment strategies, therapies, or techniques that are used to treat one or more disorders.
9. The study of the anatomy, function, and diseases of the brain and nervous system.
10. Slang term for Smoke able methamphetamine.

A. Pharmacotherapy
D. Dopamine
G. Naloxone
J. Hallucinations
M. Intervention

B. Electronic Cigarette
E. Cross Training
H. Pharmacodynamics
K. Detoxification
N. Consultation

C. Neurobiology
F. Delirium Tremens
I. Substance Use Disorders
L. Ice
O. Serotonin

7. Using the Across and Down clues, write the correct words in the numbered grid below.

ACROSS

1. A therapeutic approach that seeks to modify negative or self-defeating thoughts and behavior.
5. A period of amnesia or memory loss, typically caused by chronic, high-dose substance abuse.
6. The feelings, reactions, biases, and images from the past that the clinician may project onto the client with cod.
7. Involving a person's psychological well-being, as well as housing, employment, family, and other social aspects of life circumstances.
11. Having been diagnosed with two disorders, for example a substance use disorder and a mental health disorder.
12. The receptor in the brain that recognizes and binds cannabinoids that are produced in the brain or outside the body.
13. Synthetic substances similar to the male hormone testosterone.
14. Practices or actions through which an individual shows that he or she regards other cultures as inferior to the dominant culture.

DOWN

1. An ability, capacity, skill, or set of skills.
2. Keeping clients involved in treatment activities and receiving required services.
3. An illness whose essential feature is excessive anxiety and worry.
4. A process in which the body rids itself of a drug, or its metabolites.
8. A measure or estimate of a person's likelihood of committing suicide. A high-risk behavior associated with cod, especially (although not limited to) serious mood disorders.
9. Delusional or disordered thinking detached from reality; symptoms often include hallucinations.
10. A group of medications that reduce pain.

A. Anxiety Disorder
B. Psychosocial
C. Blackout
D. Cultural Destructiveness
E. Countertransference
F. Competency
G. Dually Disordered
H. Cannabinoid Receptor
I. Psychosis
J. Treatment Retention
K. Analgesics
L. Anabolic Androgenic Steroids
M. Detoxification
N. Cognitive Behavioral Therapy
O. Suicidality

8. Using the Across and Down clues, write the correct words in the numbered grid below.

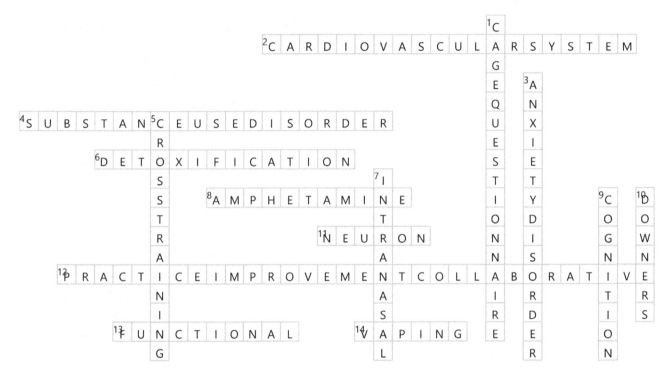

ACROSS

2. The system consisting of the heart and blood vessels. It delivers nutrients and oxygen to all cells in the body.
4. A medical illness caused by disordered use of a substance or substances.
6. A process in which the body rids itself of a drug, or its metabolites.
8. A stimulant drug that acts on the central nervous system (CNS).
11. A unique type of cell found in the brain and throughout the body that specializes in the transmission and processing of information.
12. Community-based initiatives that link treatment providers, researchers, and policymakers in order to build a strong foundation to effect action.
13. Pertaining to a person's ability to carry out tasks.
14. Inhaling the aerosol or vapor from an electronic cigarette, e-vaporizer, or other device.

DOWN

1. A brief alcoholism screening tool.
3. An illness whose essential feature is excessive anxiety and worry.
5. The simultaneous provision of material and training to persons from more than one discipline.
7. Taken through the nose.
9. Relating to the act or process of thinking, understanding, learning, and remembering.
10. Slang term for drugs that exert a depressant effect on the central nervous system. In general, downers are sedative-hypnotic drugs, such as benzodiazepines and barbiturates.

A. Functional
C. Downers
E. Cognition
G. Anxiety Disorder
I. Intranasal
K. Substance Use Disorder
M. Detoxification

B. Practice Improvement Collaborative
D. Vaping
F. Cross Training
H. Neuron
J. Cage Questionnaire
L. Cardiovascular System
N. Amphetamine

9. Using the Across and Down clues, write the correct words in the numbered grid below.

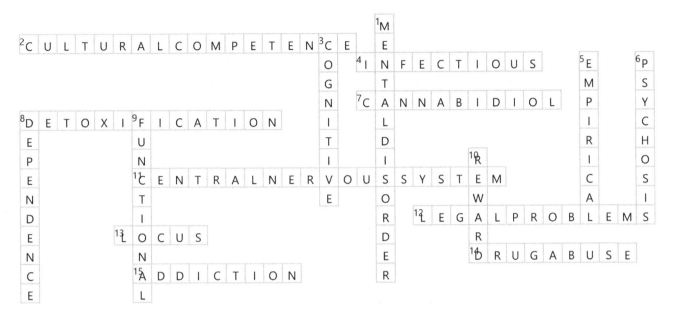

ACROSS

2. The capacity of a service provider to understand and work effectively in accordance with the cultural beliefs and practices of persons from a given ethnic
4. Able to spread by an agent such as a virus or bacterium.
7. A component of the marijuana plant without mind-altering effects that is being studied for possible medical uses.
8. A clearing of toxins from the body.
11. The system consisting of the nerves in the brain and spinal cord.
12. People who abuse substances are at a higher risk for engaging in behaviors that are high risk and illegal.
13. A place or a setting for some activity.
14. An older diagnostic term that defined use that is unsafe, use that leads a person to fail to fulfill responsibilities or gets them in legal trouble.
15. A chronic, relapsing disorder characterized by compulsive (or difficult to control) drug seeking and use despite harmful consequences, as well as long-lasting changes in the brain.

DOWN

1. A mental condition marked primarily by disorganization of personality, mind, and emotions that seriously impairs the psychological or behavioral functioning of the individual.
3. Pertaining to the mind's capacity to understand concepts and ideas.
5. Relying on observation or experience rather than theoretical principles or theory.
6. Delusional or disordered thinking detached from reality; symptoms often include hallucinations.
8. A condition that can occur with the regular use of illicit or some prescription drugs, even if taken as prescribed.
9. Pertaining to a person's ability to carry out tasks.
10. Pleasurable feelings that reinforce behavior and encourage repetition.

A. Psychosis
D. Legal Problems
G. Functional
J. Infectious
M. Detoxification
P. Locus
B. Addiction
E. Central Nervous System
H. Drug Abuse
K. Cognitive
N. Cannabidiol
C. Cultural Competence
F. Reward
I. Dependence
L. Empirical
O. Mental Disorder

10. Using the Across and Down clues, write the correct words in the numbered grid below.

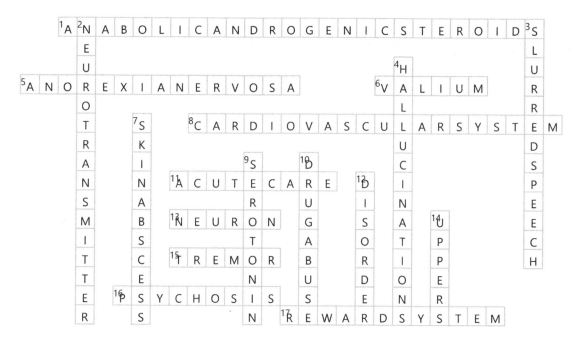

ACROSS

1. Synthetic substances similar to the male hormone testosterone.
5. A disorder in which the individual refuses to maintain a normal body weight, is afraid of gaining weight, and exhibits a significant disturbance in the perception of body shape.
6. Brand name for benzodiazepine diazepam.
8. The system consisting of the heart and blood vessels. It delivers nutrients and oxygen to all cells in the body.
11. Short-term care provided in intensive care units, brief hospital stays, and emergency rooms for those who are severely intoxicated or dangerously ill.
13. A unique type of cell found in the brain and throughout the body that specializes in the transmission and processing of information.
15. An involuntary and rhythmic movement in the muscles, most often in the hands, feet, jaw, tongue, or head.
16. A mental disorder that is characterized by distinct distortions of a person's mental capacity, ability to recognize reality, and relationships to others.
17. A brain circuit that includes the ventral tegmental area, the nucleus accumbens, and the prefrontal cortex.

DOWN

2. A chemical compound that acts as a messenger to carry signals from one nerve cell to another.
3. A sign of depressant intoxication. When people consume significant amounts of sedative-hypnotics and opioids, their speech may become garbled, mumbled, and slow.
4. Sensations, sounds and
7. A collection of pus formed as a result of bacterial infection.
9. A neurotransmitter involved in a broad range of effects on perception, movement, and emotions. Serotonin and its receptors are the targets of most hallucinogens.
10. An older diagnostic term that defined use that is unsafe, use that leads a person to fail to fulfill responsibilities or gets them in legal trouble.
12. An illness or a disruption of some mental or physical process.
14. Slang term used to describe drugs that have a stimulating effect on the central nervous system. Examples include cocaine, caffeine, and amphetamines.

A. Drug Abuse
B. Neurotransmitter
C. Disorder
D. Cardiovascular System
E. Slurred Speech
F. Skin Abscess
G. Serotonin
H. Anorexia Nervosa
I. Hallucinations
J. Valium
K. Anabolic Androgenic Steroids
L. Uppers
M. Reward System
N. Psychosis
O. Acute Care
P. Tremor
Q. Neuron

11. Using the Across and Down clues, write the correct words in the numbered grid below.

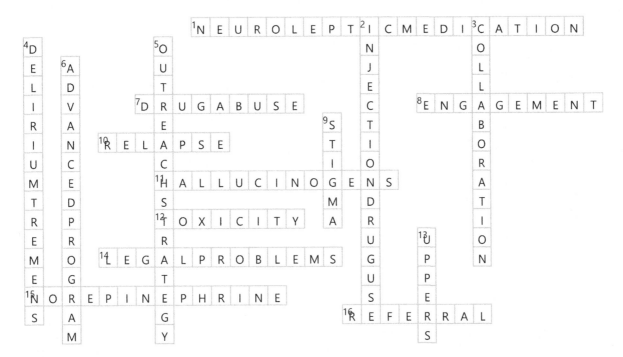

ACROSS

1. A drug used to treat psychosis, especially schizophrenia.
7. An older diagnostic term that defined use that is unsafe, use that leads a person to fail to fulfill responsibilities or gets them in legal trouble.
8. A client's commitment to and maintenance of treatment in all of its forms. A successful engagement program helps clients view the treatment facility as an important resource.
10. A breakdown or setback in a person's attempt to change or modify any particular behavior.
11. A broad group of drugs that cause distortions of sensory perception. The prototype hallucinogen is lysergic acid diethylamide (LSD).
12. Poisonous nature; poisonous quality.
14. People who abuse substances are at a higher risk for engaging in behaviors that are high risk and illegal.
15. A neurotransmitter that affects heart rate, blood pressure, stress, and attention.
16. A process for facilitating client

DOWN

2. The act of administering drugs by injection. Blood-borne viruses, like HIV and hepatitis, can be transmitted via shared needles or other drug injection equipment.
3. The action of working with someone to produce or create something.
4. A state of confusion accompanied by trembling and vivid hallucinations.
5. Approaches that actively seek out persons in a community who may have substance use disorders and engage them in substance abuse treatment.
6. A treatment program that has the capacity to provide integrated substance abuse and mental health treatment for clients with COD.
9. A negative association attached to some activity or condition. A cause of shame or embarrassment.
13. Slang term used to describe drugs that have a stimulating effect on the central nervous system. Examples include cocaine, caffeine, and amphetamines.

A. Stigma
B. Engagement
C. Toxicity
D. Delirium Tremens
E. Uppers
F. Norepinephrine
G. Outreach Strategy
H. Relapse
I. Neuroleptic Medication
J. Legal Problems
K. Hallucinogens
L. Injection Drug Use
M. Advanced Program
N. Collaboration
O. Drug Abuse
P. Referral

12. Using the Across and Down clues, write the correct words in the numbered grid below.

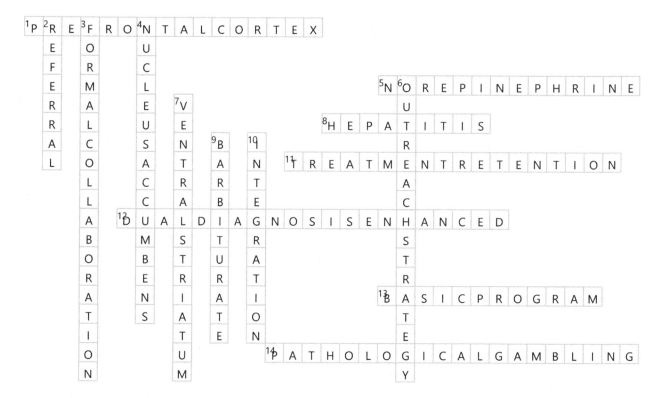

ACROSS

1. The front part of the brain responsible for reasoning, planning, problem solving, and other higher cognitive functions.
5. A neurotransmitter that affects heart rate, blood pressure, stress, and attention.
8. An inflammation of the liver, with accompanying liver cell damage and risk of death.
11. Keeping clients involved in treatment activities and receiving required services.
12. Of or pertaining to programs that have a higher than average level of integration of substance abuse and mental health treatment services.
13. A treatment program with the capacity to provide treatment for one disorder, but that also screens for other disorders and is able to access necessary consultations.
14. An illness whose essential feature is persistent and recurrent maladaptive gambling behavior that disrupts personal, family, or vocational pursuits.

DOWN

2. A process for facilitating client
3. Occurs when the nature of the client's disabilities requires more specific information and more complex and targeted intervention.
4. A brain region in the ventral striatum involved in motivation and reward.
6. Approaches that actively seek out persons in a community who may have substance use disorders and engage them in substance abuse treatment.
7. An area of the brain that is part of the basal ganglia and includes the nucleus accumbens.
9. A type of CNS depressant sometimes prescribed to promote relaxation and sleep, but more commonly used in surgical procedures and to treat seizure disorders.
10. Relationships among mental health and substance abuse providers in which both fields are moved into a single treatment setting and treatment regimen.

A. Ventral Striatum B. Integration C. Basic Program
D. Barbiturate E. Referral F. Formal Collaboration
G. Nucleus Accumbens H. Norepinephrine I. Dual Diagnosis Enhanced
J. Hepatitis K. Prefrontal Cortex L. Pathological Gambling
M. Treatment Retention N. Outreach Strategy

13. Using the Across and Down clues, write the correct words in the numbered grid below.

ACROSS

3. A tendency to act without foresight or regard for consequences and to prioritize immediate rewards over long-term goals.
4. A treatment program that focuses primarily on one disorder without substantial modification to its usual treatment.
5. Initial learning and the acquisition of skills necessary for everyday life.
7. A process of change through which people with substance use disorders improve their health and wellness, live self-directed lives, and strive to reach their full potential.
10. Pupils that have become temporarily enlarged.
12. A type of CNS depressant sometimes prescribed to promote relaxation and sleep, but more commonly used in surgical procedures and to treat seizure disorders.
13. A process in which the body rids itself of a drug, or its metabolites.
14. An area of the brain that is part of the basal ganglia and includes the nucleus accumbens.

DOWN

1. An illness or a disruption of some mental or physical process.
2. The feelings, reactions, biases, and images from the past that the client with cod may project onto the clinician.
6. A group of brain structures that process sensory information and control basic functions needed for survival such as breathing, heart rate, blood pressure, and arousal.
8. Legally forced or compelled.
9. A brand name amphetamine for treating ADHD.
11. A chemical substance that binds to and activates certain receptors on cells, causing a biological response.

A. Impulsivity
B. Habilitation
C. Ventral Striatum
D. Brainstem
E. Agonist
F. Adderall
G. Disorder
H. Recovery
I. Barbiturate
J. Transference
K. Dilated Pupils
L. Detoxification
M. Coerced
N. Intermediate Program

14. Using the Across and Down clues, write the correct words in the numbered grid below.

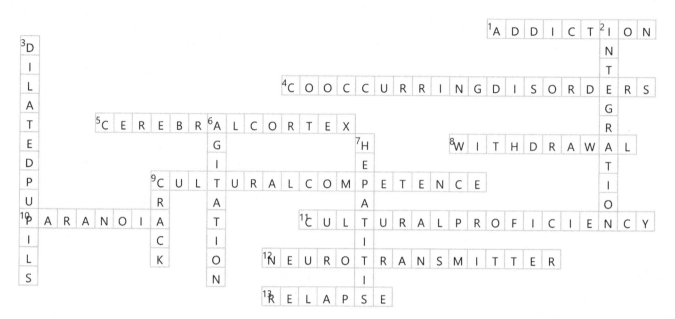

ACROSS

1. A chronic, relapsing disorder characterized by compulsive (or difficult to control) drug seeking and use despite harmful consequences, as well as long-lasting changes in the brain.
4. Refers to co-occurring substance use (abuse or dependence) and mental disorders.
5. The gray matter that covers the surface of the cerebral hemispheres, whose functions include sensory processing and motor control along with language, reasoning, and decision-making.
8. Symptoms that can occur after long-term use of a drug is reduced or stopped.
9. The capacity of a service provider to understand and work effectively in accordance with the cultural beliefs and practices of persons from a given ethnic
10. Extreme and unreasonable distrust of others.
11. The highest level of cultural capacity, which implies an ability to perceive the nuances of a culture in depth and a willingness to work to advance in proficiency through leadership.
12. A chemical compound that acts as a messenger to carry signals from one nerve cell to another.
13. In drug addiction, relapse is the return to drug use after an attempt to stop.

DOWN

2. Relationships among mental health and substance abuse providers in which both fields are moved into a single treatment setting and treatment regimen.
3. Pupils that have become temporarily enlarged.
6. A restless inability to keep still.
7. An inflammation of the liver, with accompanying liver cell damage and risk of death.
9. Cocaine that has been chemically modified so that it will become a gas vapor when heated at relatively low temperatures.

A. Agitation
D. Relapse
G. Integration
J. Cultural Competence
M. Neurotransmitter

B. Hepatitis
E. Withdrawal
H. Cerebral Cortex
K. Crack
N. Dilated Pupils

C. Paranoia
F. Co Occurring Disorders
I. Cultural Proficiency
L. Addiction

15. Using the Across and Down clues, write the correct words in the numbered grid below.

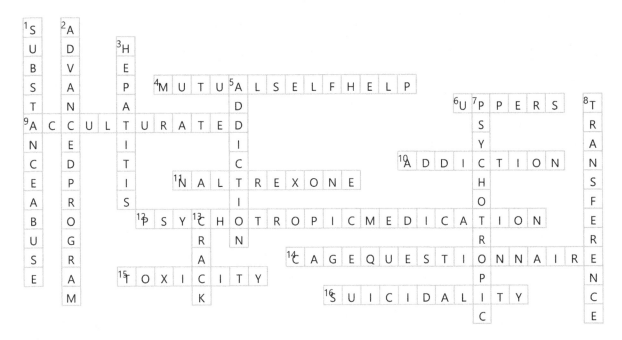

ACROSS

4. An approach to recovery from substance use disorders that emphasizes personal responsibility, self-management, and clients' helping one another.
6. Slang term used to describe drugs that have a stimulating effect on the central nervous system. Examples include cocaine, caffeine, and amphetamines.
9. Mentally and physically in harmony with and connected to the culture in which one lives.
10. Physical dependence on a substance of abuse. Inability to cease use of a substance without experiencing withdrawal symptoms.
11. A long-acting opioid antagonist medication that prevents receptors from being activated by other opioids. Naltrexone is used to treat alcohol and opioid use disorders.
12. A drug that has an effect on the mind and sometimes affects behavior as well.
14. A brief alcoholism screening tool.
15. Poisonous nature; poisonous quality.
16. A measure or estimate of a person's likelihood of committing suicide. A high-risk behavior associated with cod, especially (although not limited to) serious mood disorders.

DOWN

1. A maladaptive pattern of substance use manifested by recurrent and significant adverse consequences related to the repeated use of substances.
2. A treatment program that has the capacity to provide integrated substance abuse and mental health treatment for clients with COD.
3. An inflammation of the liver, with accompanying liver cell damage and risk of death.
5. A chronic, relapsing disorder characterized by compulsive (or difficult to control) drug seeking and use despite harmful consequences, as well as long-lasting changes in the brain.
7. Mind-altering.
8. The feelings, reactions, biases, and images from the past that the client with cod may project onto the clinician.
13. Cocaine that has been chemically modified so that it will become a gas vapor when heated at relatively low temperatures.

A. Uppers
B. Crack
C. Addiction
D. Psychotropic Medication
E. Substance Abuse
F. Toxity
G. Mutual Self Help
H. Cage Questionnaire
I. Hepatitis
J. Suicidality
K. Transference
L. Psychotropic
M. Acculturated
N. Naltrexone
O. Addiction
P. Advanced Program

16. Using the Across and Down clues, write the correct words in the numbered grid below.

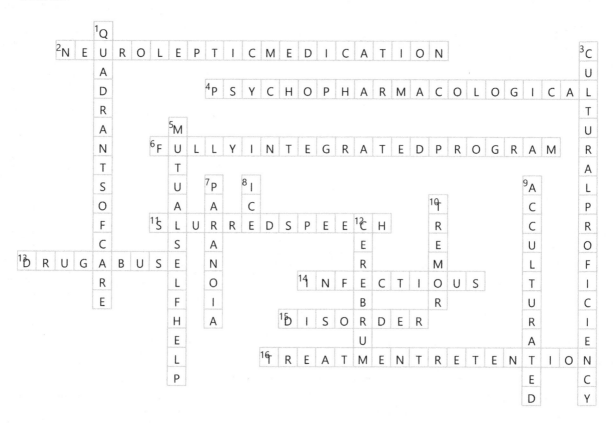

ACROSS

2. A drug used to treat psychosis, especially schizophrenia.
4. Pertaining to medications used to treat mental illnesses.
6. A treatment program that actively combines substance abuse and mental health interventions to treat disorders, related problems, and the whole person more effectively.
11. A sign of depressant intoxication. When people consume significant amounts of sedative-hypnotics and opioids, their speech may become garbled, mumbled, and slow.
13. An older diagnostic term that defined use that is unsafe, use that leads a person to fail to fulfill responsibilities or gets them in legal trouble.
14. Able to spread by an agent such as a virus or bacterium.
15. An illness or a disruption of some mental or physical process.
16. Keeping clients involved in treatment activities and receiving required services.

DOWN

1. A conceptual framework that classifies clients in four basic groups based on relative symptom severity, rather than by diagnosis.
3. The highest level of cultural capacity, which implies an ability to perceive the nuances of a culture in depth and a willingness to work to advance in proficiency through leadership.
5. An approach to recovery from substance use disorders that emphasizes personal responsibility, self-management, and clients' helping one another.
7. Extreme and unreasonable distrust of others.
8. Slang term for Smoke able methamphetamine.
9. Mentally and physically in harmony with and connected to the culture in which one lives.
10. An involuntary and rhythmic movement in the muscles, most often in the hands, feet, jaw, tongue, or head.
12. The upper part of the brain consisting of the left and right hemispheres.

A. Mutual Self Help
B. Ice
C. Treatment Retention
D. Drug Abuse
E. Tremor
F. Psychopharmacological
G. Disorder
H. Neuroleptic Medication
I. Fully Integrated Program
J. Cultural Proficiency
K. Cerebrum
L. Quadrants of Care
M. Infectious
N. Paranoia
O. Acculturated
P. Slurred Speech

17. Using the Across and Down clues, write the correct words in the numbered grid below.

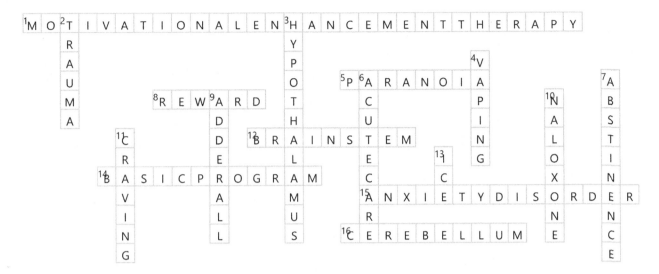

ACROSS

1. A counseling approach that uses motivational interviewing techniques to help individuals resolve any uncertainties they have about stopping their substance use.
5. Extreme and unreasonable distrust of others.
8. Pleasurable feelings that reinforce behavior and encourage repetition.
12. A group of brain structures that process sensory information and control basic functions needed for survival such as breathing, heart rate, blood pressure, and arousal.
14. A treatment program with the capacity to provide treatment for one disorder, but that also screens for other disorders and is able to access necessary consultations.
15. An illness whose essential feature is excessive anxiety and worry.
16. A part of the brain that helps regulate posture, balance, and coordination. It is also involved in the processes of emotion, motivation, memory, and thought.

DOWN

2. Violent mental or physical harm to a person, damage to an organ, etc.
3. A part of the brain that controls many bodily functions, including eating, drinking, body temperature regulation, and the release of many hormones.
4. Inhaling the aerosol or vapor from an electronic cigarette, e-vaporizer, or other device.
6. Short-term care provided in intensive care units, brief hospital stays, and emergency rooms for those who are severely intoxicated or dangerously ill.
7. Not using drugs or alcohol.
9. A brand name amphetamine for treating ADHD.
10. An opioid antagonist medication approved by the FDA to reverse an opioid overdose.
11. A powerful, often overwhelming desire to use drugs.
13. Slang term for Smoke able methamphetamine.

A. Abstinence
C. Ice
E. Basic Program
G. Craving
I. Paranoia
K. Trauma
M. Motivational Enhancement Therapy
O. Reward

B. Vaping
D. Adderall
F. Brainstem
H. Naloxone
J. Anxiety Disorder
L. Cerebellum
N. Hypothalamus
P. Acute Care

18. Using the Across and Down clues, write the correct words in the numbered grid below.

ACROSS

1. Poisonous nature; poisonous quality.
5. Any mechanism by which treatment interventions for co-occurring disorders are combined within the context of a primary treatment relationship or service setting.
8. A type of CNS depressant sometimes prescribed to promote relaxation and sleep, but more commonly used in surgical procedures and to treat seizure disorders.
11. A type of relationship between client and clinician in which both are working cooperatively toward the same goals, with mutual respect and understanding.
14. The right and left halves of the brain.
15. Interconnected brain structures that process feelings, emotions, and motivations. It is also important for learning and memory.
16. The use of strategies that soothe and distract the client who is experiencing intense pain or other strong emotions, helping the client anchor in the present and in reality.
17. Symptoms that can occur after long-term use of a drug is reduced or stopped.

DOWN

2. Keeping clients involved in treatment activities and receiving required services.
3. A brand name amphetamine for treating ADHD.
4. A treatment program that has the capacity to provide integrated substance abuse and mental health treatment for clients with COD.
6. Chemicals that bind to cannabinoid receptors in the brain.
7. A long-acting opioid antagonist medication that prevents receptors from being activated by other opioids. Naltrexone is used to treat alcohol and opioid use disorders.
9. A tendency to act without foresight or regard for consequences and to prioritize immediate rewards over long-term goals.
10. A client's commitment to and maintenance of treatment in all of its forms. A successful engagement program helps clients view the treatment facility as an important resource.
12. Able to spread by an agent such as a virus or bacterium.
13. Slang term for Smoke able methamphetamine.

A. Integrated Treatment
B. Grounding
C. Toxicity
D. Treatment Retention
E. Therapeutic Alliance
F. Cannabinoids
G. Engagement
H. Barbiturate
I. Advanced Program
J. Adderall
K. Naltrexone
L. Limbic System
M. Infectious
N. Withdrawal
O. Ice
P. Cerebral Hemispheres
Q. Impulsivity

19. Using the Across and Down clues, write the correct words in the numbered grid below.

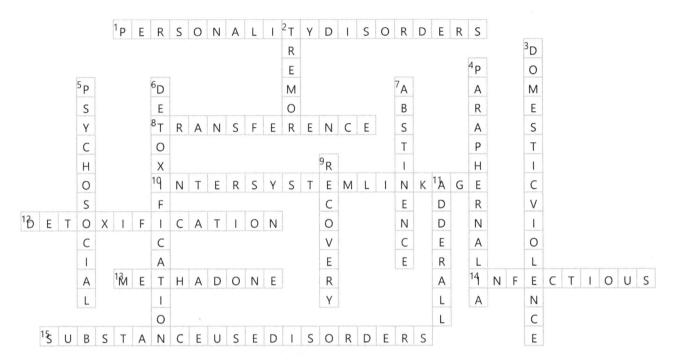

ACROSS

1. Rigid, inflexible, and maladaptive behavior patterns of sufficient severity to cause internal distress or significant impairment in functioning.
8. The feelings, reactions, biases, and images from the past that the client with cod may project onto the clinician.
10. Connections between substance abuse treatment and mental health systems that allow collaboration. Necessary because these are the primary care systems for persons with cod.
12. A clearing of toxins from the body.
13. A long-acting opioid agonist medication used for the treatment of opioid addiction and pain.
14. Able to spread by an agent such as a virus or bacterium.
15. A class of substance-related disorders that includes both substance abuse and substance dependence.

DOWN

2. An involuntary and rhythmic movement in the muscles, most often in the hands, feet, jaw, tongue, or head.
3. The use of emotional, psychological, sexual, or physical force by one family member or intimate partner to control another.
4. A broad term that describes objects used during the chemical preparation or use of drugs. These include syringes, syringe needles, roach clips, and marijuana or crack pipes.
5. Involving a person's psychological well-being, as well as housing, employment, family, and other social aspects of life circumstances.
6. A process in which the body rids itself of a drug, or its metabolites.
7. Not using drugs or alcohol.
9. A process of change through which people with substance use disorders improve their health and wellness, live self-directed lives, and strive to reach their full potential.
11. A brand name amphetamine for treating ADHD.

A. Detoxification
D. Paraphernalia
G. Personality Disorders
J. Tremor
M. Adderall
B. Substance Use Disorders
E. Transference
H. Detoxification
K. Intersystem Linkage
N. Infectious
C. Methadone
F. Recovery
I. Abstinence
L. Psychosocial
O. Domestic Violence

20. Using the Across and Down clues, write the correct words in the numbered grid below.

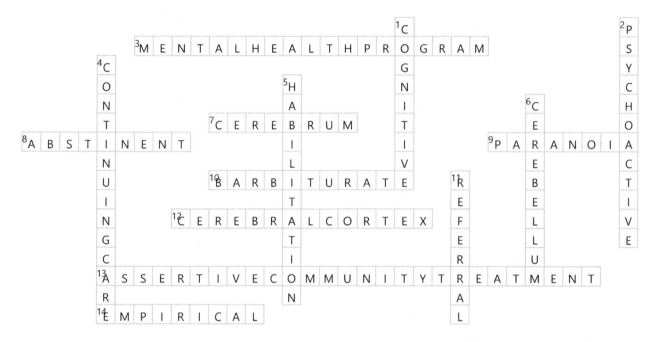

ACROSS

3. An organized array of services and interventions with a primary focus on treating mental health disorders, whether providing acute stabilization or ongoing treatment.
7. The upper part of the brain consisting of the left and right hemispheres.
8. Not using substances of abuse at any time.
9. A type of delusion, or false idea, that is unchanged by reasoned argument or proof to the contrary.
10. A type of CNS depressant sometimes prescribed to promote relaxation and sleep, but more commonly used in surgical procedures and to treat seizure disorders.
12. The gray matter that covers the surface of the cerebral hemispheres, whose functions include sensory processing and motor control along with language, reasoning, and decision-making.
13. Emphasizes shared decision making with the client as essential to the client's engagement process.
14. Relying on observation or experience rather than theoretical principles or theory.

DOWN

1. Pertaining to the mind's capacity to understand concepts and ideas.
2. Having a specific effect on the brain.
4. Care that supports a client's progress, monitors his or her condition, and can respond to a return to substance use or a return of symptoms of mental disorder.
5. Initial learning and the acquisition of skills necessary for everyday life.
6. A part of the brain that helps regulate posture, balance, and coordination. It is also involved in the processes of emotion, motivation, memory, and thought.
11. A process for facilitating client

A. Cerebral Cortex
B. Habilitation
C. Assertive Community Treatment
D. Mental Health Program
E. Cerebellum
F. Cerebrum
G. Barbiturate
H. Cognitive
I. Continuing Care
J. Empirical
K. Abstinent
L. Referral
M. Paranoia
N. Psychoactive

21. Using the Across and Down clues, write the correct words in the numbered grid below.

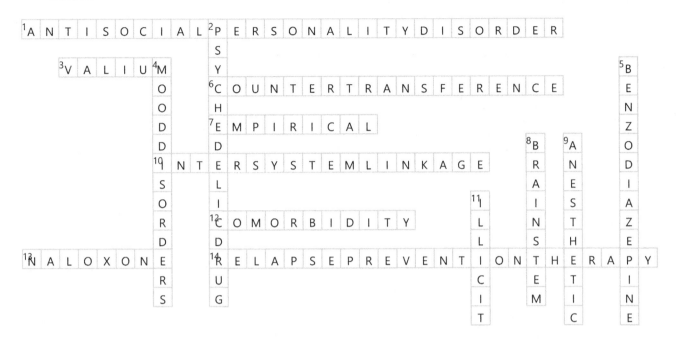

ACROSS

1. An illness whose features are a pervasive disregard for and violation of the rights of others and an inability to form meaningful interpersonal relationships.
3. Brand name for benzodiazepine diazepam.
6. The feelings, reactions, biases, and images from the past that the clinician may project onto the client with cod.
7. Relying on observation or experience rather than theoretical principles or theory.
10. Connections between substance abuse treatment and mental health systems that allow collaboration. Necessary because these are the primary care systems for persons with cod.
12. When two disorders or illnesses occur in the same person.
13. An opioid antagonist medication approved by the FDA to reverse an opioid overdose.
14. A variety of interventions designed to teach individuals who are trying to maintain health behavior changes how to anticipate and cope with the problem of relapse.

DOWN

2. A drug that distorts perception, thought, and feeling. This term is typically used to refer to drugs with hallucinogenic effects.
4. A psychological disorder characterized by the elevation or lowering of a person's mood, such as depression or bipolar disorder.
5. A type of CNS depressant sometimes prescribed to relieve anxiety, panic, or acute stress reactions. Some benzodiazepines are prescribed short-term to promote sleep.
8. A group of brain structures that process sensory information and control basic functions needed for survival such as breathing, heart rate, blood pressure, and arousal.
9. A drug that causes insensitivity to pain and is used for surgeries and other medical procedures.
11. Illegal or forbidden by law.

A. Valium
D. Anesthetic
G. Illicit
J. Relapse Prevention Therapy
M. Comorbidity

B. Naloxone
E. Antisocial Personality Disorder
H. Psychedelic Drug
K. Brainstem
N. Mood Disorders

C. Intersystem Linkage
F. Benzodiazepine
I. Countertransference
L. Empirical

22. Using the Across and Down clues, write the correct words in the numbered grid below.

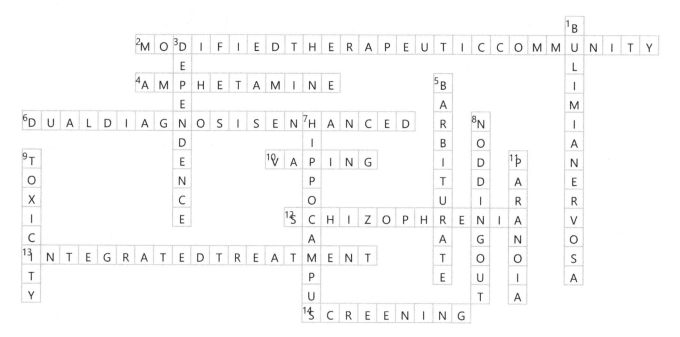

ACROSS

2. A therapeutic community whose approach to treatment adapts the principles and methods of the therapeutic community to the circumstances of the cod client.
4. A stimulant drug that acts on the central nervous system (CNS).
6. Of or pertaining to programs that have a higher than average level of integration of substance abuse and mental health treatment services.
10. Inhaling the aerosol or vapor from an electronic cigarette, e-vaporizer, or other device.
12. A type of psychosis where persons are subject to hallucinations occurring in the absence of insight into their pathological nature.
13. Any mechanism by which treatment interventions for co-occurring disorders are combined within the context of a primary treatment relationship or service setting.
14. A formal process of testing to determine whether a client warrants further attention at the current time for a particular disorder.

DOWN

1. An illness whose essential feature is binge eating and inappropriate compensatory methods to prevent weight gain.
3. A condition that can occur with the regular use of illicit or some prescription drugs, even if taken as prescribed.
5. A type of CNS depressant sometimes prescribed to promote relaxation and sleep, but more commonly used in surgical procedures and to treat seizure disorders.
7. An area of the brain crucial for learning and memory.
8. Slang term for the early stages of depressant-induced sleep.
9. Poisonous nature; poisonous quality.
11. A type of delusion, or false idea, that is unchanged by reasoned argument or proof to the contrary.

A. Integrated Treatment
C. Vaping
E. Toxicity
G. Dual Diagnosis Enhanced
I. Hippocampus
K. Amphetamine
M. Schizophrenia

B. Modified Therapeutic Community
D. Dependence
F. Paranoia
H. Screening
J. Nodding Out
L. Barbiturate
N. Bulimia Nervosa

23. Using the Across and Down clues, write the correct words in the numbered grid below.

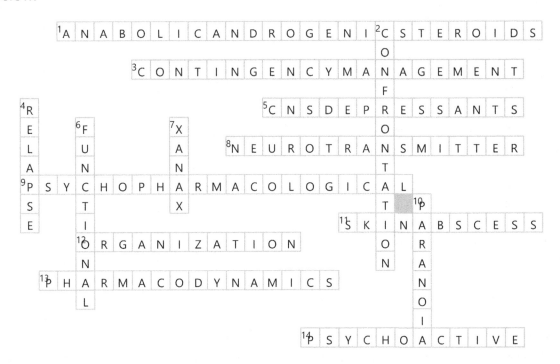

ACROSS

1. Synthetic substances similar to the male hormone testosterone.
3. A treatment approach based on providing incentives to support positive behavior change.
5. A class of drugs that include sedatives, tranquilizers, and hypnotics.
8. A chemical compound that acts as a messenger to carry signals from one nerve cell to another.
9. Pertaining to medications used to treat mental illnesses.
11. A collection of pus formed as a result of bacterial infection.
12. An entity that provides mental health services in two or three service settings and is not classified as a psychiatric or general hospital or as a residential treatment center.
13. The way a drug acts on the body.
14. Having a specific effect on the brain.

DOWN

2. A form of interpersonal exchange in which individuals present to each other their observations of, and reactions to, behaviors and attitudes that are matters of concern.
4. In drug addiction, relapse is the return to drug use after an attempt to stop.
6. Pertaining to a person's ability to carry out tasks.
7. Brand name for benzodiazepine alprazolam.
10. A type of delusion, or false idea, that is unchanged by reasoned argument or proof to the contrary.

A. Organization
D. Functional
G. Psychopharmacological
J. Confrontation
M. Anabolic Androgenic Steroids
B. CNS Depressants
E. Pharmacodynamics
H. Contingency Management
K. Paranoia
N. Skin Abscess
C. Neurotransmitter
F. Relapse
I. Psychoactive
L. Xanax

24. Using the Across and Down clues, write the correct words in the numbered grid below.

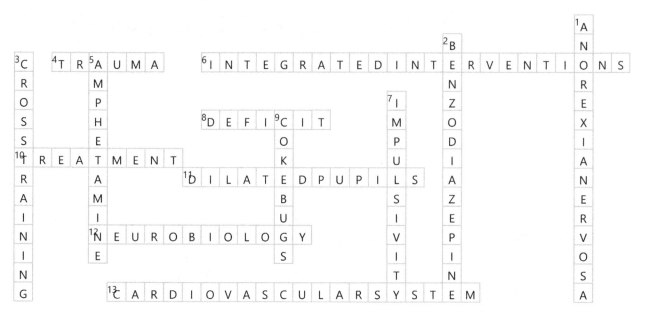

ACROSS

4. Violent mental or physical harm to a person, damage to an organ, etc.
6. Specific treatment strategies in which interventions for two or more disorders are combined in a single session or interaction, or in a series of interactions or multiple sessions.
8. In the context of substance abuse treatment, disability, or inability to function fully.
10. Substance abuse treatment is an organized array of services and interventions with a primary focus on treating substance abuse disorders.
11. Pupils that have become temporarily enlarged.
12. The study of the anatomy, function, and diseases of the brain and nervous system.
13. The system consisting of the heart and blood vessels. It delivers nutrients and oxygen to all cells in the body.

DOWN

1. A disorder in which the individual refuses to maintain a normal body weight, is afraid of gaining weight, and exhibits a significant disturbance in the perception of body shape.
2. A type of CNS depressant sometimes prescribed to relieve anxiety, panic, or acute stress reactions. Some benzodiazepines are prescribed short-term to promote sleep.
3. The simultaneous provision of material and training to persons from more than one discipline.
5. A stimulant drug that acts on the central nervous system (CNS).
7. A tendency to act without foresight or regard for consequences and to prioritize immediate rewards over long-term goals.
9. Slang term for tactile hallucinations that feel like bugs crawling on or under the skin.

A. Dilated Pupils
B. Benzodiazepine
C. Coke Bugs
D. Integrated Interventions
E. Neurobiology
F. Impulsivity
G. Amphetamine
H. Anorexia Nervosa
I. Treatment
J. Cross Training
K. Cardiovascular System
L. Trauma
M. Deficit

25. Using the Across and Down clues, write the correct words in the numbered grid below.

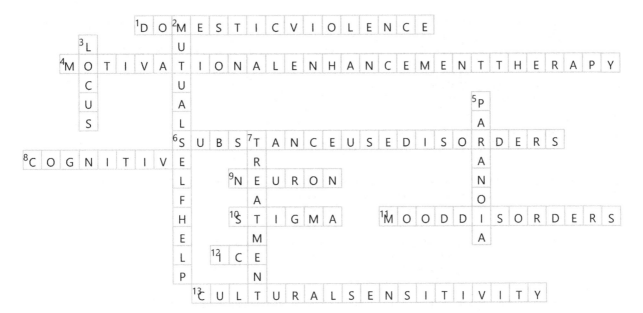

ACROSS

1. The use of emotional, psychological, sexual, or physical force by one family member or intimate partner to control another.
4. A counseling approach that uses motivational interviewing techniques to help individuals resolve any uncertainties they have about stopping their substance use.
6. A class of substance-related disorders that includes both substance abuse and substance dependence.
8. Pertaining to the mind's capacity to understand concepts and ideas.
9. A unique type of cell found in the brain and throughout the body that specializes in the transmission and processing of information.
10. A negative association attached to some activity or condition. A cause of shame or embarrassment.
11. A psychological disorder characterized by the elevation or lowering of a person's mood, such as depression or bipolar disorder.
12. Slang term for Smoke able methamphetamine.
13. The capacity and willingness of a clinician or other service provider to be open to working with issues of culture and diversity.

DOWN

2. An approach to recovery from substance use disorders that emphasizes personal responsibility, self-management, and clients' helping one another.
3. A place or a setting for some activity.
5. Extreme and unreasonable distrust of others.
7. Substance abuse treatment is an organized array of services and interventions with a primary focus on treating substance abuse disorders.

A. Mutual Self Help
B. Domestic Violence
C. Neuron
D. Mood Disorders
E. Locus
F. Cultural Sensitivity
G. Ice
H. Cognitive
I. Paranoia
J. Stigma
K. Treatment
L. Motivational Enhancement Therapy
M. Substance Use Disorders

Multiple Choice
From the words provided for each clue, provide the letter of the word which best matches the clue.

1. ____ A treatment program that actively combines substance abuse and mental health interventions to treat disorders, related problems, and the whole person more effectively.
A. Substance Dependence   B. Intersystem Linkage   C. Fully Integrated Program   D. Suicidality

2. ____ Pleasurable feelings that reinforce behavior and encourage repetition.
A. Injection Drug Use   B. Paranoia   C. Central Nervous System   D. Reward

3. ____ An ability, capacity, skill, or set of skills.
A. Competency   B. Therapeutic Alliance   C. Addiction   D. Withdrawal

4. ____ A treatment program with the capacity to provide treatment for one disorder, but that also screens for other disorders and is able to access necessary consultations.
A. System   B. Grounding   C. Barbiturate   D. Basic Program

5. ____ A long-acting opioid antagonist medication that prevents receptors from being activated by other opioids. Naltrexone is used to treat alcohol and opioid use disorders.
A. Slurred Speech   B. Brainstem   C. Naltrexone   D. Neuroleptic Medication

6. ____ A class of substance-related disorders that includes both substance abuse and substance dependence.
A. Basal Ganglia   B. Flashback   C. Substance Use Disorders   D. Practice Improvement Collaborative

7. ____ A chemical substance that binds to and blocks the activation of certain receptors on cells, preventing a biological response. Naloxone is an example of an opioid receptor antagonist.
A. Trauma   B. Cerebral Hemispheres   C. Antagonist   D. Mental Health Program

8. ____ Aspects of a treatment program that address difficult-to-treat problems, such as finding childcare while in treatment, arranging for proper housing, and finding employment.
A. Paranoia   B. Detoxification   C. Wraparound Services   D. Serotonin

9. ____ A clinician's judgment or estimate of how well a disorder will respond to treatment.
A. Ecstasy   B. Psychoactive   C. Prognosis   D. Attention Deficit Disorder

10. ____ A drug used to treat psychosis, especially schizophrenia.
A. Neuroleptic Medication   B. Withdrawal   C. Addiction Only Services   D. Cannabis

11. ____ A therapeutic community whose approach to treatment adapts the principles and methods of the therapeutic community to the circumstances of the cod client.
A. Integrated Treatment   B. Modified Therapeutic Community   C. Barbiturate   D. Prefrontal Cortex

12. ____ A therapeutic approach that seeks to modify negative or self-defeating thoughts and behavior.
A. Cultural Proficiency   B. Serotonin   C. Acculturated   D. Cognitive Behavioral Therapy

13. ____ Therapy groups in which recovery skills for co-occurring disorders are discussed.
A. Dual Recovery Groups   B. Risk Factors   C. Protease Inhibitor   D. Cognitive Behavioral Therapy

14. ____ Approaches that actively seek out persons in a community who may have substance use disorders and engage them in substance abuse treatment.
A. Serotonin   B. Ice   C. Dual Recovery Groups   D. Outreach Strategy

15. ____ A neurotransmitter involved in a broad range of effects on perception, movement, and emotions. Serotonin and its receptors are the targets of most hallucinogens.
A. Intersystem Linkage   B. Toxicity   C. Serotonin   D. Buprenorphine

16. Pupils that have become temporarily enlarged.
    A. Cage Questionnaire   B. Mutual Self Help   C. Dilated Pupils   D. Consultation

17. No one set of treatment interventions constitutes integrated treatment.
    A. Service Integration   B. Benzodiazepine   C. Pharmacotherapy   D. Receptor

18. In the context of treatment programs, consultation is a traditional type of informal relationship among treatment providers, such as a referral or a request for exchanging information.
    A. Quadrants of Care   B. Consultation   C. Treatment   D. Amphetamine

19. Legally forced or compelled.
    A. Coerced   B. Ventral Striatum   C. Cage Questionnaire   D. Injection Drug Use

20. A medical term meaning that major disease symptoms are eliminated or diminished below a pre-determined harmful level.
    A. Psychosis   B. Serotonin   C. Remission   D. Domestic Violence

21. Initial learning and the acquisition of skills necessary for everyday life.
    A. Bulimia Nervosa   B. Substance Dependence   C. Flashback   D. Habilitation

22. Mind-altering.
    A. Psychotropic   B. Toxicity   C. Neurotransmitter   D. Ventral Striatum

23. An inflammation of the liver, with accompanying liver cell damage and risk of death.
    A. Hepatitis   B. Hippocampus   C. Relapse   D. Paranoia

24. A type of relationship between client and clinician in which both are working cooperatively toward the same goals, with mutual respect and understanding.
    A. Delirium Tremens   B. Psychopharmacological   C. Therapeutic Alliance   D. Engagement

25. An approach to recovery from substance use disorders that emphasizes personal responsibility, self-management, and clients' helping one another.
    A. Mutual Self Help   B. Intranasal   C. Craving   D. Receptor

26. An area of the brain crucial for learning and memory.
    A. Consultation   B. Hippocampus   C. Cultural Proficiency   D. Tolerance

27. A brain region in the ventral striatum involved in motivation and reward.
    A. Nucleus Accumbens   B. Abstinent   C. Cognitive Behavioral Therapy   D. Assertive Community Treatment

28. A clearing of toxins from the body.
    A. Adderall   B. Comorbidity   C. Personality Disorders   D. Detoxification

29. Synthetic substances similar to the male hormone testosterone.
    A. Anabolic Androgenic Steroids   B. Treatment Retention   C. Motivational Enhancement Therapy   D. Relapse

30. Interconnected brain structures that process feelings, emotions, and motivations. It is also important for learning and memory.
    A. Cerebellum   B. Limbic System   C. Outreach Strategy   D. Ventral Striatum

31. A brief alcoholism screening tool.
    A. Pharmacotherapy   B. Cage Questionnaire   C. Toxicity   D. Modified Therapeutic Community

32. The study of the anatomy, function, and diseases of the brain and nervous system.
    A. Hallucinogens   B. Neurobiology   C. Partial Agonist   D. Modified Therapeutic Community

33. Not using substances of abuse at any time.
   A. Illicit B. Cage Questionnaire C. Abstinent D. Cannabinoids

34. An opioid partial agonist medication prescribed for the treatment of opioid addiction that relieves drug cravings without producing the high or dangerous side effects of other opioids.
   A. Competency B. Tolerance C. Buprenorphine D. Cerebral Hemispheres

35. Connections between substance abuse treatment and mental health systems that allow collaboration. Necessary because these are the primary care systems for persons with cod.
   A. Trauma B. Hippocampus C. Relapse D. Intersystem Linkage

36. Slang term for methylenedioxymethamphetamine, a member of the amphetamine family. At lower doses, MDMA causes distortions of emotional perceptions.
   A. Crack B. Practice Improvement Collaborative C. Assertive Community Treatment D. Ecstasy

37. The receptor in the brain that recognizes and binds cannabinoids that are produced in the brain or outside the body.
   A. Cage Questionnaire B. Quadrants of Care C. Cannabinoid Receptor D. Bulimia Nervosa

38. The feelings, reactions, biases, and images from the past that the client with cod may project onto the clinician.
   A. Comorbidity B. Pharmacotherapy C. Locus D. Transference

39. The act of administering drugs by injection. Blood-borne viruses, like HIV and hepatitis, can be transmitted via shared needles or other drug injection equipment.
   A. Integration B. Cognitive Behavioral Therapy C. Service Integration D. Injection Drug Use

40. A measure or estimate of a person's likelihood of committing suicide. A high-risk behavior associated with cod, especially (although not limited to) serious mood disorders.
   A. Dual Diagnosis Enhanced B. Suicidality C. Benzodiazepine D. Injection Drug Use

41. The system consisting of the nerves in the brain and spinal cord.
   A. Barbiturate B. Electronic Cigarette C. Agonist D. Central Nervous System

42. A process of change through which people with substance use disorders improve their health and wellness, live self-directed lives, and strive to reach their full potential.
   A. Co Occurring Disorders B. Recovery C. Combined Psychopharmacological Intervention D. Adderall

43. A part of the brain that controls many bodily functions, including eating, drinking, body temperature regulation, and the release of many hormones.
   A. Treatment B. Treatment Retention C. Hypothalamus D. Risk Factors

44. A broad array of services organized into programs intended to treat substance use disorders.
   A. Dual Recovery Groups B. Substance Abuse Treatment System C. System D. Cognitive

45. A formal process of testing to determine whether a client warrants further attention at the current time for a particular disorder.
   A. Central Nervous System B. Screening C. Stigma D. Benzodiazepine

46. The feelings, reactions, biases, and images from the past that the clinician may project onto the client with cod.
   A. Quadrants of Care B. Locus C. Drug Abuse D. Countertransference

47. A tendency to act without foresight or regard for consequences and to prioritize immediate rewards over long-term goals.
   A. Psychoactive B. Impulsivity C. Legal Problems D. Mood Disorders

48. In drug addiction, relapse is the return to drug use after an attempt to stop.
   A. Relapse B. Psychosocial C. Brainstem D. Cage Questionnaire

49. An illness whose essential feature is persistent and recurrent maladaptive gambling behavior that disrupts personal, family, or vocational pursuits.
A. Pathological Gambling   B. Buprenorphine   C. Functional   D. Paranoia

50. An illness whose essential feature is excessive anxiety and worry.
A. Analgesics   B. Hippocampus   C. Anxiety Disorder   D. Reward System

51. A negative association attached to some activity or condition. A cause of shame or embarrassment.
A. Stigma   B. Psychotropic Medication   C. Transference   D. Cardiovascular System

52. A brand name amphetamine for treating ADHD.
A. Psychedelic Drug   B. Psychosocial   C. Opioid   D. Adderall

53. An organized array of services and interventions with a primary focus on treating mental health disorders, whether providing acute stabilization or ongoing treatment.
A. Combined Psychopharmacological Intervention   B. Mental Health Program   C. Cognitive Behavioral Therapy   D. Schizophrenia

54. A set of negative attitudes and beliefs that motivate people to fear and discriminate against other people.
A. Stigma   B. Psychopharmacological   C. Ice   D. Cognitive Behavioral Therapy

55. The use of strategies that soothe and distract the client who is experiencing intense pain or other strong emotions, helping the client anchor in the present and in reality.
A. Grounding   B. Xanax   C. Receptor   D. Ice

56. The way a drug acts on the body.
A. Neuron   B. Pharmacodynamics   C. Limbic System   D. Ecstasy

57. A process for facilitating client
A. Cardiovascular System   B. Psychotropic Medication   C. Substance Abuse   D. Referral

58. Slang term for drugs that exert a depressant effect on the central nervous system. In general, downers are sedative-hypnotic drugs, such as benzodiazepines and barbiturates.
A. Confrontation   B. Downers   C. Fully Integrated Program   D. Consultation

59. A type of delusion, or false idea, that is unchanged by reasoned argument or proof to the contrary.
A. Delirium Tremens   B. Neurotransmitter   C. Integrated Treatment   D. Paranoia

60. A condition that can occur with the regular use of illicit or some prescription drugs, even if taken as prescribed.
A. Dependence   B. Serotonin   C. Addiction   D. Integrated Treatment

61. A mental disorder that is characterized by distinct distortions of a person's mental capacity, ability to recognize reality, and relationships to others.
A. Practice Improvement Collaborative   B. Domestic Violence   C. Psychosis   D. Single State Agency

62. A sign of depressant intoxication. When people consume significant amounts of sedative-hypnotics and opioids, their speech may become garbled, mumbled, and slow.
A. Anabolic Androgenic Steroids   B. Slurred Speech   C. Abstinent   D. Pharmacotherapy

63. Driving a vehicle while impaired due to the intoxicating effects of recent drug use.
A. Substance Use Disorders   B. Cultural Sensitivity   C. Intermediate Program   D. Drugged Driving

64. A period of amnesia or memory loss, typically caused by chronic, high-dose substance abuse.
A. Blackout   B. Recovery   C. Agitation   D. Addiction

65. An opioid antagonist medication approved by the FDA to reverse an opioid overdose.
A. Ice   B. Deficit   C. Naloxone   D. Central Nervous System

66. A symptom of a seizure, characterized by twitching and jerking of the limbs.
A. Consultation   B. Convulsions   C. Paranoia   D. Acute Care

67. Drugs that have an effect on the function of the brain and that are often used to treat psychiatric disorders.
A. Dual Diagnosis Enhanced   B. Disorder   C. Paranoia   D. Psychotherapeutics

68. A form of interpersonal exchange in which individuals present to each other their observations of, and reactions to, behaviors and attitudes that are matters of concern.
A. Coke Bugs   B. Functional   C. Confrontation   D. Motivational Enhancement Therapy

69. Poisonous nature; poisonous quality.
A. Prefrontal Cortex   B. Limbic System   C. Motivational Enhancement Therapy   D. Toxicity

70. A state in which a mental or physical disorder has been overcome or a disease process halted.
A. Formal Collaboration   B. Cannabis   C. Remission   D. Comorbidity

71. A class of drugs that include sedatives, tranquilizers, and hypnotics.
A. Abstinence   B. CNS Depressants   C. Coerced   D. Opioid

72. Hampered or held back from being able to do some mental or physical task.
A. Unsteady Gait   B. Screening   C. Overdose   D. Impaired

73. An overdose occurs when a person uses enough of a drug to produce a life-threatening reaction or death.
A. Modified Therapeutic Community   B. Mental Health Program   C. Relapse   D. Overdose

74. When two disorders or illnesses occur in the same person.
A. Anabolic Androgenic Steroids   B. Comorbidity   C. Nucleus Accumbens   D. Dependence

75. Extreme and unreasonable distrust of others.
A. Cross Training   B. Paranoia   C. Continuing Care   D. Relapse

76. A drug that has an effect on the mind and sometimes affects behavior as well.
A. Habilitation   B. Illicit   C. Psychotropic Medication   D. Paranoia

77. Mentally and physically in harmony with and connected to the culture in which one lives.
A. Psychosis   B. Acculturated   C. Legal Problems   D. Naltrexone

78. A medical illness caused by disordered use of a substance or substances.
A. Relapse Prevention Therapy   B. Drug Abuse   C. Constricted Pupils   D. Substance Use Disorder

79. A sudden but temporary recurrence of aspects of a drug experience that may occur days, weeks, or even more than a year after using drugs that cause hallucinations.
A. Mental Health Program   B. Flashback   C. CNS Depressants   D. Opioid Receptors

80. The capacity of a service provider to understand and work effectively in accordance with the cultural beliefs and practices of persons from a given ethnic
A. Cross Training   B. Transference   C. Cultural Competence   D. Functional

81. A treatment program that focuses primarily on one disorder without substantial modification to its usual treatment.
A. Treatment   B. THC   C. Intermediate Program   D. System

82. An area in the brainstem that contains dopamine neurons that make up a key part of the brain reward system, which also includes the nucleus accumbens and prefrontal cortex.
A. Ventral Tegmental Area   B. Cannabidiol   C. Attention Deficit Disorder   D. Psychotherapeutics

83. Any mechanism by which treatment interventions for co-occurring disorders are combined within the context of a primary treatment relationship or service setting.
A. Integrated Treatment   B. Intersystem Linkage   C. Psychopharmacological   D. Engagement

84. The way a drug is taken into the body. Drugs are most commonly taken by eating, drinking, inhaling, injecting, snorting, or smoking.
A. Abstinence   B. Practice Improvement Collaborative   C. Marijuana   D. Route of Administration

85. A treatment approach based on providing incentives to support positive behavior change.
A. Intranasal   B. Motivational Enhancement Therapy   C. Valium   D. Contingency Management

86. A brain chemical, classified as a neurotransmitter, found in regions of the brain that regulate movement, emotion, motivation, and reinforcement of rewarding behavior.
A. Dopamine   B. Functional   C. Habilitation   D. Cognitive Behavioral Therapy

87. A client's commitment to and maintenance of treatment in all of its forms. A successful engagement program helps clients view the treatment facility as an important resource.
A. Agonist   B. Engagement   C. Serotonin   D. Coke Bugs

88. Brand name for benzodiazepine diazepam.
A. Neurotransmitter   B. Cognitive Behavioral Therapy   C. Naloxone   D. Valium

89. Rigid, inflexible, and maladaptive behavior patterns of sufficient severity to cause internal distress or significant impairment in functioning.
A. Personality Disorders   B. Detoxification   C. Overdose   D. Xanax

90. A condition in which higher doses of a drug are required to achieve the desired effect.
A. Pharmacotherapy   B. Tolerance   C. Xanax   D. Modified Therapeutic Community

91. Specific treatment strategies in which interventions for two or more disorders are combined in a single session or interaction, or in a series of interactions or multiple sessions.
A. Integrated Interventions   B. Impulsivity   C. Injection Drug Use   D. Valium

92. An approach to treatment that maintains that the form or frequency of behavior can be altered through a planned and organized system of consequences.
A. Acculturated   B. Partial Agonist   C. Legal Problems   D. Contingency Management

93. Treatment using medications.
A. Screening   B. Contingency Management   C. CNS Depressants   D. Pharmacotherapy

94. The front part of the brain responsible for reasoning, planning, problem solving, and other higher cognitive functions.
A. Quadrants of Care   B. Electronic Cigarette   C. Substance Dependence   D. Prefrontal Cortex

95. A disorder in which the individual refuses to maintain a normal body weight, is afraid of gaining weight, and exhibits a significant disturbance in the perception of body shape.
A. Personality Disorders   B. Reward   C. Hepatitis   D. Anorexia Nervosa

96. Slang term used to describe drugs that have a stimulating effect on the central nervous system. Examples include cocaine, caffeine, and amphetamines.
A. Uppers   B. Screening   C. Psychotropic   D. Naltrexone

97. A stimulant drug that acts on the central nervous system (CNS).
A. Serotonin   B. Amphetamine   C. Disorder   D. Substance Abuse

98. Relating to the act or process of thinking, understanding, learning, and remembering.
A. Cognition   B. Ventral Tegmental Area   C. Psychotherapeutics   D. Relapse Prevention Therapy

99. The use of emotional, psychological, sexual, or physical force by one family member or intimate partner to control another.
A. Continuing Care   B. Domestic Violence   C. Antagonist   D. Concomitant Treatment

100. A chemical substance that binds to and activates certain receptors on cells, causing a biological response.
A. Co Occurring Disorders   B. Agonist   C. Deficit   D. Basic Program

From the words provided for each clue, provide the letter of the word which best matches the clue.

101. Approaches that actively seek out persons in a community who may have substance use disorders and engage them in substance abuse treatment.
A. Stigma   B. Outreach Strategy   C. Cross Training   D. Brainstem

102. A clinician's judgment or estimate of how well a disorder will respond to treatment.
A. Route of Administration   B. Blackout   C. Opioid   D. Prognosis

103. When two disorders or illnesses occur in the same person.
A. Cognitive   B. Comorbidity   C. Basal Ganglia   D. Neuroleptic Medication

104. An involuntary and rhythmic movement in the muscles, most often in the hands, feet, jaw, tongue, or head.
A. Nodding Out   B. Tremor   C. Quadrants of Care   D. Domestic Violence

105. Not using drugs or alcohol.
A. Abstinence   B. Legal Problems   C. Cannabis   D. Combined Psychopharmacological Intervention

106. A measure or estimate of a person's likelihood of committing suicide. A high-risk behavior associated with cod, especially (although not limited to) serious mood disorders.
A. Psychosis   B. Mental Disorder   C. Ice   D. Suicidality

107. A state of confusion accompanied by trembling and vivid hallucinations.
A. Neurobiology   B. Delirium Tremens   C. Outreach Strategy   D. Toxicity

108. A part of the brain that helps regulate posture, balance, and coordination. It is also involved in the processes of emotion, motivation, memory, and thought.
A. Transference   B. Cannabinoids   C. Practice Improvement Collaborative   D. Cerebellum

109. Pleasurable feelings that reinforce behavior and encourage repetition.
A. Therapeutic Community   B. Xanax   C. Reward   D. Psychotropic

110. Illegal or forbidden by law.
A. Psychopharmacological   B. Therapeutic Alliance   C. Illicit   D. Countertransference

111. A maladaptive pattern of substance use leading to clinically significant impairment or distress.
A. Substance Dependence   B. Screening   C. Grounding   D. Antagonist

112. A conceptual framework that classifies clients in four basic groups based on relative symptom severity, rather than by diagnosis.
A. Quadrants of Care   B. Consultation   C. Trauma   D. Route of Administration

113. Slang term for methylenedioxymethamphetamine, a member of the amphetamine family. At lower doses, MDMA causes distortions of emotional perceptions.
A. Remission   B. Ecstasy   C. Anesthetic   D. Hallucinations

114. Another name for the marijuana plant, cannabis sativa.
A. Recovery B. Mutual Self Help C. Cannabis D. Advanced Program

115. Encompasses the specific treatment strategies, therapies, or techniques that are used to treat one or more disorders.
A. Substance Use Disorders B. Intervention C. Anxiety Disorder D. Tremor

116. A group of medications that reduce pain.
A. Withdrawal B. Substance Abuse Treatment System C. Opioid Receptors D. Analgesics

117. Relating to the act or process of thinking, understanding, learning, and remembering.
A. Cultural Destructiveness B. Cognition C. Substance Abuse Treatment System D. Paranoia

118. Mentally and physically in harmony with and connected to the culture in which one lives.
A. Serotonin B. Acculturated C. Buprenorphine D. Paranoia

119. Brand name for benzodiazepine diazepam.
A. Valium B. Blackout C. Substance Use Disorders D. Neuron

120. A type of delusion, or false idea, that is unchanged by reasoned argument or proof to the contrary.
A. Remission B. Barbiturate C. Psychoactive D. Paranoia

121. A powerful, often overwhelming desire to use drugs.
A. Treatment B. Craving C. Abstinent D. Tolerance

122. Occurs when the nature of the client's disabilities requires more specific information and more complex and targeted intervention.
A. Competency B. Blackout C. Acculturated D. Formal Collaboration

123. A clearing of toxins from the body.
A. Cannabinoid Receptor B. Practice Improvement Collaborative C. Wraparound Services D. Detoxification

124. A treatment program that focuses primarily on one disorder without substantial modification to its usual treatment.
A. Brainstem B. Intermediate Program C. Confrontation D. Therapeutic Alliance

125. A condition in which higher doses of a drug are required to achieve the desired effect.
A. Methadone B. Tolerance C. Flashback D. Ice

126. A unique type of cell found in the brain and throughout the body that specializes in the transmission and processing of information.
A. Overdose B. Neuron C. Electronic Cigarette D. Xanax

127. A restless inability to keep still.
A. Drug Abuse B. Addiction C. Agitation D. Therapeutic Community

128. A class of drugs that include sedatives, tranquilizers, and hypnotics.
A. Cognitive B. CNS Depressants C. Intranasal D. Cannabinoids

129. A stimulant drug that acts on the central nervous system (CNS).
A. Amphetamine B. Wraparound Services C. Uppers D. Downers

130. The feelings, reactions, biases, and images from the past that the client with cod may project onto the clinician.
A. Drugged Driving B. Transference C. Consultation D. Treatment Retention

131. A molecule located on the surface of a cell that recognizes specific chemicals and transmits the chemical message into the cell.
A. Psychotropic Medication   B. Craving   C. Cerebral Cortex   D. Receptor

132. An approach to recovery from substance use disorders that emphasizes personal responsibility, self-management, and clients' helping one another.
A. Suicidality   B. Mutual Self Help   C. Drugged Driving   D. CNS Depressants

133. Programs that by law or regulation, by choice, or for lack of resources cannot accommodate patients who have psychiatric illnesses that require ongoing treatment.
A. Vaping   B. Cultural Competence   C. Addiction Only Services   D. Psychosis

134. A counseling approach that uses motivational interviewing techniques to help individuals resolve any uncertainties they have about stopping their substance use.
A. Relapse Prevention Therapy   B. Neuroleptic Medication   C. Motivational Enhancement Therapy   D. Detoxification

135. The Indian hemp plant cannabis sativa; also called "pot" and "weed."
A. Marijuana   B. Advanced Program   C. Reward   D. Relapse Prevention Therapy

136. A brain circuit that includes the ventral tegmental area, the nucleus accumbens, and the prefrontal cortex.
A. Risk Factors   B. Reward System   C. Concomitant Treatment   D. Neuroleptic Medication

137. A sudden but temporary recurrence of aspects of a drug experience that may occur days, weeks, or even more than a year after using drugs that cause hallucinations.
A. Dependence   B. Fully Integrated Program   C. Flashback   D. Naloxone

138. Cocaine that has been chemically modified so that it will become a gas vapor when heated at relatively low temperatures.
A. Psychotherapeutics   B. Convulsions   C. Crack   D. Paranoia

139. Delta-9-tetrahydrocannabinol; the main mind-altering ingredient in marijuana.
A. Empirical   B. Coke Bugs   C. Cannabidiol   D. THC

140. Keeping clients involved in treatment activities and receiving required services.
A. Treatment Retention   B. Anabolic Androgenic Steroids   C. Relapse   D. Psychoactive

141. Connections between substance abuse treatment and mental health systems that allow collaboration. Necessary because these are the primary care systems for persons with cod.
A. Toxicity   B. Intersystem Linkage   C. Cultural Sensitivity   D. Wraparound Services

142. A place or a setting for some activity.
A. Locus   B. Abstinent   C. Competency   D. Recovery

143. The front part of the brain responsible for reasoning, planning, problem solving, and other higher cognitive functions.
A. Psychotherapeutics   B. Schizophrenia   C. Prefrontal Cortex   D. Contingency Management

144. A medical term meaning that major disease symptoms are eliminated or diminished below a pre-determined harmful level.
A. Intervention   B. Outreach Strategy   C. Ventral Striatum   D. Remission

145. A brand name amphetamine for treating ADHD.
A. Route of Administration   B. Convulsions   C. Adderall   D. Valium

146. _____ A broad group of drugs that cause distortions of sensory perception. The prototype hallucinogen is lysergic acid diethylamide (LSD).
A. Hallucinogens   B. Benzodiazepine   C. Empirical   D. Psychotropic Medication

147. _____ The gray matter that covers the surface of the cerebral hemispheres, whose functions include sensory processing and motor control along with language, reasoning, and decision-making.
A. Locus   B. Buprenorphine   C. Cerebral Cortex   D. Substance Abuse Treatment System

148. _____ The study of the anatomy, function, and diseases of the brain and nervous system.
A. Serotonin   B. Neurobiology   C. Co Occurring Disorders   D. Abstinence

149. _____ A chemical substance that binds to and blocks the activation of certain receptors on cells, preventing a biological response. Naloxone is an example of an opioid receptor antagonist.
A. Countertransference   B. Antagonist   C. Toxicity   D. Serotonin

150. _____ The use of emotional, psychological, sexual, or physical force by one family member or intimate partner to control another.
A. Abstinent   B. Electronic Cigarette   C. Domestic Violence   D. Cognitive Behavioral Therapy

151. _____ Able to spread by an agent such as a virus or bacterium.
A. Antagonist   B. Infectious   C. Locus   D. Reward System

152. _____ A disorder in which the individual refuses to maintain a normal body weight, is afraid of gaining weight, and exhibits a significant disturbance in the perception of body shape.
A. Toxicity   B. Psychotropic   C. Anorexia Nervosa   D. Grounding

153. _____ A drug used to treat psychosis, especially schizophrenia.
A. Quadrants of Care   B. Contingency Management   C. Neuroleptic Medication   D. Therapeutic Alliance

154. _____ Substance abuse treatment is an organized array of services and interventions with a primary focus on treating substance abuse disorders.
A. Ventral Tegmental Area   B. Treatment   C. Neurotransmitter   D. Functional

155. _____ Practices or actions through which an individual shows that he or she regards other cultures as inferior to the dominant culture.
A. Mental Disorder   B. Cultural Sensitivity   C. Cultural Destructiveness   D. Acculturated

156. _____ In the context of treatment programs, consultation is a traditional type of informal relationship among treatment providers, such as a referral or a request for exchanging information.
A. Impulsivity   B. Consultation   C. Intersystem Linkage   D. Acute Care

157. _____ Legally forced or compelled.
A. Coerced   B. Brainstem   C. Psychosocial   D. Intranasal

158. _____ A drug that distorts perception, thought, and feeling. This term is typically used to refer to drugs with hallucinogenic effects.
A. Receptor   B. Pharmacotherapy   C. Anorexia Nervosa   D. Psychedelic Drug

159. _____ The simultaneous provision of material and training to persons from more than one discipline.
A. Intranasal   B. Habilitation   C. Abstinent   D. Cross Training

160. _____ Crooked, meandering, and uncoordinated walk, typical of alcohol-impaired people.
A. Comorbidity   B. Modified Therapeutic Community   C. Unsteady Gait   D. Hippocampus

161. _____ A set of negative attitudes and beliefs that motivate people to fear and discriminate against other people.
A. Screening   B. Substance Dependence   C. Substance Use Disorders   D. Stigma

162. Slang term used to describe drugs that have a stimulating effect on the central nervous system. Examples include cocaine, caffeine, and amphetamines.
A. Uppers   B. Flashback   C. Grounding   D. Paranoia

163. Not using substances of abuse at any time.
A. Abstinent   B. Basic Program   C. Countertransference   D. Substance Dependence

164. A treatment program that actively combines substance abuse and mental health interventions to treat disorders, related problems, and the whole person more effectively.
A. Flashback   B. Competency   C. Fully Integrated Program   D. Cannabis

165. Community-based initiatives that link treatment providers, researchers, and policymakers in order to build a strong foundation to effect action.
A. Habilitation   B. Practice Improvement Collaborative   C. Dilated Pupils   D. Benzodiazepine

166. A symptom of a seizure, characterized by twitching and jerking of the limbs.
A. Convulsions   B. Nodding Out   C. Risk Factors   D. Abstinent

167. Treatment episodes in which a client receives medications both to reduce cravings for substances and to medicate a mental disorder.
A. Paraphernalia   B. Combined Psychopharmacological Intervention   C. Treatment   D. Neuron

168. An area of the brain crucial for learning and memory.
A. Agitation   B. Wraparound Services   C. Hippocampus   D. Route of Administration

169. The capacity and willingness of a clinician or other service provider to be open to working with issues of culture and diversity.
A. Treatment   B. Cultural Sensitivity   C. Treatment Retention   D. Psychedelic Drug

170. A therapeutic approach that seeks to modify negative or self-defeating thoughts and behavior.
A. Injection Drug Use   B. Cognitive Behavioral Therapy   C. Substance Dependence   D. Coerced

171. A type of relationship between client and clinician in which both are working cooperatively toward the same goals, with mutual respect and understanding.
A. Serotonin   B. Therapeutic Alliance   C. Continuing Care   D. Reward

172. Treatment of two or more mental or physical disorders at the same time.
A. Dopamine   B. Concomitant Treatment   C. Craving   D. Ecstasy

173. Pertaining to a person's ability to carry out tasks.
A. Functional   B. Impaired   C. Relapse   D. Xanax

174. A therapeutic community whose approach to treatment adapts the principles and methods of the therapeutic community to the circumstances of the cod client.
A. Wraparound Services   B. Modified Therapeutic Community   C. Intranasal   D. Opioid Receptors

175. A type of psychosis where persons are subject to hallucinations occurring in the absence of insight into their pathological nature.
A. Schizophrenia   B. Continuing Care   C. Cognition   D. Referral

176. Inhaling the aerosol or vapor from an electronic cigarette, e-vaporizer, or other device.
A. Cultural Destructiveness   B. Remission   C. Mutual Self Help   D. Vaping

177. Driving a vehicle while impaired due to the intoxicating effects of recent drug use.
A. Skin Abscess   B. Drugged Driving   C. Modified Therapeutic Community   D. Psychotherapeutics

178. Relationships among mental health and substance abuse providers in which both fields are moved into a single treatment setting and treatment regimen.
A. Dual Diagnosis Enhanced   B. Dilated Pupils   C. Integration   D. Recovery

179. A battery-operated device that people use to inhale an aerosol, which typically contains nicotine, flavorings, and other chemicals.
A. Practice Improvement Collaborative   B. Cannabinoids   C. Psychedelic Drug   D. Electronic Cigarette

180. A part of the brain that controls many bodily functions, including eating, drinking, body temperature regulation, and the release of many hormones.
A. Hypothalamus   B. Cannabidiol   C. Competency   D. Cognitive Behavioral Therapy

181. A mental disorder that is characterized by distinct distortions of a person's mental capacity, ability to recognize reality, and relationships to others.
A. Wraparound Services   B. Hallucinogens   C. Psychosis   D. Opioid

182. Pupils that have become temporarily enlarged.
A. Cultural Proficiency   B. Motivational Enhancement Therapy   C. Dilated Pupils   D. Paranoia

183. A process in which the body rids itself of a drug, or its metabolites.
A. Empirical   B. Infectious   C. Detoxification   D. Abstinence

184. A type of CNS depressant sometimes prescribed to relieve anxiety, panic, or acute stress reactions. Some benzodiazepines are prescribed short-term to promote sleep.
A. Mental Disorder   B. Cerebral Cortex   C. Benzodiazepine   D. Intersystem Linkage

185. The evaluation or estimation of the nature, quality, or ability of someone or something.
A. Psychoactive   B. Assessment   C. Comorbidity   D. Partial Agonist

186. A type of CNS depressant sometimes prescribed to promote relaxation and sleep, but more commonly used in surgical procedures and to treat seizure disorders.
A. Fully Integrated Program   B. Screening   C. Habilitation   D. Barbiturate

187. A group of brain structures that process sensory information and control basic functions needed for survival such as breathing, heart rate, blood pressure, and arousal.
A. Modified Therapeutic Community   B. Anesthetic   C. Brainstem   D. Neuroleptic Medication

188. The act of administering drugs by injection. Blood-borne viruses, like HIV and hepatitis, can be transmitted via shared needles or other drug injection equipment.
A. Cognitive Behavioral Therapy   B. Injection Drug Use   C. Hypothalamus   D. Intervention

189. Poisonous nature; poisonous quality.
A. Limbic System   B. Ice   C. Neuron   D. Toxicity

190. The area of the brain that plays an important role in positive forms of motivation, including the pleasurable effects of healthy activities like eating, socializing, and sex.
A. Basal Ganglia   B. Antisocial Personality Disorder   C. Xanax   D. Detoxification

191. Rigid, inflexible, and maladaptive behavior patterns of sufficient severity to cause internal distress or significant impairment in functioning.
A. Continuing Care   B. Cannabinoids   C. Serotonin   D. Personality Disorders

192. Interconnected brain structures that process feelings, emotions, and motivations. It is also important for learning and memory.
A. Cerebellum   B. Hypothalamus   C. Limbic System   D. Culturally Competent

193. A brain chemical, classified as a neurotransmitter, found in regions of the brain that regulate movement, emotion, motivation, and reinforcement of rewarding behavior.
A. Xanax   B. Dopamine   C. Domestic Violence   D. Grounding

194. Therapy groups in which recovery skills for co-occurring disorders are discussed.
A. Combined Psychopharmacological Intervention   B. Psychopharmacological   C. Psychotherapeutics   D. Dual Recovery Groups

195. Synthetic substances similar to the male hormone testosterone.
A. Therapeutic Alliance   B. Tolerance   C. Anabolic Androgenic Steroids   D. Coke Bugs

196. In drug addiction, relapse is the return to drug use after an attempt to stop.
A. Hallucinogens   B. Collaboration   C. Relapse   D. Ice

197. An illness whose features are a pervasive disregard for and violation of the rights of others and an inability to form meaningful interpersonal relationships.
A. Single State Agency   B. Antisocial Personality Disorder   C. Acculturated   D. Attention Deficit Disorder

198. An older diagnostic term that defined use that is unsafe, use that leads a person to fail to fulfill responsibilities or gets them in legal trouble.
A. Dually Disordered   B. Drug Abuse   C. Assertive Community Treatment   D. Recovery

199. Proteins on the surface of neurons, or other cells, that are activated by endogenous opioids, such as endorphins, and opioid drugs, such as heroin.
A. Stigma   B. Opioid Receptors   C. Domestic Violence   D. Intersystem Linkage

200. An opioid partial agonist medication prescribed for the treatment of opioid addiction that relieves drug cravings without producing the high or dangerous side effects of other opioids.
A. Cannabidiol   B. Anesthetic   C. Buprenorphine   D. Legal Problems

From the words provided for each clue, provide the letter of the word which best matches the clue.

1. __C__ A treatment program that actively combines substance abuse and mental health interventions to treat disorders, related problems, and the whole person more effectively.
   A. Substance Dependence   B. Intersystem Linkage   C. Fully Integrated Program   D. Suicidality

2. __D__ Pleasurable feelings that reinforce behavior and encourage repetition.
   A. Injection Drug Use   B. Paranoia   C. Central Nervous System   D. Reward

3. __A__ An ability, capacity, skill, or set of skills.
   A. Competency   B. Therapeutic Alliance   C. Addiction   D. Withdrawal

4. __D__ A treatment program with the capacity to provide treatment for one disorder, but that also screens for other disorders and is able to access necessary consultations.
   A. System   B. Grounding   C. Barbiturate   D. Basic Program

5. __C__ A long-acting opioid antagonist medication that prevents receptors from being activated by other opioids. Naltrexone is used to treat alcohol and opioid use disorders.
   A. Slurred Speech   B. Brainstem   C. Naltrexone   D. Neuroleptic Medication

6. __C__ A class of substance-related disorders that includes both substance abuse and substance dependence.
   A. Basal Ganglia   B. Flashback   C. Substance Use Disorders   D. Practice Improvement Collaborative

7. __C__ A chemical substance that binds to and blocks the activation of certain receptors on cells, preventing a biological response. Naloxone is an example of an opioid receptor antagonist.
   A. Trauma   B. Cerebral Hemispheres   C. Antagonist   D. Mental Health Program

8. __C__ Aspects of a treatment program that address difficult-to-treat problems, such as finding childcare while in treatment, arranging for proper housing, and finding employment.
   A. Paranoia   B. Detoxification   C. Wraparound Services   D. Serotonin

9. __C__ A clinician's judgment or estimate of how well a disorder will respond to treatment.
   A. Ecstasy   B. Psychoactive   C. Prognosis   D. Attention Deficit Disorder

10. __A__ A drug used to treat psychosis, especially schizophrenia.
    A. Neuroleptic Medication   B. Withdrawal   C. Addiction Only Services   D. Cannabis

11. __B__ A therapeutic community whose approach to treatment adapts the principles and methods of the therapeutic community to the circumstances of the cod client.
    A. Integrated Treatment   B. Modified Therapeutic Community   C. Barbiturate   D. Prefrontal Cortex

12. __D__ A therapeutic approach that seeks to modify negative or self-defeating thoughts and behavior.
    A. Cultural Proficiency   B. Serotonin   C. Acculturated   D. Cognitive Behavioral Therapy

13. __A__ Therapy groups in which recovery skills for co-occurring disorders are discussed.
    A. Dual Recovery Groups   B. Risk Factors   C. Protease Inhibitor   D. Cognitive Behavioral Therapy

14. __D__ Approaches that actively seek out persons in a community who may have substance use disorders and engage them in substance abuse treatment.
    A. Serotonin   B. Ice   C. Dual Recovery Groups   D. Outreach Strategy

15. __C__ A neurotransmitter involved in a broad range of effects on perception, movement, and emotions. Serotonin and its receptors are the targets of most hallucinogens.
    A. Intersystem Linkage   B. Toxicity   C. Serotonin   D. Buprenorphine

16. __C__ Pupils that have become temporarily enlarged.
A. Cage Questionnaire B. Mutual Self Help C. Dilated Pupils D. Consultation

17. __A__ No one set of treatment interventions constitutes integrated treatment.
A. Service Integration B. Benzodiazepine C. Pharmacotherapy D. Receptor

18. __B__ In the context of treatment programs, consultation is a traditional type of informal relationship among treatment providers, such as a referral or a request for exchanging information.
A. Quadrants of Care B. Consultation C. Treatment D. Amphetamine

19. __A__ Legally forced or compelled.
A. Coerced B. Ventral Striatum C. Cage Questionnaire D. Injection Drug Use

20. __C__ A medical term meaning that major disease symptoms are eliminated or diminished below a pre-determined harmful level.
A. Psychosis B. Serotonin C. Remission D. Domestic Violence

21. __D__ Initial learning and the acquisition of skills necessary for everyday life.
A. Bulimia Nervosa B. Substance Dependence C. Flashback D. Habilitation

22. __A__ Mind-altering.
A. Psychotropic B. Toxicity C. Neurotransmitter D. Ventral Striatum

23. __A__ An inflammation of the liver, with accompanying liver cell damage and risk of death.
A. Hepatitis B. Hippocampus C. Relapse D. Paranoia

24. __C__ A type of relationship between client and clinician in which both are working cooperatively toward the same goals, with mutual respect and understanding.
A. Delirium Tremens B. Psychopharmacological C. Therapeutic Alliance D. Engagement

25. __A__ An approach to recovery from substance use disorders that emphasizes personal responsibility, self-management, and clients' helping one another.
A. Mutual Self Help B. Intranasal C. Craving D. Receptor

26. __B__ An area of the brain crucial for learning and memory.
A. Consultation B. Hippocampus C. Cultural Proficiency D. Tolerance

27. __A__ A brain region in the ventral striatum involved in motivation and reward.
A. Nucleus Accumbens B. Abstinent C. Cognitive Behavioral Therapy D. Assertive Community Treatment

28. __D__ A clearing of toxins from the body.
A. Adderall B. Comorbidity C. Personality Disorders D. Detoxification

29. __A__ Synthetic substances similar to the male hormone testosterone.
A. Anabolic Androgenic Steroids B. Treatment Retention C. Motivational Enhancement Therapy D. Relapse

30. __B__ Interconnected brain structures that process feelings, emotions, and motivations. It is also important for learning and memory.
A. Cerebellum B. Limbic System C. Outreach Strategy D. Ventral Striatum

31. __B__ A brief alcoholism screening tool.
A. Pharmacotherapy B. Cage Questionnaire C. Toxicity D. Modified Therapeutic Community

32. __B__ The study of the anatomy, function, and diseases of the brain and nervous system.
A. Hallucinogens B. Neurobiology C. Partial Agonist D. Modified Therapeutic Community

33. __C__ Not using substances of abuse at any time.
A. Illicit B. Cage Questionnaire C. Abstinent D. Cannabinoids

34. __C__ An opioid partial agonist medication prescribed for the treatment of opioid addiction that relieves drug cravings without producing the high or dangerous side effects of other opioids.
A. Competency B. Tolerance C. Buprenorphine D. Cerebral Hemispheres

35. __D__ Connections between substance abuse treatment and mental health systems that allow collaboration. Necessary because these are the primary care systems for persons with cod.
A. Trauma B. Hippocampus C. Relapse D. Intersystem Linkage

36. __D__ Slang term for methylenedioxymethamphetamine, a member of the amphetamine family. At lower doses, MDMA causes distortions of emotional perceptions.
A. Crack B. Practice Improvement Collaborative C. Assertive Community Treatment D. Ecstasy

37. __C__ The receptor in the brain that recognizes and binds cannabinoids that are produced in the brain or outside the body.
A. Cage Questionnaire B. Quadrants of Care C. Cannabinoid Receptor D. Bulimia Nervosa

38. __D__ The feelings, reactions, biases, and images from the past that the client with cod may project onto the clinician.
A. Comorbidity B. Pharmacotherapy C. Locus D. Transference

39. __D__ The act of administering drugs by injection. Blood-borne viruses, like HIV and hepatitis, can be transmitted via shared needles or other drug injection equipment.
A. Integration B. Cognitive Behavioral Therapy C. Service Integration D. Injection Drug Use

40. __B__ A measure or estimate of a person's likelihood of committing suicide. A high-risk behavior associated with cod, especially (although not limited to) serious mood disorders.
A. Dual Diagnosis Enhanced B. Suicidality C. Benzodiazepine D. Injection Drug Use

41. __D__ The system consisting of the nerves in the brain and spinal cord.
A. Barbiturate B. Electronic Cigarette C. Agonist D. Central Nervous System

42. __B__ A process of change through which people with substance use disorders improve their health and wellness, live self-directed lives, and strive to reach their full potential.
A. Co Occurring Disorders B. Recovery C. Combined Psychopharmacological Intervention D. Adderall

43. __C__ A part of the brain that controls many bodily functions, including eating, drinking, body temperature regulation, and the release of many hormones.
A. Treatment B. Treatment Retention C. Hypothalamus D. Risk Factors

44. __B__ A broad array of services organized into programs intended to treat substance use disorders.
A. Dual Recovery Groups B. Substance Abuse Treatment System C. System D. Cognitive

45. __B__ A formal process of testing to determine whether a client warrants further attention at the current time for a particular disorder.
A. Central Nervous System B. Screening C. Stigma D. Benzodiazepine

46. __D__ The feelings, reactions, biases, and images from the past that the clinician may project onto the client with cod.
A. Quadrants of Care B. Locus C. Drug Abuse D. Countertransference

47. __B__ A tendency to act without foresight or regard for consequences and to prioritize immediate rewards over long-term goals.
A. Psychoactive B. Impulsivity C. Legal Problems D. Mood Disorders

48. __A__ In drug addiction, relapse is the return to drug use after an attempt to stop.
A. Relapse B. Psychosocial C. Brainstem D. Cage Questionnaire

49. __A__ An illness whose essential feature is persistent and recurrent maladaptive gambling behavior that disrupts personal, family, or vocational pursuits.
A. Pathological Gambling B. Buprenorphine C. Functional D. Paranoia

50. __C__ An illness whose essential feature is excessive anxiety and worry.
A. Analgesics B. Hippocampus C. Anxiety Disorder D. Reward System

51. __A__ A negative association attached to some activity or condition. A cause of shame or embarrassment.
A. Stigma B. Psychotropic Medication C. Transference D. Cardiovascular System

52. __D__ A brand name amphetamine for treating ADHD.
A. Psychedelic Drug B. Psychosocial C. Opioid D. Adderall

53. __B__ An organized array of services and interventions with a primary focus on treating mental health disorders, whether providing acute stabilization or ongoing treatment.
A. Combined Psychopharmacological Intervention B. Mental Health Program C. Cognitive Behavioral Therapy D. Schizophrenia

54. __A__ A set of negative attitudes and beliefs that motivate people to fear and discriminate against other people.
A. Stigma B. Psychopharmacological C. Ice D. Cognitive Behavioral Therapy

55. __A__ The use of strategies that soothe and distract the client who is experiencing intense pain or other strong emotions, helping the client anchor in the present and in reality.
A. Grounding B. Xanax C. Receptor D. Ice

56. __B__ The way a drug acts on the body.
A. Neuron B. Pharmacodynamics C. Limbic System D. Ecstasy

57. __D__ A process for facilitating client
A. Cardiovascular System B. Psychotropic Medication C. Substance Abuse D. Referral

58. __B__ Slang term for drugs that exert a depressant effect on the central nervous system. In general, downers are sedative-hypnotic drugs, such as benzodiazepines and barbiturates.
A. Confrontation B. Downers C. Fully Integrated Program D. Consultation

59. __D__ A type of delusion, or false idea, that is unchanged by reasoned argument or proof to the contrary.
A. Delirium Tremens B. Neurotransmitter C. Integrated Treatment D. Paranoia

60. __A__ A condition that can occur with the regular use of illicit or some prescription drugs, even if taken as prescribed.
A. Dependence B. Serotonin C. Addiction D. Integrated Treatment

61. __C__ A mental disorder that is characterized by distinct distortions of a person's mental capacity, ability to recognize reality, and relationships to others.
A. Practice Improvement Collaborative B. Domestic Violence C. Psychosis D. Single State Agency

62. __B__ A sign of depressant intoxication. When people consume significant amounts of sedative-hypnotics and opioids, their speech may become garbled, mumbled, and slow.
A. Anabolic Androgenic Steroids B. Slurred Speech C. Abstinent D. Pharmacotherapy

63. __D__ Driving a vehicle while impaired due to the intoxicating effects of recent drug use.
A. Substance Use Disorders B. Cultural Sensitivity C. Intermediate Program D. Drugged Driving

64. __A__ A period of amnesia or memory loss, typically caused by chronic, high-dose substance abuse.
A. Blackout B. Recovery C. Agitation D. Addiction

65. __C__ An opioid antagonist medication approved by the FDA to reverse an opioid overdose.
A. Ice B. Deficit C. Naloxone D. Central Nervous System

66. __B__ A symptom of a seizure, characterized by twitching and jerking of the limbs.
A. Consultation   B. Convulsions   C. Paranoia   D. Acute Care

67. __D__ Drugs that have an effect on the function of the brain and that are often used to treat psychiatric disorders.
A. Dual Diagnosis Enhanced   B. Disorder   C. Paranoia   D. Psychotherapeutics

68. __C__ A form of interpersonal exchange in which individuals present to each other their observations of, and reactions to, behaviors and attitudes that are matters of concern.
A. Coke Bugs   B. Functional   C. Confrontation   D. Motivational Enhancement Therapy

69. __D__ Poisonous nature; poisonous quality.
A. Prefrontal Cortex   B. Limbic System   C. Motivational Enhancement Therapy   D. Toxicity

70. __C__ A state in which a mental or physical disorder has been overcome or a disease process halted.
A. Formal Collaboration   B. Cannabis   C. Remission   D. Comorbidity

71. __B__ A class of drugs that include sedatives, tranquilizers, and hypnotics.
A. Abstinence   B. CNS Depressants   C. Coerced   D. Opioid

72. __D__ Hampered or held back from being able to do some mental or physical task.
A. Unsteady Gait   B. Screening   C. Overdose   D. Impaired

73. __D__ An overdose occurs when a person uses enough of a drug to produce a life-threatening reaction or death.
A. Modified Therapeutic Community   B. Mental Health Program   C. Relapse   D. Overdose

74. __B__ When two disorders or illnesses occur in the same person.
A. Anabolic Androgenic Steroids   B. Comorbidity   C. Nucleus Accumbens   D. Dependence

75. __B__ Extreme and unreasonable distrust of others.
A. Cross Training   B. Paranoia   C. Continuing Care   D. Relapse

76. __C__ A drug that has an effect on the mind and sometimes affects behavior as well.
A. Habilitation   B. Illicit   C. Psychotropic Medication   D. Paranoia

77. __B__ Mentally and physically in harmony with and connected to the culture in which one lives.
A. Psychosis   B. Acculturated   C. Legal Problems   D. Naltrexone

78. __D__ A medical illness caused by disordered use of a substance or substances.
A. Relapse Prevention Therapy   B. Drug Abuse   C. Constricted Pupils   D. Substance Use Disorder

79. __B__ A sudden but temporary recurrence of aspects of a drug experience that may occur days, weeks, or even more than a year after using drugs that cause hallucinations.
A. Mental Health Program   B. Flashback   C. CNS Depressants   D. Opioid Receptors

80. __C__ The capacity of a service provider to understand and work effectively in accordance with the cultural beliefs and practices of persons from a given ethnic
A. Cross Training   B. Transference   C. Cultural Competence   D. Functional

81. __C__ A treatment program that focuses primarily on one disorder without substantial modification to its usual treatment.
A. Treatment   B. THC   C. Intermediate Program   D. System

82. __A__ An area in the brainstem that contains dopamine neurons that make up a key part of the brain reward system, which also includes the nucleus accumbens and prefrontal cortex.
A. Ventral Tegmental Area   B. Cannabidiol   C. Attention Deficit Disorder   D. Psychotherapeutics

83. A Any mechanism by which treatment interventions for co-occurring disorders are combined within the context of a primary treatment relationship or service setting.
A. Integrated Treatment   B. Intersystem Linkage   C. Psychopharmacological   D. Engagement

84. D The way a drug is taken into the body. Drugs are most commonly taken by eating, drinking, inhaling, injecting, snorting, or smoking.
A. Abstinence   B. Practice Improvement Collaborative   C. Marijuana   D. Route of Administration

85. D A treatment approach based on providing incentives to support positive behavior change.
A. Intranasal   B. Motivational Enhancement Therapy   C. Valium   D. Contingency Management

86. A A brain chemical, classified as a neurotransmitter, found in regions of the brain that regulate movement, emotion, motivation, and reinforcement of rewarding behavior.
A. Dopamine   B. Functional   C. Habilitation   D. Cognitive Behavioral Therapy

87. B A client's commitment to and maintenance of treatment in all of its forms. A successful engagement program helps clients view the treatment facility as an important resource.
A. Agonist   B. Engagement   C. Serotonin   D. Coke Bugs

88. D Brand name for benzodiazepine diazepam.
A. Neurotransmitter   B. Cognitive Behavioral Therapy   C. Naloxone   D. Valium

89. A Rigid, inflexible, and maladaptive behavior patterns of sufficient severity to cause internal distress or significant impairment in functioning.
A. Personality Disorders   B. Detoxification   C. Overdose   D. Xanax

90. B A condition in which higher doses of a drug are required to achieve the desired effect.
A. Pharmacotherapy   B. Tolerance   C. Xanax   D. Modified Therapeutic Community

91. A Specific treatment strategies in which interventions for two or more disorders are combined in a single session or interaction, or in a series of interactions or multiple sessions.
A. Integrated Interventions   B. Impulsivity   C. Injection Drug Use   D. Valium

92. D An approach to treatment that maintains that the form or frequency of behavior can be altered through a planned and organized system of consequences.
A. Acculturated   B. Partial Agonist   C. Legal Problems   D. Contingency Management

93. D Treatment using medications.
A. Screening   B. Contingency Management   C. CNS Depressants   D. Pharmacotherapy

94. D The front part of the brain responsible for reasoning, planning, problem solving, and other higher cognitive functions.
A. Quadrants of Care   B. Electronic Cigarette   C. Substance Dependence   D. Prefrontal Cortex

95. D A disorder in which the individual refuses to maintain a normal body weight, is afraid of gaining weight, and exhibits a significant disturbance in the perception of body shape.
A. Personality Disorders   B. Reward   C. Hepatitis   D. Anorexia Nervosa

96. A Slang term used to describe drugs that have a stimulating effect on the central nervous system. Examples include cocaine, caffeine, and amphetamines.
A. Uppers   B. Screening   C. Psychotropic   D. Naltrexone

97. B A stimulant drug that acts on the central nervous system (CNS).
A. Serotonin   B. Amphetamine   C. Disorder   D. Substance Abuse

98. A Relating to the act or process of thinking, understanding, learning, and remembering.
A. Cognition   B. Ventral Tegmental Area   C. Psychotherapeutics   D. Relapse Prevention Therapy

99. __B__ The use of emotional, psychological, sexual, or physical force by one family member or intimate partner to control another.
A. Continuing Care   B. Domestic Violence   C. Antagonist   D. Concomitant Treatment

100. __B__ A chemical substance that binds to and activates certain receptors on cells, causing a biological response.
A. Co Occurring Disorders   B. Agonist   C. Deficit   D. Basic Program

From the words provided for each clue, provide the letter of the word which best matches the clue.

101. __B__ Approaches that actively seek out persons in a community who may have substance use disorders and engage them in substance abuse treatment.
A. Stigma   B. Outreach Strategy   C. Cross Training   D. Brainstem

102. __D__ A clinician's judgment or estimate of how well a disorder will respond to treatment.
A. Route of Administration   B. Blackout   C. Opioid   D. Prognosis

103. __B__ When two disorders or illnesses occur in the same person.
A. Cognitive   B. Comorbidity   C. Basal Ganglia   D. Neuroleptic Medication

104. __B__ An involuntary and rhythmic movement in the muscles, most often in the hands, feet, jaw, tongue, or head.
A. Nodding Out   B. Tremor   C. Quadrants of Care   D. Domestic Violence

105. __A__ Not using drugs or alcohol.
A. Abstinence   B. Legal Problems   C. Cannabis   D. Combined Psychopharmacological Intervention

106. __D__ A measure or estimate of a person's likelihood of committing suicide. A high-risk behavior associated with cod, especially (although not limited to) serious mood disorders.
A. Psychosis   B. Mental Disorder   C. Ice   D. Suicidality

107. __B__ A state of confusion accompanied by trembling and vivid hallucinations.
A. Neurobiology   B. Delirium Tremens   C. Outreach Strategy   D. Toxicity

108. __D__ A part of the brain that helps regulate posture, balance, and coordination. It is also involved in the processes of emotion, motivation, memory, and thought.
A. Transference   B. Cannabinoids   C. Practice Improvement Collaborative   D. Cerebellum

109. __C__ Pleasurable feelings that reinforce behavior and encourage repetition.
A. Therapeutic Community   B. Xanax   C. Reward   D. Psychotropic

110. __C__ Illegal or forbidden by law.
A. Psychopharmacological   B. Therapeutic Alliance   C. Illicit   D. Countertransference

111. __A__ A maladaptive pattern of substance use leading to clinically significant impairment or distress.
A. Substance Dependence   B. Screening   C. Grounding   D. Antagonist

112. __A__ A conceptual framework that classifies clients in four basic groups based on relative symptom severity, rather than by diagnosis.
A. Quadrants of Care   B. Consultation   C. Trauma   D. Route of Administration

113. __B__ Slang term for methylenedioxymethamphetamine, a member of the amphetamine family. At lower doses, MDMA causes distortions of emotional perceptions.
A. Remission   B. Ecstasy   C. Anesthetic   D. Hallucinations

114. __C__ Another name for the marijuana plant, cannabis sativa.
A. Recovery   B. Mutual Self Help   C. Cannabis   D. Advanced Program

115. __B__ Encompasses the specific treatment strategies, therapies, or techniques that are used to treat one or more disorders.
A. Substance Use Disorders   B. Intervention   C. Anxiety Disorder   D. Tremor

116. __D__ A group of medications that reduce pain.
A. Withdrawal   B. Substance Abuse Treatment System   C. Opioid Receptors   D. Analgesics

117. __B__ Relating to the act or process of thinking, understanding, learning, and remembering.
A. Cultural Destructiveness   B. Cognition   C. Substance Abuse Treatment System   D. Paranoia

118. __B__ Mentally and physically in harmony with and connected to the culture in which one lives.
A. Serotonin   B. Acculturated   C. Buprenorphine   D. Paranoia

119. __A__ Brand name for benzodiazepine diazepam.
A. Valium   B. Blackout   C. Substance Use Disorders   D. Neuron

120. __D__ A type of delusion, or false idea, that is unchanged by reasoned argument or proof to the contrary.
A. Remission   B. Barbiturate   C. Psychoactive   D. Paranoia

121. __B__ A powerful, often overwhelming desire to use drugs.
A. Treatment   B. Craving   C. Abstinent   D. Tolerance

122. __D__ Occurs when the nature of the client's disabilities requires more specific information and more complex and targeted intervention.
A. Competency   B. Blackout   C. Acculturated   D. Formal Collaboration

123. __D__ A clearing of toxins from the body.
A. Cannabinoid Receptor   B. Practice Improvement Collaborative   C. Wraparound Services   D. Detoxification

124. __B__ A treatment program that focuses primarily on one disorder without substantial modification to its usual treatment.
A. Brainstem   B. Intermediate Program   C. Confrontation   D. Therapeutic Alliance

125. __B__ A condition in which higher doses of a drug are required to achieve the desired effect.
A. Methadone   B. Tolerance   C. Flashback   D. Ice

126. __B__ A unique type of cell found in the brain and throughout the body that specializes in the transmission and processing of information.
A. Overdose   B. Neuron   C. Electronic Cigarette   D. Xanax

127. __C__ A restless inability to keep still.
A. Drug Abuse   B. Addiction   C. Agitation   D. Therapeutic Community

128. __B__ A class of drugs that include sedatives, tranquilizers, and hypnotics.
A. Cognitive   B. CNS Depressants   C. Intranasal   D. Cannabinoids

129. __A__ A stimulant drug that acts on the central nervous system (CNS).
A. Amphetamine   B. Wraparound Services   C. Uppers   D. Downers

130. __B__ The feelings, reactions, biases, and images from the past that the client with cod may project onto the clinician.
A. Drugged Driving   B. Transference   C. Consultation   D. Treatment Retention

131. __D__ A molecule located on the surface of a cell that recognizes specific chemicals and transmits the chemical message into the cell.
A. Psychotropic Medication   B. Craving   C. Cerebral Cortex   D. Receptor

132. __B__ An approach to recovery from substance use disorders that emphasizes personal responsibility, self-management, and clients' helping one another.
A. Suicidality   B. Mutual Self Help   C. Drugged Driving   D. CNS Depressants

133. __C__ Programs that by law or regulation, by choice, or for lack of resources cannot accommodate patients who have psychiatric illnesses that require ongoing treatment.
A. Vaping   B. Cultural Competence   C. Addiction Only Services   D. Psychosis

134. __C__ A counseling approach that uses motivational interviewing techniques to help individuals resolve any uncertainties they have about stopping their substance use.
A. Relapse Prevention Therapy   B. Neuroleptic Medication   C. Motivational Enhancement Therapy   D. Detoxification

135. __A__ The Indian hemp plant cannabis sativa; also called "pot" and "weed."
A. Marijuana   B. Advanced Program   C. Reward   D. Relapse Prevention Therapy

136. __B__ A brain circuit that includes the ventral tegmental area, the nucleus accumbens, and the prefrontal cortex.
A. Risk Factors   B. Reward System   C. Concomitant Treatment   D. Neuroleptic Medication

137. __C__ A sudden but temporary recurrence of aspects of a drug experience that may occur days, weeks, or even more than a year after using drugs that cause hallucinations.
A. Dependence   B. Fully Integrated Program   C. Flashback   D. Naloxone

138. __C__ Cocaine that has been chemically modified so that it will become a gas vapor when heated at relatively low temperatures.
A. Psychotherapeutics   B. Convulsions   C. Crack   D. Paranoia

139. __D__ Delta-9-tetrahydrocannabinol; the main mind-altering ingredient in marijuana.
A. Empirical   B. Coke Bugs   C. Cannabidiol   D. THC

140. __A__ Keeping clients involved in treatment activities and receiving required services.
A. Treatment Retention   B. Anabolic Androgenic Steroids   C. Relapse   D. Psychoactive

141. __B__ Connections between substance abuse treatment and mental health systems that allow collaboration. Necessary because these are the primary care systems for persons with cod.
A. Toxicity   B. Intersystem Linkage   C. Cultural Sensitivity   D. Wraparound Services

142. __A__ A place or a setting for some activity.
A. Locus   B. Abstinent   C. Competency   D. Recovery

143. __C__ The front part of the brain responsible for reasoning, planning, problem solving, and other higher cognitive functions.
A. Psychotherapeutics   B. Schizophrenia   C. Prefrontal Cortex   D. Contingency Management

144. __D__ A medical term meaning that major disease symptoms are eliminated or diminished below a pre-determined harmful level.
A. Intervention   B. Outreach Strategy   C. Ventral Striatum   D. Remission

145. __C__ A brand name amphetamine for treating ADHD.
A. Route of Administration   B. Convulsions   C. Adderall   D. Valium

146. __A__ A broad group of drugs that cause distortions of sensory perception. The prototype hallucinogen is lysergic acid diethylamide (LSD).
A. Hallucinogens   B. Benzodiazepine   C. Empirical   D. Psychotropic Medication

147. __C__ The gray matter that covers the surface of the cerebral hemispheres, whose functions include sensory processing and motor control along with language, reasoning, and decision-making.
A. Locus   B. Buprenorphine   C. Cerebral Cortex   D. Substance Abuse Treatment System

148. __B__ The study of the anatomy, function, and diseases of the brain and nervous system.
A. Serotonin   B. Neurobiology   C. Co Occurring Disorders   D. Abstinence

149. __B__ A chemical substance that binds to and blocks the activation of certain receptors on cells, preventing a biological response. Naloxone is an example of an opioid receptor antagonist.
A. Countertransference   B. Antagonist   C. Toxicity   D. Serotonin

150. __C__ The use of emotional, psychological, sexual, or physical force by one family member or intimate partner to control another.
A. Abstinent   B. Electronic Cigarette   C. Domestic Violence   D. Cognitive Behavioral Therapy

151. __B__ Able to spread by an agent such as a virus or bacterium.
A. Antagonist   B. Infectious   C. Locus   D. Reward System

152. __C__ A disorder in which the individual refuses to maintain a normal body weight, is afraid of gaining weight, and exhibits a significant disturbance in the perception of body shape.
A. Toxicity   B. Psychotropic   C. Anorexia Nervosa   D. Grounding

153. __C__ A drug used to treat psychosis, especially schizophrenia.
A. Quadrants of Care   B. Contingency Management   C. Neuroleptic Medication   D. Therapeutic Alliance

154. __B__ Substance abuse treatment is an organized array of services and interventions with a primary focus on treating substance abuse disorders.
A. Ventral Tegmental Area   B. Treatment   C. Neurotransmitter   D. Functional

155. __C__ Practices or actions through which an individual shows that he or she regards other cultures as inferior to the dominant culture.
A. Mental Disorder   B. Cultural Sensitivity   C. Cultural Destructiveness   D. Acculturated

156. __B__ In the context of treatment programs, consultation is a traditional type of informal relationship among treatment providers, such as a referral or a request for exchanging information.
A. Impulsivity   B. Consultation   C. Intersystem Linkage   D. Acute Care

157. __A__ Legally forced or compelled.
A. Coerced   B. Brainstem   C. Psychosocial   D. Intranasal

158. __D__ A drug that distorts perception, thought, and feeling. This term is typically used to refer to drugs with hallucinogenic effects.
A. Receptor   B. Pharmacotherapy   C. Anorexia Nervosa   D. Psychedelic Drug

159. __D__ The simultaneous provision of material and training to persons from more than one discipline.
A. Intranasal   B. Habilitation   C. Abstinent   D. Cross Training

160. __C__ Crooked, meandering, and uncoordinated walk, typical of alcohol-impaired people.
A. Comorbidity   B. Modified Therapeutic Community   C. Unsteady Gait   D. Hippocampus

161. __D__ A set of negative attitudes and beliefs that motivate people to fear and discriminate against other people.
A. Screening   B. Substance Dependence   C. Substance Use Disorders   D. Stigma

162. __A__ Slang term used to describe drugs that have a stimulating effect on the central nervous system. Examples include cocaine, caffeine, and amphetamines.
A. Uppers B. Flashback C. Grounding D. Paranoia

163. __A__ Not using substances of abuse at any time.
A. Abstinent B. Basic Program C. Countertransference D. Substance Dependence

164. __C__ A treatment program that actively combines substance abuse and mental health interventions to treat disorders, related problems, and the whole person more effectively.
A. Flashback B. Competency C. Fully Integrated Program D. Cannabis

165. __B__ Community-based initiatives that link treatment providers, researchers, and policymakers in order to build a strong foundation to effect action.
A. Habilitation B. Practice Improvement Collaborative C. Dilated Pupils D. Benzodiazepine

166. __A__ A symptom of a seizure, characterized by twitching and jerking of the limbs.
A. Convulsions B. Nodding Out C. Risk Factors D. Abstinent

167. __B__ Treatment episodes in which a client receives medications both to reduce cravings for substances and to medicate a mental disorder.
A. Paraphernalia B. Combined Psychopharmacological Intervention C. Treatment D. Neuron

168. __C__ An area of the brain crucial for learning and memory.
A. Agitation B. Wraparound Services C. Hippocampus D. Route of Administration

169. __B__ The capacity and willingness of a clinician or other service provider to be open to working with issues of culture and diversity.
A. Treatment B. Cultural Sensitivity C. Treatment Retention D. Psychedelic Drug

170. __B__ A therapeutic approach that seeks to modify negative or self-defeating thoughts and behavior.
A. Injection Drug Use B. Cognitive Behavioral Therapy C. Substance Dependence D. Coerced

171. __B__ A type of relationship between client and clinician in which both are working cooperatively toward the same goals, with mutual respect and understanding.
A. Serotonin B. Therapeutic Alliance C. Continuing Care D. Reward

172. __B__ Treatment of two or more mental or physical disorders at the same time.
A. Dopamine B. Concomitant Treatment C. Craving D. Ecstasy

173. __A__ Pertaining to a person's ability to carry out tasks.
A. Functional B. Impaired C. Relapse D. Xanax

174. __B__ A therapeutic community whose approach to treatment adapts the principles and methods of the therapeutic community to the circumstances of the cod client.
A. Wraparound Services B. Modified Therapeutic Community C. Intranasal D. Opioid Receptors

175. __A__ A type of psychosis where persons are subject to hallucinations occurring in the absence of insight into their pathological nature.
A. Schizophrenia B. Continuing Care C. Cognition D. Referral

176. __D__ Inhaling the aerosol or vapor from an electronic cigarette, e-vaporizer, or other device.
A. Cultural Destructiveness B. Remission C. Mutual Self Help D. Vaping

177. __B__ Driving a vehicle while impaired due to the intoxicating effects of recent drug use.
A. Skin Abscess B. Drugged Driving C. Modified Therapeutic Community D. Psychotherapeutics

178. __C__ Relationships among mental health and substance abuse providers in which both fields are moved into a single treatment setting and treatment regimen.
A. Dual Diagnosis Enhanced   B. Dilated Pupils   C. Integration   D. Recovery

179. __D__ A battery-operated device that people use to inhale an aerosol, which typically contains nicotine, flavorings, and other chemicals.
A. Practice Improvement Collaborative   B. Cannabinoids   C. Psychedelic Drug   D. Electronic Cigarette

180. __A__ A part of the brain that controls many bodily functions, including eating, drinking, body temperature regulation, and the release of many hormones.
A. Hypothalamus   B. Cannabidiol   C. Competency   D. Cognitive Behavioral Therapy

181. __C__ A mental disorder that is characterized by distinct distortions of a person's mental capacity, ability to recognize reality, and relationships to others.
A. Wraparound Services   B. Hallucinogens   C. Psychosis   D. Opioid

182. __C__ Pupils that have become temporarily enlarged.
A. Cultural Proficiency   B. Motivational Enhancement Therapy   C. Dilated Pupils   D. Paranoia

183. __C__ A process in which the body rids itself of a drug, or its metabolites.
A. Empirical   B. Infectious   C. Detoxification   D. Abstinence

184. __C__ A type of CNS depressant sometimes prescribed to relieve anxiety, panic, or acute stress reactions. Some benzodiazepines are prescribed short-term to promote sleep.
A. Mental Disorder   B. Cerebral Cortex   C. Benzodiazepine   D. Intersystem Linkage

185. __B__ The evaluation or estimation of the nature, quality, or ability of someone or something.
A. Psychoactive   B. Assessment   C. Comorbidity   D. Partial Agonist

186. __D__ A type of CNS depressant sometimes prescribed to promote relaxation and sleep, but more commonly used in surgical procedures and to treat seizure disorders.
A. Fully Integrated Program   B. Screening   C. Habilitation   D. Barbiturate

187. __C__ A group of brain structures that process sensory information and control basic functions needed for survival such as breathing, heart rate, blood pressure, and arousal.
A. Modified Therapeutic Community   B. Anesthetic   C. Brainstem   D. Neuroleptic Medication

188. __B__ The act of administering drugs by injection. Blood-borne viruses, like HIV and hepatitis, can be transmitted via shared needles or other drug injection equipment.
A. Cognitive Behavioral Therapy   B. Injection Drug Use   C. Hypothalamus   D. Intervention

189. __D__ Poisonous nature; poisonous quality.
A. Limbic System   B. Ice   C. Neuron   D. Toxicity

190. __A__ The area of the brain that plays an important role in positive forms of motivation, including the pleasurable effects of healthy activities like eating, socializing, and sex.
A. Basal Ganglia   B. Antisocial Personality Disorder   C. Xanax   D. Detoxification

191. __D__ Rigid, inflexible, and maladaptive behavior patterns of sufficient severity to cause internal distress or significant impairment in functioning.
A. Continuing Care   B. Cannabinoids   C. Serotonin   D. Personality Disorders

192. __C__ Interconnected brain structures that process feelings, emotions, and motivations. It is also important for learning and memory.
A. Cerebellum   B. Hypothalamus   C. Limbic System   D. Culturally Competent

193. __B__ A brain chemical, classified as a neurotransmitter, found in regions of the brain that regulate movement, emotion, motivation, and reinforcement of rewarding behavior.
A. Xanax   B. Dopamine   C. Domestic Violence   D. Grounding

194. __D__ Therapy groups in which recovery skills for co-occurring disorders are discussed.
A. Combined Psychopharmacological Intervention   B. Psychopharmacological   C. Psychotherapeutics   D. Dual Recovery Groups

195. __C__ Synthetic substances similar to the male hormone testosterone.
A. Therapeutic Alliance   B. Tolerance   C. Anabolic Androgenic Steroids   D. Coke Bugs

196. __C__ In drug addiction, relapse is the return to drug use after an attempt to stop.
A. Hallucinogens   B. Collaboration   C. Relapse   D. Ice

197. __B__ An illness whose features are a pervasive disregard for and violation of the rights of others and an inability to form meaningful interpersonal relationships.
A. Single State Agency   B. Antisocial Personality Disorder   C. Acculturated   D. Attention Deficit Disorder

198. __B__ An older diagnostic term that defined use that is unsafe, use that leads a person to fail to fulfill responsibilities or gets them in legal trouble.
A. Dually Disordered   B. Drug Abuse   C. Assertive Community Treatment   D. Recovery

199. __B__ Proteins on the surface of neurons, or other cells, that are activated by endogenous opioids, such as endorphins, and opioid drugs, such as heroin.
A. Stigma   B. Opioid Receptors   C. Domestic Violence   D. Intersystem Linkage

200. __C__ An opioid partial agonist medication prescribed for the treatment of opioid addiction that relieves drug cravings without producing the high or dangerous side effects of other opioids.
A. Cannabidiol   B. Anesthetic   C. Buprenorphine   D. Legal Problems

Matching

Provide the word that best matches each clue.

1. _____ — The act of administering drugs by injection. Blood-borne viruses, like HIV and hepatitis, can be transmitted via shared needles or other drug injection equipment.

2. _____ — A client-centered, directive method for enhancing intrinsic motivation to change by exploring and resolving ambivalence.

3. _____ — Brand name for benzodiazepine diazepam.

4. _____ — The feelings, reactions, biases, and images from the past that the clinician may project onto the client with cod.

5. _____ — Biopsychosocial or other treatment that is adapted to suit the special cultural beliefs, practices, and needs of a client.

6. _____ — A brand name amphetamine for treating ADHD.

7. _____ — Extreme and unreasonable distrust of others.

8. _____ — Approaches that actively seek out persons in a community who may have substance use disorders and engage them in substance abuse treatment.

9. _____ — Refers to co-occurring substance use (abuse or dependence) and mental disorders.

10. _____ — People who abuse substances are at a higher risk for engaging in behaviors that are high risk and illegal.

11. _____ Treatment episodes in which a client receives medications both to reduce cravings for substances and to medicate a mental disorder.

12. _____ Care that supports a client's progress, monitors his or her condition, and can respond to a return to substance use or a return of symptoms of mental disorder.

13. _____ A neurotransmitter involved in a broad range of effects on perception, movement, and emotions. Serotonin and its receptors are the targets of most hallucinogens.

14. _____ A powerful, often overwhelming desire to use drugs.

15. _____ Relating to the act or process of thinking, understanding, learning, and remembering.

16. _____ A measure or estimate of a person's likelihood of committing suicide. A high-risk behavior associated with cod, especially (although not limited to) serious mood disorders.

17. _____ The right and left halves of the brain.

18. _____ In drug addiction, relapse is the return to drug use after an attempt to stop.

19. _____ A period of amnesia or memory loss, typically caused by chronic, high-dose substance abuse.

20. _____ A substance that binds to and activates a receptor to a lesser degree than a full agonist.

21. _____ Not using drugs or alcohol.

22. _____ Hampered or held back from being able to do some mental or physical task.

23. _____ The evaluation or estimation of the nature, quality, or ability of someone or something.

24. _____ Symptoms that can occur after long-term use of a drug is reduced or stopped.

25. _____ An illness whose essential feature is excessive anxiety and worry.

A. Partial Agonist
B. Legal Problems
C. Culturally Competent
D. Motivational Interviewing
E. Injection Drug Use
F. Anxiety Disorder
G. Cognition
H. Withdrawal
I. Cerebral Hemispheres
J. Continuing Care
K. Suicidality
L. Abstinence
M. Relapse
N. Serotonin
O. Blackout
P. Adderall
Q. Valium
R. Combined Psychopharmacological Intervention
S. Outreach Strategy
T. Countertransference
U. Craving
V. Impaired
W. Assessment
X. Paranoia
Y. Co Occurring Disorders

Provide the word that best matches each clue.

26. _____ Initial learning and the acquisition of skills necessary for everyday life.

27. _____ An entity that provides mental health services in two or three service settings and is not classified as a psychiatric or general hospital or as a residential treatment center.

28. _____ A client's commitment to and maintenance of treatment in all of its forms. A successful engagement program helps clients view the treatment facility as an important resource.

29. _____ Chemicals that bind to cannabinoid receptors in the brain.

30. _____ A place or a setting for some activity.

31. _____ Rigid, inflexible, and maladaptive behavior patterns of sufficient severity to cause internal distress or significant impairment in functioning.

32. _____ Delusional or disordered thinking detached from reality; symptoms often include hallucinations.

33. _____ Pleasurable feelings that reinforce behavior and encourage repetition.

34. _____ When two disorders or illnesses occur in the same person.

35. _____ Relationships among mental health and substance abuse providers in which both fields are moved into a single treatment setting and treatment regimen.

36. _____ A long-acting opioid antagonist medication that prevents receptors from being activated by other opioids. Naltrexone is used to treat alcohol and opioid use disorders.

37. _____ A conceptual framework that classifies clients in four basic groups based on relative symptom severity, rather than by diagnosis.

38. _____ A sudden but temporary recurrence of aspects of a drug experience that may occur days, weeks, or even more than a year after using drugs that cause hallucinations.

39. _____ Driving a vehicle while impaired due to the intoxicating effects of recent drug use.

40. _____ The use of strategies that soothe and distract the client who is experiencing intense pain or other strong emotions, helping the client anchor in the present and in reality.

41. _Treatment Retention_ — Keeping clients involved in treatment activities and receiving required services.

42. _Benzodiazepine_ — A type of CNS depressant sometimes prescribed to relieve anxiety, panic, or acute stress reactions. Some benzodiazepines are prescribed short-term to promote sleep.

43. _Recovery_ — A process of change through which people with substance use disorders improve their health and wellness, live self-directed lives, and strive to reach their full potential.

44. _Anesthetic_ — A drug that causes insensitivity to pain and is used for surgeries and other medical procedures.

45. _Cerebrum_ — The upper part of the brain consisting of the left and right hemispheres.

46. _Functional_ — Pertaining to a person's ability to carry out tasks.

47. _Skin Abscess_ — A collection of pus formed as a result of bacterial infection.

48. _Transference_ — The feelings, reactions, biases, and images from the past that the client with cod may project onto the clinician.

49. _Suicidality_ — A measure or estimate of a person's likelihood of committing suicide. A high-risk behavior associated with cod, especially (although not limited to) serious mood disorders.

50. _Engagement_ — Emphasizes shared decision making with the client as essential to the client's engagement process.

A. Skin Abscess
B. Comorbidity
C. Naltrexone
D. Quadrants of Care
E. Functional
F. Treatment Retention
G. Reward
H. Cannabinoids
I. Drugged Driving
J. Cerebrum
K. Organization
L. Suicidality
M. Personality Disorders
N. Transference
O. Integration
P. Locus
Q. Anesthetic
R. Psychosis
S. Flashback
T. Recovery
U. Engagement
V. Assertive Community Treatment
W. Grounding
X. Habilitation
Y. Benzodiazepine

Provide the word that best matches each clue.

51. _____ Treatment of two or more mental or physical disorders at the same time.

52. _____ A brain chemical, classified as a neurotransmitter, found in regions of the brain that regulate movement, emotion, motivation, and reinforcement of rewarding behavior.

53. _____ A treatment program with the capacity to provide treatment for one disorder, but that also screens for other disorders and is able to access necessary consultations.

54. _____ A unique type of cell found in the brain and throughout the body that specializes in the transmission and processing of information.

55. _____ The area of the brain that plays an important role in positive forms of motivation, including the pleasurable effects of healthy activities like eating, socializing, and sex.

56. _____ A process in which the body rids itself of a drug, or its metabolites.

57. _____ An illness whose features are a pervasive disregard for and violation of the rights of others and an inability to form meaningful interpersonal relationships.

58. _____ No one set of treatment interventions constitutes integrated treatment.

59. _____ A component of the marijuana plant without mind-altering effects that is being studied for possible medical uses.

60. _____ The evaluation or estimation of the nature, quality, or ability of someone or something.

61. _____ Rigid, inflexible, and maladaptive behavior patterns of sufficient severity to cause internal distress or significant impairment in functioning.

62. _____ Slang term used to describe drugs that have a stimulating effect on the central nervous system. Examples include cocaine, caffeine, and amphetamines.

63. _____ A tendency to act without foresight or regard for consequences and to prioritize immediate rewards over long-term goals.

64. _____ Not using substances of abuse at any time.

65. _____ Of or pertaining to programs that have a higher than average level of integration of substance abuse and mental health treatment services.

66. _____ Systems that organize statewide services.

67. _____ A sign of depressant intoxication. When people consume significant amounts of sedative-hypnotics and opioids, their speech may become garbled, mumbled, and slow.

68. _____ A brand name amphetamine for treating ADHD.

69. _____ The right and left halves of the brain.

70. _____ A collection of pus formed as a result of bacterial infection.

71. _____ Initial learning and the acquisition of skills necessary for everyday life.

72. _____ A maladaptive pattern of substance use manifested by recurrent and significant adverse consequences related to the repeated use of substances.

73. _____ An approach to recovery from substance use disorders that emphasizes personal responsibility, self-management, and clients' helping one another.

74. _____ An approach to treatment that maintains that the form or frequency of behavior can be altered through a planned and organized system of consequences.

75. _____ Slang term for Smoke able methamphetamine.

A. Cannabidiol
B. Assessment
C. Mutual Self Help
D. Substance Abuse
E. Impulsivity
F. Neuron
G. Single State Agency
H. Ice
I. Detoxification
J. Personality Disorders
K. Dopamine
L. Service Integration
M. Basal Ganglia
N. Slurred Speech
O. Uppers
P. Adderall
Q. Habilitation
R. Antisocial Personality Disorder

S. Dual Diagnosis Enhanced
T. Skin Abscess
U. Contingency Management
V. Abstinent
W. Concomitant Treatment
X. Cerebral Hemispheres
Y. Basic Program

Provide the word that best matches each clue.

76. _____ Rigid, inflexible, and maladaptive behavior patterns of sufficient severity to cause internal distress or significant impairment in functioning.

77. _____ The front part of the brain responsible for reasoning, planning, problem solving, and other higher cognitive functions.

78. _____ Pertaining to a person's ability to carry out tasks.

79. _____ A substance that binds to and activates a receptor to a lesser degree than a full agonist.

80. _____ A unique type of cell found in the brain and throughout the body that specializes in the transmission and processing of information.

81. _____ Sensations, sounds and

82. _____ An overdose occurs when a person uses enough of a drug to produce a life-threatening reaction or death.

83. _____ A period of amnesia or memory loss, typically caused by chronic, high-dose substance abuse.

84. _____ Pertaining to medications used to treat mental illnesses.

85. _____ People who abuse substances are at a higher risk for engaging in behaviors that are high risk and illegal.

86. _____ A drug used to treat psychosis, especially schizophrenia.

87. _____ A therapeutic approach that seeks to modify negative or self-defeating thoughts and behavior.

88. _____ A treatment program with the capacity to provide treatment for one disorder, but that also screens for other disorders and is able to access necessary consultations.

89. _____ Encompasses the specific treatment strategies, therapies, or techniques that are used to treat one or more disorders.

90. _____ A process in which the body rids itself of a drug, or its metabolites.

91. _____ A maladaptive pattern of substance use leading to clinically significant impairment or distress.

92. _____ In the context of treatment programs, consultation is a traditional type of informal relationship among treatment providers, such as a referral or a request for exchanging information.

93. _____ When two disorders or illnesses occur in the same person.

94. _____ A condition in which higher doses of a drug are required to achieve the desired effect.

95. _____ An older diagnostic term that defined use that is unsafe, use that leads a person to fail to fulfill responsibilities or gets them in legal trouble.

96. _____ Poisonous nature; poisonous quality.

97. _____ Emphasizes shared decision making with the client as essential to the client's engagement process.

98. _____ A therapeutic community whose approach to treatment adapts the principles and methods of the therapeutic community to the circumstances of the cod client.

99. _____ A disorder in which the individual refuses to maintain a normal body weight, is afraid of gaining weight, and exhibits a significant disturbance in the perception of body shape.

100. _____ A treatment program that focuses primarily on one disorder without substantial modification to its usual treatment.

A. Functional
B. Intervention
C. Personality Disorders
D. Overdose
E. Basic Program
F. Legal Problems
G. Cognitive Behavioral Therapy
H. Prefrontal Cortex
I. Partial Agonist
J. Psychopharmacological

K. Tolerance
L. Consultation
M. Blackout
N. Modified Therapeutic Community
O. Neuroleptic Medication
P. Detoxification
Q. Drug Abuse
R. Neuron
S. Substance Dependence
T. Hallucinations
U. Comorbidity
V. Intermediate Program
W. Assertive Community Treatment
X. Toxicity
Y. Anorexia Nervosa

Provide the word that best matches each clue.

101. _____ An organized array of services and interventions with a primary focus on treating mental health disorders, whether providing acute stabilization or ongoing treatment.

102. _____ What the body does to a drug after it has been taken, including how rapidly the drug is absorbed, broken down, and processed by the body.

103. _____ Slang term for Smoke able methamphetamine.

104. _____ The area of the brain that plays an important role in positive forms of motivation, including the pleasurable effects of healthy activities like eating, socializing, and sex.

105. _____ The gray matter that covers the surface of the cerebral hemispheres, whose functions include sensory processing and motor control along with language, reasoning, and decision-making.

106. _____ A class of drugs that include sedatives, tranquilizers, and hypnotics.

107. _____ An overdose occurs when a person uses enough of a drug to produce a life-threatening reaction or death.

108. _____ The use of strategies that soothe and distract the client who is experiencing intense pain or other strong emotions, helping the client anchor in the present and in reality.

109. _____ An organization of a number of different treatment programs and related services in order to implement a specific mission and common goals.

110. _____ A broad array of services organized into programs intended to treat substance use disorders.

111. _____ An approach to recovery from substance use disorders that emphasizes personal responsibility, self-management, and clients' helping one another.

112. _____ A measure or estimate of a person's likelihood of committing suicide. A high-risk behavior associated with cod, especially (although not limited to) serious mood disorders.

113. _____ The right and left halves of the brain.

114. _____ Slang term for methylenedioxymethamphetamine, a member of the amphetamine family. At lower doses, MDMA causes distortions of emotional perceptions.

115. _____ A drug that causes insensitivity to pain and is used for surgeries and other medical procedures.

116. _____ A neurotransmitter that affects heart rate, blood pressure, stress, and attention.

117. _____ Keeping clients involved in treatment activities and receiving required services.

118. _____ A treatment program that has the capacity to provide integrated substance abuse and mental health treatment for clients with COD.

119. _____ A chemical compound that acts as a messenger to carry signals from one nerve cell to another.

120. _____ A treatment program that actively combines substance abuse and mental health interventions to treat disorders, related problems, and the whole person more effectively.

121. _____ A negative association attached to some activity or condition. A cause of shame or embarrassment.

122. _____ Slang term for the early stages of depressant-induced sleep.

123. _____ Slang term for tactile hallucinations that feel like bugs crawling on or under the skin.

124. _____ The way a drug is taken into the body. Drugs are most commonly taken by eating, drinking, inhaling, injecting, snorting, or smoking.

125. _____ A consciously designed social environment or residential treatment setting in which the social and group process is harnessed with therapeutic intent.

A. System
C. Pharmacokinetics
E. Neurotransmitter
G. Grounding
I. Route of Administration
K. Ice
M. Cerebral Cortex
O. Stigma
Q. Treatment Retention
S. Advanced Program
U. Basal Ganglia
W. Therapeutic Community
Y. Suicidality

B. Mutual Self Help
D. Mental Health Program
F. Fully Integrated Program
H. Anesthetic
J. Cerebral Hemispheres
L. Ecstasy
N. Coke Bugs
P. CNS Depressants
R. Norepinephrine
T. Nodding Out
V. Substance Abuse Treatment System
X. Overdose

Provide the word that best matches each clue.

126. _____ A type of delusion, or false idea, that is unchanged by reasoned argument or proof to the contrary.

127. _____ The capacity and willingness of a clinician or other service provider to be open to working with issues of culture and diversity.

128. _____ An organization of a number of different treatment programs and related services in order to implement a specific mission and common goals.

129. _____ A tendency to act without foresight or regard for consequences and to prioritize immediate rewards over long-term goals.

130. _____ An illness or a disruption of some mental or physical process.

131. _____ A negative association attached to some activity or condition. A cause of shame or embarrassment.

132. _____ Sensations, sounds and

133. _____ Therapy groups in which recovery skills for co-occurring disorders are discussed.

134. _____ Poisonous nature; poisonous quality.

135. _____ A powerful, often overwhelming desire to use drugs.

136. _____ The study of the anatomy, function, and diseases of the brain and nervous system.

137. _____ Violent mental or physical harm to a person, damage to an organ, etc.

138. _____ Pertaining to a person's ability to carry out tasks.

139. _____ A maladaptive pattern of substance use leading to clinically significant impairment or distress.

140. _____ The simultaneous provision of material and training to persons from more than one discipline.

141. _____ Legally forced or compelled.

142. _____ A neurotransmitter that affects heart rate, blood pressure, stress, and attention.

143. _____ Slang term for drugs that exert a depressant effect on the central nervous system. In general, downers are sedative-hypnotic drugs, such as benzodiazepines and barbiturates.

144. _____ The use of strategies that soothe and distract the client who is experiencing intense pain or other strong emotions, helping the client anchor in the present and in reality.

145. _____ Synthetic substances similar to the male hormone testosterone.

146. _____ Not using drugs or alcohol.

147. _____ Drugs that have an effect on the function of the brain and that are often used to treat psychiatric disorders.

148. _____ Treatment of two or more mental or physical disorders at the same time.

149. _____ What the body does to a drug after it has been taken, including how rapidly the drug is absorbed, broken down, and processed by the body.

150. _____ A collection of pus formed as a result of bacterial infection.

A. Trauma
C. Abstinence
E. Coerced
G. Paranoia
I. Neurobiology
K. Substance Dependence
M. Psychotherapeutics
O. Hallucinations
Q. Concomitant Treatment
S. Stigma
U. Impulsivity
W. Disorder
Y. Grounding

B. Dual Recovery Groups
D. System
F. Pharmacokinetics
H. Downers
J. Cultural Sensitivity
L. Norepinephrine
N. Toxicity
P. Cross Training
R. Skin Abscess
T. Anabolic Androgenic Steroids
V. Craving
X. Functional

Provide the word that best matches each clue.

151. _____ In the context of substance abuse treatment, disability, or inability to function fully.

152. _____ Pleasurable feelings that reinforce behavior and encourage repetition.

153. _____ The simultaneous provision of material and training to persons from more than one discipline.

154. _____ A maladaptive pattern of substance use leading to clinically significant impairment or distress.

155. _____ Treatment using medications.

156. _____ A condition in which higher doses of a drug are required to achieve the desired effect.

157. _____ A brain region in the ventral striatum involved in motivation and reward.

158. _____ Brand name for benzodiazepine alprazolam.

159. _____ Mind-altering.

160. _____ An area in the brainstem that contains dopamine neurons that make up a key part of the brain reward system, which also includes the nucleus accumbens and prefrontal cortex.

161. _____ Involving a person's psychological well-being, as well as housing, employment, family, and other social aspects of life circumstances.

162. _____ The evaluation or estimation of the nature, quality, or ability of someone or something.

163. _____ Substance abuse treatment is an organized array of services and interventions with a primary focus on treating substance abuse disorders.

164. _____ A class of substance-related disorders that includes both substance abuse and substance dependence.

165. _____ Relationships among mental health and substance abuse providers in which both fields are moved into a single treatment setting and treatment regimen.

166. _____ A treatment program that has the capacity to provide integrated substance abuse and mental health treatment for clients with COD.

167. _____ A persistent pattern of inattention and hyperactivity-impulsivity that is more frequently displayed and more serious than is typically observed in comparable individuals.

168. _____ The act of administering drugs by injection. Blood-borne viruses, like HIV and hepatitis, can be transmitted via shared needles or other drug injection equipment.

169. _____ Having been diagnosed with two disorders, for example a substance use disorder and a mental health disorder.

170. _____ Taken through the nose.

171. _____ Initial learning and the acquisition of skills necessary for everyday life.

172. _____ Inhaling the aerosol or vapor from an electronic cigarette, e-vaporizer, or other device.

173. _____ A broad group of drugs that cause distortions of sensory perception. The prototype hallucinogen is lysergic acid diethylamide (LSD).

174. _____ Legally forced or compelled.

175. _____ A form of psychotherapy that teaches people strategies to identify and correct problematic associations among thoughts, emotions, and behaviors.

A. Ventral Tegmental Area
B. Hallucinogens
C. Reward
D. Attention Deficit Disorder
E. Coerced
F. Vaping
G. Injection Drug Use
H. Pharmacotherapy
I. Cognitive Behavioral Therapy
J. Psychosocial
K. Nucleus Accumbens
L. Deficit
M. Dually Disordered
N. Xanax
O. Tolerance
P. Assessment
Q. Habilitation
R. Intranasal
S. Advanced Program
T. Cross Training
U. Substance Dependence
V. Integration
W. Treatment
X. Substance Use Disorders
Y. Psychotropic

Provide the word that best matches each clue.

176. _____ A client's commitment to and maintenance of treatment in all of its forms. A successful engagement program helps clients view the treatment facility as an important resource.

177. _____ Interconnected brain structures that process feelings, emotions, and motivations. It is also important for learning and memory.

178. _____ People who abuse substances are at a higher risk for engaging in behaviors that are high risk and illegal.

179. _____ An illness or a disruption of some mental or physical process.

180. _____ Slang term for drugs that exert a depressant effect on the central nervous system. In general, downers are sedative-hypnotic drugs, such as benzodiazepines and barbiturates.

181. _____ Synthetic substances similar to the male hormone testosterone.

182. _____ An organized array of services and interventions with a primary focus on treating mental health disorders, whether providing acute stabilization or ongoing treatment.

183. _____ Having a specific effect on the brain.

184. _____ Biopsychosocial or other treatment that is adapted to suit the special cultural beliefs, practices, and needs of a client.

185. _____ Extreme and unreasonable distrust of others.

186. _____ Occurs when the nature of the client's disabilities requires more specific information and more complex and targeted intervention.

187. _____ A battery-operated device that people use to inhale an aerosol, which typically contains nicotine, flavorings, and other chemicals.

188. _____ An illness whose features are a pervasive disregard for and violation of the rights of others and an inability to form meaningful interpersonal relationships.

189. _____ Slang term for the early stages of depressant-induced sleep.

190. _____ The way a drug is taken into the body. Drugs are most commonly taken by eating, drinking, inhaling, injecting, snorting, or smoking.

191. _____ The highest level of cultural capacity, which implies an ability to perceive the nuances of a culture in depth and a willingness to work to advance in proficiency through leadership.

192. _____ The system consisting of the nerves in the brain and spinal cord.

193. _____ Legally forced or compelled.

194. _____ A restless inability to keep still.

195. _____ A component of the marijuana plant without mind-altering effects that is being studied for possible medical uses.

196. _____ An approach to recovery from substance use disorders that emphasizes personal responsibility, self-management, and clients' helping one another.

197. _____ Poisonous nature; poisonous quality.

198. _____ A persistent pattern of inattention and hyperactivity-impulsivity that is more frequently displayed and more serious than is typically observed in comparable individuals.

199. _____ A form of interpersonal exchange in which individuals present to each other their observations of, and reactions to, behaviors and attitudes that are matters of concern.

200. _____ Another name for the marijuana plant, cannabis sativa.

A. Downers
B. Culturally Competent
C. Paranoia
D. Confrontation
E. Antisocial Personality Disorder
F. Formal Collaboration
G. Legal Problems
H. Psychoactive
I. Nodding Out
J. Central Nervous System
K. Anabolic Androgenic Steroids
L. Route of Administration
M. Toxicity
N. Agitation
O. Attention Deficit Disorder
P. Cultural Proficiency
Q. Limbic System
R. Cannabis
S. Disorder
T. Mutual Self Help
U. Cannabidiol
V. Mental Health Program
W. Engagement
X. Coerced
Y. Electronic Cigarette

Provide the word that best matches each clue.

1. INJECTION DRUG USE — The act of administering drugs by injection. Blood-borne viruses, like HIV and hepatitis, can be transmitted via shared needles or other drug injection equipment.

2. MOTIVATIONAL INTERVIEWING — A client-centered, directive method for enhancing intrinsic motivation to change by exploring and resolving ambivalence.

3. VALIUM — Brand name for benzodiazepine diazepam.

4. COUNTERTRANSFERENCE — The feelings, reactions, biases, and images from the past that the clinician may project onto the client with cod.

5. CULTURALLY COMPETENT — Biopsychosocial or other treatment that is adapted to suit the special cultural beliefs, practices, and needs of a client.

6. ADDERALL — A brand name amphetamine for treating ADHD.

7. PARANOIA — Extreme and unreasonable distrust of others.

8. OUTREACH STRATEGY — Approaches that actively seek out persons in a community who may have substance use disorders and engage them in substance abuse treatment.

9. CO OCCURRING DISORDERS — Refers to co-occurring substance use (abuse or dependence) and mental disorders.

10. LEGAL PROBLEMS — People who abuse substances are at a higher risk for engaging in behaviors that are high risk and illegal.

11.	COMBINED PSYCHOPHARMACOLOGICAL INTERVENTION	Treatment episodes in which a client receives medications both to reduce cravings for substances and to medicate a mental disorder.
12.	CONTINUING CARE	Care that supports a client's progress, monitors his or her condition, and can respond to a return to substance use or a return of symptoms of mental disorder.
13.	SEROTONIN	A neurotransmitter involved in a broad range of effects on perception, movement, and emotions. Serotonin and its receptors are the targets of most hallucinogens.
14.	CRAVING	A powerful, often overwhelming desire to use drugs.
15.	COGNITION	Relating to the act or process of thinking, understanding, learning, and remembering.
16.	SUICIDALITY	A measure or estimate of a person's likelihood of committing suicide. A high-risk behavior associated with cod, especially (although not limited to) serious mood disorders.
17.	CEREBRAL HEMISPHERES	The right and left halves of the brain.
18.	RELAPSE	In drug addiction, relapse is the return to drug use after an attempt to stop.
19.	BLACKOUT	A period of amnesia or memory loss, typically caused by chronic, high-dose substance abuse.
20.	PARTIAL AGONIST	A substance that binds to and activates a receptor to a lesser degree than a full agonist.
21.	ABSTINENCE	Not using drugs or alcohol.

22. IMPAIRED _____ Hampered or held back from being able to do some mental or physical task.

23. ASSESSMENT _____ The evaluation or estimation of the nature, quality, or ability of someone or something.

24. WITHDRAWAL _____ Symptoms that can occur after long-term use of a drug is reduced or stopped.

25. ANXIETY DISORDER _____ An illness whose essential feature is excessive anxiety and worry.

A. Partial Agonist
B. Legal Problems
C. Culturally Competent
D. Motivational Interviewing
E. Injection Drug Use
F. Anxiety Disorder
G. Cognition
H. Withdrawal
I. Cerebral Hemispheres
J. Continuing Care
K. Suicidality
L. Abstinence
M. Relapse
N. Serotonin
O. Blackout
P. Adderall
Q. Valium
R. Combined Psychopharmacological Intervention
S. Outreach Strategy
T. Countertransference
U. Craving
V. Impaired
W. Assessment
X. Paranoia
Y. Co Occurring Disorders

Provide the word that best matches each clue.

26. HABILITATION _____ Initial learning and the acquisition of skills necessary for everyday life.

27.	ORGANIZATION	An entity that provides mental health services in two or three service settings and is not classified as a psychiatric or general hospital or as a residential treatment center.
28.	ENGAGEMENT	A client's commitment to and maintenance of treatment in all of its forms. A successful engagement program helps clients view the treatment facility as an important resource.
29.	CANNABINOIDS	Chemicals that bind to cannabinoid receptors in the brain.
30.	LOCUS	A place or a setting for some activity.
31.	PERSONALITY DISORDERS	Rigid, inflexible, and maladaptive behavior patterns of sufficient severity to cause internal distress or significant impairment in functioning.
32.	PSYCHOSIS	Delusional or disordered thinking detached from reality; symptoms often include hallucinations.
33.	REWARD	Pleasurable feelings that reinforce behavior and encourage repetition.
34.	COMORBIDITY	When two disorders or illnesses occur in the same person.
35.	INTEGRATION	Relationships among mental health and substance abuse providers in which both fields are moved into a single treatment setting and treatment regimen.
36.	NALTREXONE	A long-acting opioid antagonist medication that prevents receptors from being activated by other opioids. Naltrexone is used to treat alcohol and opioid use disorders.
37.	QUADRANTS OF CARE	A conceptual framework that classifies clients in four basic groups based on relative symptom severity, rather than by diagnosis.
38.	FLASHBACK	A sudden but temporary recurrence of aspects of a drug experience that may occur days, weeks, or even more than a year after using drugs that cause hallucinations.
39.	DRUGGED DRIVING	Driving a vehicle while impaired due to the intoxicating effects of recent drug use.
40.	GROUNDING	The use of strategies that soothe and distract the client who is experiencing intense pain or other strong emotions, helping the client anchor in the present and in reality.

41. TREATMENT RETENTION — Keeping clients involved in treatment activities and receiving required services.

42. BENZODIAZEPINE — A type of CNS depressant sometimes prescribed to relieve anxiety, panic, or acute stress reactions. Some benzodiazepines are prescribed short-term to promote sleep.

43. RECOVERY — A process of change through which people with substance use disorders improve their health and wellness, live self-directed lives, and strive to reach their full potential.

44. ANESTHETIC — A drug that causes insensitivity to pain and is used for surgeries and other medical procedures.

45. CEREBRUM — The upper part of the brain consisting of the left and right hemispheres.

46. FUNCTIONAL — Pertaining to a person's ability to carry out tasks.

47. SKIN ABSCESS — A collection of pus formed as a result of bacterial infection.

48. TRANSFERENCE — The feelings, reactions, biases, and images from the past that the client with cod may project onto the clinician.

49. SUICIDALITY — A measure or estimate of a person's likelihood of committing suicide. A high-risk behavior associated with cod, especially (although not limited to) serious mood disorders.

50. ASSERTIVE COMMUNITY TREATMENT — Emphasizes shared decision making with the client as essential to the client's engagement process.

- A. Skin Abscess
- B. Comorbidity
- C. Naltrexone
- D. Quadrants of Care
- E. Functional
- F. Treatment Retention
- G. Reward
- H. Cannabinoids
- I. Drugged Driving
- J. Cerebrum
- K. Organization
- L. Suicidality
- M. Personality Disorders
- N. Transference
- O. Integration
- P. Locus
- Q. Anesthetic
- R. Psychosis
- S. Flashback
- T. Recovery
- U. Engagement
- V. Assertive Community Treatment
- W. Grounding
- X. Habilitation
- Y. Benzodiazepine

Provide the word that best matches each clue.

51. **CONCOMITANT TREATMENT** — Treatment of two or more mental or physical disorders at the same time.

52. **DOPAMINE** — A brain chemical, classified as a neurotransmitter, found in regions of the brain that regulate movement, emotion, motivation, and reinforcement of rewarding behavior.

53. **BASIC PROGRAM** — A treatment program with the capacity to provide treatment for one disorder, but that also screens for other disorders and is able to access necessary consultations.

54. **NEURON** — A unique type of cell found in the brain and throughout the body that specializes in the transmission and processing of information.

55. **BASAL GANGLIA** — The area of the brain that plays an important role in positive forms of motivation, including the pleasurable effects of healthy activities like eating, socializing, and sex.

56. **DETOXIFICATION** — A process in which the body rids itself of a drug, or its metabolites.

57. **ANTISOCIAL PERSONALITY DISORDER** — An illness whose features are a pervasive disregard for and violation of the rights of others and an inability to form meaningful interpersonal relationships.

58. **SERVICE INTEGRATION** — No one set of treatment interventions constitutes integrated treatment.

59. **CANNABIDIOL** — A component of the marijuana plant without mind-altering effects that is being studied for possible medical uses.

60. **ASSESSMENT** — The evaluation or estimation of the nature, quality, or ability of someone or something.

61. **PERSONALITY DISORDERS** — Rigid, inflexible, and maladaptive behavior patterns of sufficient severity to cause internal distress or significant impairment in functioning.

62. **UPPERS** — Slang term used to describe drugs that have a stimulating effect on the central nervous system. Examples include cocaine, caffeine, and amphetamines.

63. IMPULSIVITY — A tendency to act without foresight or regard for consequences and to prioritize immediate rewards over long-term goals.

64. ABSTINENT — Not using substances of abuse at any time.

65. DUAL DIAGNOSIS ENHANCED — Of or pertaining to programs that have a higher than average level of integration of substance abuse and mental health treatment services.

66. SINGLE STATE AGENCY — Systems that organize statewide services.

67. SLURRED SPEECH — A sign of depressant intoxication. When people consume significant amounts of sedative-hypnotics and opioids, their speech may become garbled, mumbled, and slow.

68. ADDERALL — A brand name amphetamine for treating ADHD.

69. CEREBRAL HEMISPHERES — The right and left halves of the brain.

70. SKIN ABSCESS — A collection of pus formed as a result of bacterial infection.

71. HABILITATION — Initial learning and the acquisition of skills necessary for everyday life.

72. SUBSTANCE ABUSE — A maladaptive pattern of substance use manifested by recurrent and significant adverse consequences related to the repeated use of substances.

73. MUTUAL SELF HELP — An approach to recovery from substance use disorders that emphasizes personal responsibility, self-management, and clients' helping one another.

74. CONTINGENCY MANAGEMENT — An approach to treatment that maintains that the form or frequency of behavior can be altered through a planned and organized system of consequences.

75. ICE — Slang term for Smoke able methamphetamine.

A. Cannabidiol
B. Assessment
C. Mutual Self Help
D. Substance Abuse
E. Impulsivity
F. Neuron
G. Single State Agency
H. Ice
I. Detoxification
J. Personality Disorders
K. Dopamine
L. Service Integration
M. Basal Ganglia
N. Slurred Speech
O. Uppers
P. Adderall
Q. Habilitation
R. Antisocial Personality Disorder

S. Dual Diagnosis Enhanced
T. Skin Abscess
U. Contingency Management
V. Abstinent
W. Concomitant Treatment
X. Cerebral Hemispheres
Y. Basic Program

Provide the word that best matches each clue.

76. PERSONALITY DISORDERS — Rigid, inflexible, and maladaptive behavior patterns of sufficient severity to cause internal distress or significant impairment in functioning.

77. PREFRONTAL CORTEX — The front part of the brain responsible for reasoning, planning, problem solving, and other higher cognitive functions.

78. FUNCTIONAL — Pertaining to a person's ability to carry out tasks.

79. PARTIAL AGONIST — A substance that binds to and activates a receptor to a lesser degree than a full agonist.

80. NEURON — A unique type of cell found in the brain and throughout the body that specializes in the transmission and processing of information.

81. HALLUCINATIONS — Sensations, sounds and

82. OVERDOSE — An overdose occurs when a person uses enough of a drug to produce a life-threatening reaction or death.

83. BLACKOUT — A period of amnesia or memory loss, typically caused by chronic, high-dose substance abuse.

84. PSYCHOPHARMACOLOGICAL — Pertaining to medications used to treat mental illnesses.

85. LEGAL PROBLEMS — People who abuse substances are at a higher risk for engaging in behaviors that are high risk and illegal.

86. NEUROLEPTIC MEDICATION — A drug used to treat psychosis, especially schizophrenia.

87. COGNITIVE BEHAVIORAL THERAPY — A therapeutic approach that seeks to modify negative or self-defeating thoughts and behavior.

88. BASIC PROGRAM — A treatment program with the capacity to provide treatment for one disorder, but that also screens for other disorders and is able to access necessary consultations.

89. INTERVENTION _____ Encompasses the specific treatment strategies, therapies, or techniques that are used to treat one or more disorders.

90. DETOXIFICATION _____ A process in which the body rids itself of a drug, or its metabolites.

91. SUBSTANCE DEPENDENCE _____ A maladaptive pattern of substance use leading to clinically significant impairment or distress.

92. CONSULTATION _____ In the context of treatment programs, consultation is a traditional type of informal relationship among treatment providers, such as a referral or a request for exchanging information.

93. COMORBIDITY _____ When two disorders or illnesses occur in the same person.

94. TOLERANCE _____ A condition in which higher doses of a drug are required to achieve the desired effect.

95. DRUG ABUSE _____ An older diagnostic term that defined use that is unsafe, use that leads a person to fail to fulfill responsibilities or gets them in legal trouble.

96. TOXICITY _____ Poisonous nature; poisonous quality.

97. ASSERTIVE COMMUNITY TREATMENT _____ Emphasizes shared decision making with the client as essential to the client's engagement process.

98. MODIFIED THERAPEUTIC COMMUNITY _____ A therapeutic community whose approach to treatment adapts the principles and methods of the therapeutic community to the circumstances of the cod client.

99. ANOREXIA NERVOSA _____ A disorder in which the individual refuses to maintain a normal body weight, is afraid of gaining weight, and exhibits a significant disturbance in the perception of body shape.

100. INTERMEDIATE PROGRAM _____ A treatment program that focuses primarily on one disorder without substantial modification to its usual treatment.

A. Functional
B. Intervention
C. Personality Disorders
D. Overdose
E. Basic Program
F. Legal Problems
G. Cognitive Behavioral Therapy
H. Prefrontal Cortex
I. Partial Agonist
J. Psychopharmacological

K. Tolerance
L. Consultation
M. Blackout
N. Modified Therapeutic Community
O. Neuroleptic Medication
P. Detoxification
Q. Drug Abuse
R. Neuron
S. Substance Dependence
T. Hallucinations
U. Comorbidity
V. Intermediate Program
W. Assertive Community Treatment
X. Toxicity
Y. Anorexia Nervosa

Provide the word that best matches each clue.

101. MENTAL HEALTH PROGRAM — An organized array of services and interventions with a primary focus on treating mental health disorders, whether providing acute stabilization or ongoing treatment.

102. PHARMACOKINETICS — What the body does to a drug after it has been taken, including how rapidly the drug is absorbed, broken down, and processed by the body.

103. ICE — Slang term for Smoke able methamphetamine.

104. BASAL GANGLIA — The area of the brain that plays an important role in positive forms of motivation, including the pleasurable effects of healthy activities like eating, socializing, and sex.

105. CEREBRAL CORTEX — The gray matter that covers the surface of the cerebral hemispheres, whose functions include sensory processing and motor control along with language, reasoning, and decision-making.

106. CNS DEPRESSANTS — A class of drugs that include sedatives, tranquilizers, and hypnotics.

107. OVERDOSE — An overdose occurs when a person uses enough of a drug to produce a life-threatening reaction or death.

108. GROUNDING — The use of strategies that soothe and distract the client who is experiencing intense pain or other strong emotions, helping the client anchor in the present and in reality.

109. SYSTEM — An organization of a number of different treatment programs and related services in order to implement a specific mission and common goals.

110.	SUBSTANCE ABUSE TREATMENT SYSTEM	A broad array of services organized into programs intended to treat substance use disorders.
111.	MUTUAL SELF HELP	An approach to recovery from substance use disorders that emphasizes personal responsibility, self-management, and clients' helping one another.
112.	SUICIDALITY	A measure or estimate of a person's likelihood of committing suicide. A high-risk behavior associated with cod, especially (although not limited to) serious mood disorders.
113.	CEREBRAL HEMISPHERES	The right and left halves of the brain.
114.	ECSTASY	Slang term for methylenedioxymethamphetamine, a member of the amphetamine family. At lower doses, MDMA causes distortions of emotional perceptions.
115.	ANESTHETIC	A drug that causes insensitivity to pain and is used for surgeries and other medical procedures.
116.	NOREPINEPHRINE	A neurotransmitter that affects heart rate, blood pressure, stress, and attention.
117.	TREATMENT RETENTION	Keeping clients involved in treatment activities and receiving required services.
118.	ADVANCED PROGRAM	A treatment program that has the capacity to provide integrated substance abuse and mental health treatment for clients with COD.
119.	NEUROTRANSMITTER	A chemical compound that acts as a messenger to carry signals from one nerve cell to another.
120.	FULLY INTEGRATED PROGRAM	A treatment program that actively combines substance abuse and mental health interventions to treat disorders, related problems, and the whole person more effectively.
121.	STIGMA	A negative association attached to some activity or condition. A cause of shame or embarrassment.
122.	NODDING OUT	Slang term for the early stages of depressant-induced sleep.
123.	COKE BUGS	Slang term for tactile hallucinations that feel like bugs crawling on or under the skin.

124. ROUTE OF ADMINISTRATION — The way a drug is taken into the body. Drugs are most commonly taken by eating, drinking, inhaling, injecting, snorting, or smoking.

125. THERAPEUTIC COMMUNITY — A consciously designed social environment or residential treatment setting in which the social and group process is harnessed with therapeutic intent.

A. System
B. Mutual Self Help
C. Pharmacokinetics
D. Mental Health Program
E. Neurotransmitter
F. Fully Integrated Program
G. Grounding
H. Anesthetic
I. Route of Administration
J. Cerebral Hemispheres
K. Ice
L. Ecstasy
M. Cerebral Cortex
N. Coke Bugs
O. Stigma
P. CNS Depressants
Q. Treatment Retention
R. Norepinephrine
S. Advanced Program
T. Nodding Out
U. Basal Ganglia
V. Substance Abuse Treatment System
W. Therapeutic Community
X. Overdose
Y. Suicidality

Provide the word that best matches each clue.

126. PARANOIA — A type of delusion, or false idea, that is unchanged by reasoned argument or proof to the contrary.

127. CULTURAL SENSITIVITY — The capacity and willingness of a clinician or other service provider to be open to working with issues of culture and diversity.

128. SYSTEM — An organization of a number of different treatment programs and related services in order to implement a specific mission and common goals.

129. IMPULSIVITY — A tendency to act without foresight or regard for consequences and to prioritize immediate rewards over long-term goals.

130. DISORDER — An illness or a disruption of some mental or physical process.

131. STIGMA — A negative association attached to some activity or condition. A cause of shame or embarrassment.

132. HALLUCINATIONS — Sensations, sounds and

133.	DUAL RECOVERY GROUPS	Therapy groups in which recovery skills for co-occurring disorders are discussed.
134.	TOXICITY	Poisonous nature; poisonous quality.
135.	CRAVING	A powerful, often overwhelming desire to use drugs.
136.	NEUROBIOLOGY	The study of the anatomy, function, and diseases of the brain and nervous system.
137.	TRAUMA	Violent mental or physical harm to a person, damage to an organ, etc.
138.	FUNCTIONAL	Pertaining to a person's ability to carry out tasks.
139.	SUBSTANCE DEPENDENCE	A maladaptive pattern of substance use leading to clinically significant impairment or distress.
140.	CROSS TRAINING	The simultaneous provision of material and training to persons from more than one discipline.
141.	COERCED	Legally forced or compelled.
142.	NOREPINEPHRINE	A neurotransmitter that affects heart rate, blood pressure, stress, and attention.
143.	DOWNERS	Slang term for drugs that exert a depressant effect on the central nervous system. In general, downers are sedative-hypnotic drugs, such as benzodiazepines and barbiturates.
144.	GROUNDING	The use of strategies that soothe and distract the client who is experiencing intense pain or other strong emotions, helping the client anchor in the present and in reality.
145.	ANABOLIC ANDROGENIC STEROIDS	Synthetic substances similar to the male hormone testosterone.
146.	ABSTINENCE	Not using drugs or alcohol.
147.	PSYCHOTHERAPEUTICS	Drugs that have an effect on the function of the brain and that are often used to treat psychiatric disorders.
148.	CONCOMITANT TREATMENT	Treatment of two or more mental or physical disorders at the same time.

149. PHARMACOKINETICS — What the body does to a drug after it has been taken, including how rapidly the drug is absorbed, broken down, and processed by the body.

150. SKIN ABSCESS — A collection of pus formed as a result of bacterial infection.

A. Trauma
C. Abstinence
E. Coerced
G. Paranoia
I. Neurobiology
K. Substance Dependence
M. Psychotherapeutics
O. Hallucinations
Q. Concomitant Treatment
S. Stigma
U. Impulsivity
W. Disorder
Y. Grounding
B. Dual Recovery Groups
D. System
F. Pharmacokinetics
H. Downers
J. Cultural Sensitivity
L. Norepinephrine
N. Toxicity
P. Cross Training
R. Skin Abscess
T. Anabolic Androgenic Steroids
V. Craving
X. Functional

Provide the word that best matches each clue.

151. DEFICIT — In the context of substance abuse treatment, disability, or inability to function fully.

152. REWARD — Pleasurable feelings that reinforce behavior and encourage repetition.

153. CROSS TRAINING — The simultaneous provision of material and training to persons from more than one discipline.

154. SUBSTANCE DEPENDENCE — A maladaptive pattern of substance use leading to clinically significant impairment or distress.

155. PHARMACOTHERAPY — Treatment using medications.

156. TOLERANCE — A condition in which higher doses of a drug are required to achieve the desired effect.

157. NUCLEUS ACCUMBENS — A brain region in the ventral striatum involved in motivation and reward.

158. XANAX — Brand name for benzodiazepine alprazolam.

159. PSYCHOTROPIC — Mind-altering.

160.	VENTRAL TEGMENTAL AREA	An area in the brainstem that contains dopamine neurons that make up a key part of the brain reward system, which also includes the nucleus accumbens and prefrontal cortex.
161.	PSYCHOSOCIAL	Involving a person's psychological well-being, as well as housing, employment, family, and other social aspects of life circumstances.
162.	ASSESSMENT	The evaluation or estimation of the nature, quality, or ability of someone or something.
163.	TREATMENT	Substance abuse treatment is an organized array of services and interventions with a primary focus on treating substance abuse disorders.
164.	SUBSTANCE USE DISORDERS	A class of substance-related disorders that includes both substance abuse and substance dependence.
165.	INTEGRATION	Relationships among mental health and substance abuse providers in which both fields are moved into a single treatment setting and treatment regimen.
166.	ADVANCED PROGRAM	A treatment program that has the capacity to provide integrated substance abuse and mental health treatment for clients with COD.
167.	ATTENTION DEFICIT DISORDER	A persistent pattern of inattention and hyperactivity-impulsivity that is more frequently displayed and more serious than is typically observed in comparable individuals.
168.	INJECTION DRUG USE	The act of administering drugs by injection. Blood-borne viruses, like HIV and hepatitis, can be transmitted via shared needles or other drug injection equipment.
169.	DUALLY DISORDERED	Having been diagnosed with two disorders, for example a substance use disorder and a mental health disorder.
170.	INTRANASAL	Taken through the nose.
171.	HABILITATION	Initial learning and the acquisition of skills necessary for everyday life.
172.	VAPING	Inhaling the aerosol or vapor from an electronic cigarette, e-vaporizer, or other device.
173.	HALLUCINOGENS	A broad group of drugs that cause distortions of sensory perception. The prototype hallucinogen is lysergic acid diethylamide (LSD).

174. COERCED — Legally forced or compelled.

175. COGNITIVE BEHAVIORAL THERAPY — A form of psychotherapy that teaches people strategies to identify and correct problematic associations among thoughts, emotions, and behaviors.

A. Ventral Tegmental Area
B. Hallucinogens
C. Reward
D. Attention Deficit Disorder
E. Coerced
F. Vaping
G. Injection Drug Use
H. Pharmacotherapy
I. Cognitive Behavioral Therapy
J. Psychosocial
K. Nucleus Accumbens
L. Deficit
M. Dually Disordered
N. Xanax
O. Tolerance
P. Assessment
Q. Habilitation
R. Intranasal
S. Advanced Program
T. Cross Training
U. Substance Dependence
V. Integration
W. Treatment
X. Substance Use Disorders
Y. Psychotropic

Provide the word that best matches each clue.

176. ENGAGEMENT — A client's commitment to and maintenance of treatment in all of its forms. A successful engagement program helps clients view the treatment facility as an important resource.

177. LIMBIC SYSTEM — Interconnected brain structures that process feelings, emotions, and motivations. It is also important for learning and memory.

178. LEGAL PROBLEMS — People who abuse substances are at a higher risk for engaging in behaviors that are high risk and illegal.

179. DISORDER — An illness or a disruption of some mental or physical process.

180. DOWNERS — Slang term for drugs that exert a depressant effect on the central nervous system. In general, downers are sedative-hypnotic drugs, such as benzodiazepines and barbiturates.

181. ANABOLIC ANDROGENIC STEROIDS — Synthetic substances similar to the male hormone testosterone.

182.	MENTAL HEALTH PROGRAM	An organized array of services and interventions with a primary focus on treating mental health disorders, whether providing acute stabilization or ongoing treatment.
183.	PSYCHOACTIVE	Having a specific effect on the brain.
184.	CULTURALLY COMPETENT	Biopsychosocial or other treatment that is adapted to suit the special cultural beliefs, practices, and needs of a client.
185.	PARANOIA	Extreme and unreasonable distrust of others.
186.	FORMAL COLLABORATION	Occurs when the nature of the client's disabilities requires more specific information and more complex and targeted intervention.
187.	ELECTRONIC CIGARETTE	A battery-operated device that people use to inhale an aerosol, which typically contains nicotine, flavorings, and other chemicals.
188.	ANTISOCIAL PERSONALITY DISORDER	An illness whose features are a pervasive disregard for and violation of the rights of others and an inability to form meaningful interpersonal relationships.
189.	NODDING OUT	Slang term for the early stages of depressant-induced sleep.
190.	ROUTE OF ADMINISTRATION	The way a drug is taken into the body. Drugs are most commonly taken by eating, drinking, inhaling, injecting, snorting, or smoking.
191.	CULTURAL PROFICIENCY	The highest level of cultural capacity, which implies an ability to perceive the nuances of a culture in depth and a willingness to work to advance in proficiency through leadership.
192.	CENTRAL NERVOUS SYSTEM	The system consisting of the nerves in the brain and spinal cord.
193.	COERCED	Legally forced or compelled.
194.	AGITATION	A restless inability to keep still.
195.	CANNABIDIOL	A component of the marijuana plant without mind-altering effects that is being studied for possible medical uses.

196. MUTUAL SELF HELP — An approach to recovery from substance use disorders that emphasizes personal responsibility, self-management, and clients' helping one another.

197. TOXICITY — Poisonous nature; poisonous quality.

198. ATTENTION DEFICIT DISORDER — A persistent pattern of inattention and hyperactivity-impulsivity that is more frequently displayed and more serious than is typically observed in comparable individuals.

199. CONFRONTATION — A form of interpersonal exchange in which individuals present to each other their observations of, and reactions to, behaviors and attitudes that are matters of concern.

200. CANNABIS — Another name for the marijuana plant, cannabis sativa.

- A. Downers
- B. Culturally Competent
- C. Paranoia
- D. Confrontation
- E. Antisocial Personality Disorder
- F. Formal Collaboration
- G. Legal Problems
- H. Psychoactive
- I. Nodding Out
- J. Central Nervous System
- K. Anabolic Androgenic Steroids
- L. Route of Administration
- M. Toxicity
- N. Agitation
- O. Attention Deficit Disorder
- P. Cultural Proficiency
- Q. Limbic System
- R. Cannabis
- S. Disorder
- T. Mutual Self Help
- U. Cannabidiol
- V. Mental Health Program
- W. Engagement
- X. Coerced
- Y. Electronic Cigarette

Word Search

1. Find the hidden words. The words have been placed horizontally, vertically, or diagonally. When you locate a word, draw an ellipse around it.

V	E	A	J	Q	H	V	R	E	P	A	T	C	R	A	V	I	N	G	M	A	Q	F
J	I	N	C	A	R	D	I	O	V	A	S	C	U	L	A	R	S	Y	S	T	E	M
X	D	X	R	F	S	I	G	B	A	Z	J	E	S	V	S	S	K	A	A	Q	T	M
Z	E	I	I	G	I	N	J	E	C	T	I	O	N	D	R	U	G	U	S	E	N	U
A	T	E	S	S	I	C	O	N	S	T	R	I	C	T	E	D	P	U	P	I	L	S
K	O	T	K	N	N	O	I	R	D	P	K	V	Z	N	P	D	J	R	X	R	Y	J
X	X	Y	F	D	H	I	N	L	Z	Z	M	X	J	R	S	Y	H	O	S	P	M	W
P	I	D	A	I	B	R	T	D	I	A	O	A	N	B	P	D	I	J	W	V	Q	V
B	F	I	C	S	B	B	R	N	P	G	F	D	G	C	E	R	E	B	R	U	M	G
T	I	S	T	O	C	B	A	F	B	O	L	O	T	F	A	B	X	R	T	Z	U	K
M	C	O	O	R	Y	W	N	T	A	N	I	W	W	C	R	S	R	O	K	I	Z	V
L	A	R	R	D	X	P	A	L	Z	I	I	N	Z	E	K	D	I	U	X	Z	B	B
H	T	D	S	E	R	B	S	R	J	S	N	E	F	K	G	Y	O	I	T	E	U	R
C	I	E	C	R	F	W	A	K	I	T	K	R	E	Y	R	I	X	Z	B	F	R	R
P	O	R	G	S	H	I	L	M	Y	S	E	S	F	A	T	Q	K	F	I	Q	S	V
T	N	F	R	Z	S	U	I	C	I	D	A	L	I	T	Y	G	X	S	S	E	I	K

1. Slang term for drugs that exert a depressant effect on the central nervous system. In general, downers are sedative-hypnotic drugs, such as benzodiazepines and barbiturates.
2. Pupils that are temporarily narrowed or closed. This is usually a sign of opioid abuse.
3. Taken through the nose.
4. An illness or a disruption of some mental or physical process.
5. A powerful, often overwhelming desire to use drugs.
6. An illness whose essential feature is excessive anxiety and worry.
7. The act of administering drugs by injection. Blood-borne viruses, like HIV and hepatitis, can be transmitted via shared needles or other drug injection equipment.
8. The system consisting of the heart and blood vessels. It delivers nutrients and oxygen to all cells in the body.
9. A process in which the body rids itself of a drug, or its metabolites.
10. The upper part of the brain consisting of the left and right hemispheres.
11. A chemical substance that binds to and activates certain receptors on cells, causing a biological response.
12. A measure or estimate of a person's likelihood of committing suicide. A high-risk behavior associated with cod, especially (although not limited to) serious mood disorders.
13. Factors that increase the likelihood of beginning substance use, of regular and harmful use, and of other behavioral health problems associated with use.

A. Cerebrum
B. Cardiovascular System
C. Suicidality
D. Anxiety Disorder
E. Craving
F. Agonist
G. Disorder
H. Injection Drug Use
I. Constricted Pupils
J. Intranasal
K. Detoxification
L. Downers
M. Risk Factors

2. Find the hidden words. The words have been placed horizontally, vertically, or diagonally. When you locate a word, draw an ellipse around it.

O	C	A	H	R	O	P	B	J	F	J	Q	S	D	L	Q	P	U	D	D	W	D	J
W	E	I	M	E	N	T	A	L	D	I	S	O	R	D	E	R	B	Q	M	A	U	L
I	R	E	S	I	U	Q	Y	Z	K	K	H	D	X	Q	D	B	H	R	B	V	A	N
T	E	R	D	R	U	G	A	B	U	S	E	R	A	L	N	A	B	P	F	W	L	G
H	B	Y	Q	O	V	E	R	D	O	S	E	F	O	E	X	S	R	W	P	A	L	T
D	R	E	A	G	H	Q	G	N	T	C	Q	A	U	Z	I	A	T	D	G	V	Y	S
R	A	A	T	C	A	N	E	S	T	H	E	T	I	C	E	L	L	Q	Y	J	D	L
A	L	F	P	V	M	M	A	R	I	J	U	A	N	A	V	G	T	N	R	T	I	D
W	C	W	V	C	M	E	U	H	A	L	L	U	C	I	N	A	T	I	O	N	S	P
A	O	X	V	F	F	T	N	A	L	O	X	O	N	E	L	N	T	L	B	W	O	Z
L	R	A	C	W	V	H	Q	S	W	B	N	N	V	O	Z	G	G	V	C	K	R	C
Z	T	W	Y	H	H	A	O	N	V	T	E	A	M	D	T	L	P	V	T	K	D	V
Y	E	M	D	Z	A	D	Z	H	U	J	W	Z	J	I	J	I	I	B	Z	B	E	T
U	X	H	I	V	Y	O	S	A	A	J	B	Z	D	M	K	A	H	M	Q	V	R	X
X	I	A	U	D	Y	N	U	U	S	D	V	S	P	U	A	Q	N	Q	R	E	E	G
A	Y	Y	S	K	T	E	M	Z	B	F	L	A	S	H	B	A	C	K	W	S	D	F

1. The gray matter that covers the surface of the cerebral hemispheres, whose functions include sensory processing and motor control along with language, reasoning, and decision-making.
2. The area of the brain that plays an important role in positive forms of motivation, including the pleasurable effects of healthy activities like eating, socializing, and sex.
3. An overdose occurs when a person uses enough of a drug to produce a life-threatening reaction or death.
4. A mental condition marked primarily by disorganization of personality, mind, and emotions that seriously impairs the psychological or behavioral functioning of the individual.
5. An older diagnostic term that defined use that is unsafe, use that leads a person to fail to fulfill responsibilities or gets them in legal trouble.
6. The Indian hemp plant cannabis sativa; also called "pot" and "weed."
7. A drug that causes insensitivity to pain and is used for surgeries and other medical procedures.
8. A long-acting opioid agonist medication used for the treatment of opioid addiction and pain.
9. Having been diagnosed with two disorders, for example a substance use disorder and a mental health disorder.
10. A sudden but temporary recurrence of aspects of a drug experience that may occur days, weeks, or even more than a year after using drugs that cause hallucinations.
11. Sensations, sounds and
12. Symptoms that can occur after long-term use of a drug is reduced or stopped.
13. An opioid antagonist medication approved by the FDA to reverse an opioid overdose.

A. Withdrawal
B. Drug Abuse
C. Hallucinations
D. Flashback
E. Marijuana
F. Naloxone
G. Dually Disordered
H. Anesthetic
I. Mental Disorder
J. Overdose
K. Basal Ganglia
L. Methadone
M. Cerebral Cortex

3. Find the hidden words. The words have been placed horizontally, vertically, or diagonally. When you locate a word, draw an ellipse around it.

B	B	D	L	U	M	E	W	E	Y	I	I	N	T	E	R	V	E	N	T	I	O	N
A	X	N	P	S	Y	C	H	O	T	H	E	R	A	P	E	U	T	I	C	S	J	J
S	I	M	U	T	V	Z	Q	R	X	J	B	B	T	F	H	U	Q	G	D	M	N	R
A	P	V	A	M	U	A	A	N	A	L	G	E	S	I	C	S	I	R	B	K	J	A
L	T	H	E	R	A	P	E	U	T	I	C	C	O	M	M	U	N	I	T	Y	R	K
G	Z	E	I	A	T	P	K	F	B	S	L	K	Q	X	D	R	Q	J	X	V	E	Q
A	X	Y	S	J	A	G	O	N	I	S	T	E	Q	I	G	I	R	R	S	V	W	I
N	Q	I	F	K	X	D	M	N	D	P	B	D	D	F	Z	K	B	M	E	U	A	B
G	F	P	P	S	Y	C	H	O	A	C	T	I	V	E	R	O	Y	C	Y	S	R	B
L	H	A	L	L	U	C	I	N	A	T	I	O	N	S	T	R	V	O	N	J	D	L
I	Z	Z	S	D	K	V	D	I	R	E	M	I	S	S	I	O	N	B	N	D	S	G
A	Y	P	F	N	A	G	K	T	O	W	Y	A	N	V	B	V	J	H	O	S	Y	Q
V	E	N	T	R	A	L	T	E	G	M	E	N	T	A	L	A	R	E	A	Y	S	C
P	S	Y	C	H	O	P	H	A	R	M	A	C	O	L	O	G	I	C	A	L	T	M
M	Q	R	K	L	I	M	L	M	O	O	D	D	I	S	O	R	D	E	R	S	E	Y
C	O	N	T	I	N	G	E	N	C	Y	M	A	N	A	G	E	M	E	N	T	M	S

1. Sensations, sounds and
2. Having a specific effect on the brain.
3. A brain circuit that includes the ventral tegmental area, the nucleus accumbens, and the prefrontal cortex.
4. The area of the brain that plays an important role in positive forms of motivation, including the pleasurable effects of healthy activities like eating, socializing, and sex.
5. A medical term meaning that major disease symptoms are eliminated or diminished below a pre-determined harmful level.
6. Encompasses the specific treatment strategies, therapies, or techniques that are used to treat one or more disorders.
7. A consciously designed social environment or residential treatment setting in which the social and group process is harnessed with therapeutic intent.
8. A chemical substance that binds to and activates certain receptors on cells, causing a biological response.
9. A psychological disorder characterized by the elevation or lowering of a person's mood, such as depression or bipolar disorder.
10. An area in the brainstem that contains dopamine neurons that make up a key part of the brain reward system, which also includes the nucleus accumbens and prefrontal cortex.
11. Pertaining to medications used to treat mental illnesses.
12. A group of medications that reduce pain.
13. Drugs that have an effect on the function of the brain and that are often used to treat psychiatric disorders.
14. A treatment approach based on providing incentives to support positive behavior change.

A. Mood Disorders
B. Therapeutic Community
C. Basal Ganglia
D. Contingency Management
E. Psychopharmacological
F. Reward System
G. Psychoactive
H. Hallucinations
I. Remission
J. Analgesics
K. Agonist
L. Ventral Tegmental Area
M. Psychotherapeutics
N. Intervention

4. Find the hidden words. The words have been placed horizontally, vertically, or diagonally. When you locate a word, draw an ellipse around it.

P	R	O	T	E	A	S	E	I	N	H	I	B	I	T	O	R	C	U	L	P	O	D
C	A	N	N	A	B	I	N	O	I	D	S	E	D	U	I	C	O	Q	W	R	C	U
B	R	Q	P	T	H	Y	U	Z	K	Q	Z	C	N	S	B	K	N	O	Z	O	H	A
F	J	O	N	B	V	A	Q	H	F	M	F	S	P	Z	C	Z	T	L	U	G	Z	L
C	C	R	Q	E	K	S	L	O	B	U	X	T	V	C	K	T	I	C	I	N	R	L
S	R	G	N	A	P	U	O	D	A	S	H	A	T	V	Q	X	N	O	H	O	H	Y
K	A	A	M	M	J	D	V	R	B	N	U	S	G	S	L	D	U	C	M	S	M	D
Q	C	N	K	P	G	X	E	F	O	M	D	Y	R	K	S	S	I	K	W	I	J	I
O	K	I	V	H	Z	H	I	N	T	R	A	N	A	S	A	L	N	T	F	S	V	S
B	M	Z	C	E	E	M	P	I	R	I	C	A	L	A	H	L	G	O	P	F	H	O
I	A	A	M	T	H	R	E	C	E	P	T	O	R	K	C	F	C	Y	W	Z	D	R
G	J	T	U	A	P	S	Y	C	H	O	A	C	T	I	V	E	A	J	J	I	X	D
I	D	I	F	M	T	L	P	F	L	C	E	G	B	O	C	F	R	L	K	K	K	E
C	E	O	S	I	T	J	W	G	R	U	C	H	R	Y	C	R	E	G	C	C	P	R
P	X	N	B	N	Y	A	B	R	U	K	B	B	Y	K	Y	Z	F	T	P	J	V	E
W	E	Y	L	E	I	V	A	D	D	I	C	T	I	O	N	M	I	Y	X	V	C	D

1. Care that supports a client's progress, monitors his or her condition, and can respond to a return to substance use or a return of symptoms of mental disorder.
2. Slang term for methylenedioxymethamphetamine, a member of the amphetamine family. At lower doses, MDMA causes distortions of emotional perceptions.
3. Relying on observation or experience rather than theoretical principles or theory.
4. Chemicals that bind to cannabinoid receptors in the brain.
5. Having been diagnosed with two disorders, for example a substance use disorder and a mental health disorder.
6. A stimulant drug that acts on the central nervous system (CNS).
7. Cocaine that has been chemically modified so that it will become a gas vapor when heated at relatively low temperatures.
8. Physical dependence on a substance of abuse. Inability to cease use of a substance without experiencing withdrawal symptoms.
9. An entity that provides mental health services in two or three service settings and is not classified as a psychiatric or general hospital or as a residential treatment center.
10. Having a specific effect on the brain.
11. Taken through the nose.
12. Medications used to treat HIV; they interfere with the action of this enzyme, thus interfering with viral reproduction.
13. A molecule located on the surface of a cell that recognizes specific chemicals and transmits the chemical message into the cell.
14. A clinician's judgment or estimate of how well a disorder will respond to treatment.

A. Intranasal
B. Receptor
C. Dually Disordered
D. Amphetamine
E. Continuing Care
F. Prognosis
G. Psychoactive
H. Cannabinoids
I. Crack
J. Organization
K. Addiction
L. Protease Inhibitor
M. Ecstasy
N. Empirical

5. Find the hidden words. The words have been placed horizontally, vertically, or diagonally. When you locate a word, draw an ellipse around it.

I	V	V	P	A	T	H	O	L	O	G	I	C	A	L	G	A	M	B	L	I	N	G
N	B	F	D	E	L	I	R	I	U	M	T	R	E	M	E	N	S	S	S	R	B	V
Q	S	E	W	S	Y	W	X	R	S	G	S	K	Z	P	Q	E	O	I	V	N	F	Y
P	P	D	M	C	U	L	T	U	R	A	L	S	E	N	S	I	T	I	V	I	T	Y
E	O	X	R	E	U	J	H	T	D	Y	U	J	B	Z	E	J	C	C	L	O	L	O
N	D	I	A	M	P	H	E	T	A	M	I	N	E	G	I	K	T	P	H	P	M	S
J	F	U	L	L	Y	I	N	T	E	G	R	A	T	E	D	P	R	O	G	R	A	M
T	D	O	W	N	E	R	S	B	D	E	T	O	X	I	F	I	C	A	T	I	O	N
C	Y	A	R	W	N	G	U	Z	T	N	B	O	M	V	N	R	X	S	Z	J	N	V
C	O	N	T	I	N	G	E	N	C	Y	M	A	N	A	G	E	M	E	N	T	O	A
X	Z	O	R	E	W	J	Q	U	P	P	E	R	S	P	L	I	A	D	K	X	O	B
H	J	J	M	V	J	F	C	T	X	P	Z	J	J	I	O	H	J	Z	T	X	Y	O
P	C	K	C	A	G	E	Q	U	E	S	T	I	O	N	N	A	I	R	E	W	Q	G
M	I	N	T	E	R	V	E	N	T	I	O	N	J	G	H	A	E	Y	C	E	L	C
I	N	T	E	G	R	A	T	E	D	I	N	T	E	R	V	E	N	T	I	O	N	S
C	O	N	C	O	M	I	T	A	N	T	T	R	E	A	T	M	E	N	T	F	O	T

1. A treatment program that actively combines substance abuse and mental health interventions to treat disorders, related problems, and the whole person more effectively.
2. A clearing of toxins from the body.
3. An illness whose essential feature is persistent and recurrent maladaptive gambling behavior that disrupts personal, family, or vocational pursuits.
4. The capacity and willingness of a clinician or other service provider to be open to working with issues of culture and diversity.
5. Specific treatment strategies in which interventions for two or more disorders are combined in a single session or interaction, or in a series of interactions or multiple sessions.
6. Inhaling the aerosol or vapor from an electronic cigarette, e-vaporizer, or other device.
7. A stimulant drug that acts on the central nervous system (CNS).
8. Encompasses the specific treatment strategies, therapies, or techniques that are used to treat one or more disorders.
9. Slang term used to describe drugs that have a stimulating effect on the central nervous system. Examples include cocaine, caffeine, and amphetamines.
10. A brief alcoholism screening tool.
11. A treatment approach based on providing incentives to support positive behavior change.
12. A state of confusion accompanied by trembling and vivid hallucinations.
13. Treatment of two or more mental or physical disorders at the same time.
14. Slang term for drugs that exert a depressant effect on the central nervous system. In general, downers are sedative-hypnotic drugs, such as benzodiazepines and barbiturates.

A. Concomitant Treatment
B. Amphetamine
C. Delirium Tremens
D. Downers
E. Integrated Interventions
F. Fully Integrated Program
G. Cultural Sensitivity
H. Contingency Management
I. Vaping
J. Intervention
K. Pathological Gambling
L. Uppers
M. Detoxification
N. Cage Questionnaire

6. Find the hidden words. The words have been placed horizontally, vertically, or diagonally. When you locate a word, draw an ellipse around it.

A	M	P	H	E	T	A	M	I	N	E	E	T	R	C	K	U	Q	M	H	V	P	F
V	U	S	D	F	I	X	O	P	C	H	K	O	E	E	A	Z	T	N	G	H	T	J
W	E	D	J	W	T	K	T	M	Z	G	I	E	Y	P	T	Z	W	C	O	C	M	H
D	E	T	O	X	I	F	I	C	A	T	I	O	N	O	G	Q	Q	N	O	H	I	X
C	L	W	E	L	E	C	T	R	O	N	I	C	C	I	G	A	R	E	T	T	E	Y
C	Z	A	V	F	I	U	K	C	I	W	Z	C	J	Z	N	K	F	F	G	J	X	P
C	G	C	X	F	F	R	I	O	G	T	B	R	R	E	C	O	V	E	R	Y	R	A
C	E	N	T	R	A	L	N	E	R	V	O	U	S	S	Y	S	T	E	M	V	H	I
U	R	W	G	K	Q	O	E	R	O	T	Y	S	X	F	M	B	M	W	U	S	I	D
O	V	E	R	D	O	S	E	C	P	T	Z	P	G	A	S	I	N	O	Y	W	M	R
A	J	S	P	N	S	R	L	E	S	P	J	O	P	P	F	D	A	O	A	Q	C	D
G	U	J	O	L	G	F	J	D	U	S	U	I	C	I	D	A	L	I	T	Y	A	S
U	A	D	D	A	D	D	E	R	A	L	L	E	E	P	M	E	A	J	G	S	L	C
D	C	A	R	D	I	O	V	A	S	C	U	L	A	R	S	Y	S	T	E	M	K	N
P	S	Y	C	H	O	T	R	O	P	I	C	M	E	D	I	C	A	T	I	O	N	J
P	S	Y	C	H	O	P	H	A	R	M	A	C	O	L	O	G	I	C	A	L	V	V

1. A process of change through which people with substance use disorders improve their health and wellness, live self-directed lives, and strive to reach their full potential.
2. Legally forced or compelled.
3. A battery-operated device that people use to inhale an aerosol, which typically contains nicotine, flavorings, and other chemicals.
4. A brand name amphetamine for treating ADHD.
5. A drug that has an effect on the mind and sometimes affects behavior as well.
6. An overdose occurs when a person uses enough of a drug to produce a life-threatening reaction or death.
7. A process in which the body rids itself of a drug, or its metabolites.
8. The system consisting of the nerves in the brain and spinal cord.
9. Pertaining to medications used to treat mental illnesses.
10. The system consisting of the heart and blood vessels. It delivers nutrients and oxygen to all cells in the body.
11. A measure or estimate of a person's likelihood of committing suicide. A high-risk behavior associated with cod, especially (although not limited to) serious mood disorders.
12. A stimulant drug that acts on the central nervous system (CNS).

A. Overdose
D. Adderall
G. Psychotropic Medication
J. Suicidality
B. Detoxification
E. Electronic Cigarette
H. Central Nervous System
K. Psychopharmacological
C. Recovery
F. Coerced
I. Cardiovascular System
L. Amphetamine

7. Find the hidden words. The words have been placed horizontally, vertically, or diagonally. When you locate a word, draw an ellipse around it.

P	X	C	Y	G	Z	C	A	G	E	Q	U	E	S	T	I	O	N	N	A	I	R	E
H	K	F	J	D	E	T	O	X	I	F	I	C	A	T	I	O	N	V	I	V	U	O
B	Z	W	J	L	E	Y	C	X	N	R	B	A	S	I	C	P	R	O	G	R	A	M
D	J	C	O	N	T	I	N	G	E	N	C	Y	M	A	N	A	G	E	M	E	N	T
C	S	U	B	S	T	A	N	C	E	U	S	E	D	I	S	O	R	D	E	R	V	V
K	F	I	X	F	D	B	F	T	O	L	E	R	A	N	C	E	Y	F	I	B	Y	R
N	Y	M	M	X	Q	N	B	L	R	Z	J	R	R	U	E	L	O	W	X	I	J	N
L	C	P	E	Y	O	L	A	T	X	E	D	C	Z	L	J	O	U	M	V	B	K	D
K	W	U	T	F	O	J	W	U	J	R	E	W	A	R	D	I	K	T	O	D	C	W
Z	C	L	H	C	B	R	T	V	G	O	I	N	T	E	R	V	E	N	T	I	O	N
R	I	S	A	V	W	U	K	B	G	Z	J	A	G	S	A	B	D	Z	O	W	T	J
K	I	I	D	G	S	V	J	T	Z	T	K	P	Q	Q	W	B	A	X	P	Y	I	M
P	T	V	O	C	Q	G	C	A	X	R	F	Z	M	F	G	Z	P	E	Z	A	I	G
F	Z	I	N	K	Q	C	A	N	N	A	B	I	N	O	I	D	S	C	D	A	D	B
Z	X	T	E	K	W	V	O	D	B	O	H	S	C	B	E	Q	D	K	P	B	L	T
P	X	Y	Z	G	J	T	S	Z	E	Z	A	U	Q	G	B	C	J	L	K	L	C	K

1. A treatment approach based on providing incentives to support positive behavior change.
2. A long-acting opioid agonist medication used for the treatment of opioid addiction and pain.
3. A clearing of toxins from the body.
4. A treatment program with the capacity to provide treatment for one disorder, but that also screens for other disorders and is able to access necessary consultations.
5. Pleasurable feelings that reinforce behavior and encourage repetition.
6. Encompasses the specific treatment strategies, therapies, or techniques that are used to treat one or more disorders.
7. Chemicals that bind to cannabinoid receptors in the brain.
8. A brief alcoholism screening tool.
9. A condition in which higher doses of a drug are required to achieve the desired effect.
10. A medical illness caused by disordered use of a substance or substances.
11. A tendency to act without foresight or regard for consequences and to prioritize immediate rewards over long-term goals.

A. Reward
D. Intervention
G. Impulsivity
J. Cage Questionnaire
B. Contingency Management
E. Methadone
H. Cannabinoids
K. Substance Use Disorder
C. Basic Program
F. Detoxification
I. Tolerance

8. Find the hidden words. The words have been placed horizontally, vertically, or diagonally. When you locate a word, draw an ellipse around it.

P	T	Q	E	D	V	C	O	G	N	I	T	I	O	N	T	N	R	N	Y	R	I	J
S	A	K	Q	A	B	S	T	I	N	E	N	T	L	U	K	C	K	I	R	H	L	C
Y	X	P	B	B	E	Q	Z	R	E	E	J	B	F	Y	Y	M	M	L	C	C	H	O
C	W	A	R	T	A	P	B	A	Z	K	Y	W	S	X	D	M	Q	J	H	S	P	M
H	Q	E	W	Q	U	A	D	R	A	N	T	S	O	F	C	A	R	E	B	O	S	P
O	F	D	E	L	I	R	I	U	M	T	R	E	M	E	N	S	W	L	P	Y	Y	E
S	W	P	F	D	B	O	J	H	D	A	Y	Q	E	T	K	F	N	B	V	A	C	T
I	W	C	U	J	R	S	E	Q	E	U	T	P	K	B	O	J	R	O	W	P	H	E
S	C	I	F	H	U	A	A	C	Q	J	R	U	Q	O	C	T	V	V	M	I	O	N
J	T	D	I	L	A	T	E	D	P	U	P	I	L	S	C	J	H	J	G	D	S	C
E	B	N	Z	F	F	Y	N	X	M	P	R	S	C	Z	V	C	Z	Y	V	Z	I	Y
U	N	W	X	B	N	F	I	F	W	A	L	T	W	X	O	V	S	O	L	Q	S	O
W	I	F	A	V	Q	P	A	R	T	I	A	L	A	G	O	N	I	S	T	H	T	H
G	H	L	N	K	I	M	P	U	L	S	I	V	I	T	Y	D	K	N	R	X	S	A
P	H	B	A	I	N	T	E	G	R	A	T	E	D	T	R	E	A	T	M	E	N	T
M	E	X	X	V	E	N	T	R	A	L	S	T	R	I	A	T	U	M	V	E	L	A

1. Any mechanism by which treatment interventions for co-occurring disorders are combined within the context of a primary treatment relationship or service setting.
2. Relating to the act or process of thinking, understanding, learning, and remembering.
3. Pupils that have become temporarily enlarged.
4. Brand name for benzodiazepine alprazolam.
5. A state of confusion accompanied by trembling and vivid hallucinations.
6. A tendency to act without foresight or regard for consequences and to prioritize immediate rewards over long-term goals.
7. A substance that binds to and activates a receptor to a lesser degree than a full agonist.
8. Not using substances of abuse at any time.
9. An area of the brain that is part of the basal ganglia and includes the nucleus accumbens.
10. Delusional or disordered thinking detached from reality; symptoms often include hallucinations.
11. A mental disorder that is characterized by distinct distortions of a person's mental capacity, ability to recognize reality, and relationships to others.
12. A conceptual framework that classifies clients in four basic groups based on relative symptom severity, rather than by diagnosis.
13. An ability, capacity, skill, or set of skills.

A. Delirium Tremens
B. Ventral Striatum
C. Xanax
D. Partial Agonist
E. Psychosis
F. Dilated Pupils
G. Competency
H. Quadrants of Care
I. Cognition
J. Abstinent
K. Psychosis
L. Integrated Treatment
M. Impulsivity

9. Find the hidden words. The words have been placed horizontally, vertically, or diagonally. When you locate a word, draw an ellipse around it.

1. A drug that has an effect on the mind and sometimes affects behavior as well.
2. Drugs that have an effect on the function of the brain and that are often used to treat psychiatric disorders.
3. Having been diagnosed with two disorders, for example a substance use disorder and a mental health disorder.
4. Taken through the nose.
5. A type of CNS depressant sometimes prescribed to relieve anxiety, panic, or acute stress reactions. Some benzodiazepines are prescribed short-term to promote sleep.
6. A type of delusion, or false idea, that is unchanged by reasoned argument or proof to the contrary.
7. An older diagnostic term that defined use that is unsafe, use that leads a person to fail to fulfill responsibilities or gets them in legal trouble.
8. Keeping clients involved in treatment activities and receiving required services.
9. In drug addiction, relapse is the return to drug use after an attempt to stop.
10. An inflammation of the liver, with accompanying liver cell damage and risk of death.
11. The feelings, reactions, biases, and images from the past that the clinician may project onto the client with cod.
12. Of or pertaining to programs that have a higher than average level of integration of substance abuse and mental health treatment services.
13. The system consisting of the nerves in the brain and spinal cord.

A. Treatment Retention
B. Drug Abuse
C. Relapse
D. Psychotropic Medication
E. Paranoia
F. Psychotherapeutics
G. Benzodiazepine
H. Dual Diagnosis Enhanced
I. Countertransference
J. Dually Disordered
K. Intranasal
L. Hepatitis
M. Central Nervous System

10. Find the hidden words. The words have been placed horizontally, vertically, or diagonally. When you locate a word, draw an ellipse around it.

M	A	T	U	F	E	D	H	E	B	A	N	Y	C	E	R	E	B	R	U	M	W	U
L	N	R	B	F	U	N	C	T	I	O	N	A	L	Y	E	E	I	W	W	H	G	E
I	O	I	I	W	Y	D	S	K	Y	L	Q	O	A	L	M	T	W	W	Y	R	W	Y
F	R	T	P	U	T	I	D	S	P	Q	X	N	Z	A	V	Z	W	F	B	E	J	G
L	E	V	Z	A	M	Y	T	S	S	P	A	Z	I	K	F	C	P	S	B	W	E	V
O	X	R	I	O	C	P	Z	Q	Y	M	X	Q	U	P	P	M	J	T	P	A	I	V
P	I	P	S	Y	C	H	O	A	C	T	I	V	E	L	C	Q	X	E	P	R	U	S
K	A	D	E	X	N	R	T	N	H	L	Y	X	E	C	S	T	A	S	Y	D	Y	D
F	N	S	P	A	T	H	O	L	O	G	I	C	A	L	G	A	M	B	L	I	N	G
J	E	E	T	U	T	T	V	D	T	S	J	G	D	O	S	Q	X	Z	F	X	C	T
M	R	X	B	X	S	W	H	R	R	L	W	L	F	K	G	T	L	V	B	Z	O	A
L	V	N	H	O	E	U	V	A	O	X	S	F	D	Y	W	H	S	W	A	W	O	M
H	O	M	U	Y	E	L	X	M	P	E	E	Y	O	T	B	J	T	J	N	C	M	Q
N	S	D	G	B	P	A	R	T	I	A	L	A	G	O	N	I	S	T	M	K	M	S
Y	A	A	C	A	N	P	S	Y	C	H	E	D	E	L	I	C	D	R	U	G	D	B
M	P	E	R	S	O	N	A	L	I	T	Y	D	I	S	O	R	D	E	R	S	Q	A

1. The upper part of the brain consisting of the left and right hemispheres.
2. A disorder in which the individual refuses to maintain a normal body weight, is afraid of gaining weight, and exhibits a significant disturbance in the perception of body shape.
3. Mind-altering.
4. Pleasurable feelings that reinforce behavior and encourage repetition.
5. Rigid, inflexible, and maladaptive behavior patterns of sufficient severity to cause internal distress or significant impairment in functioning.
6. Pertaining to a person's ability to carry out tasks.
7. Having a specific effect on the brain.
8. Slang term for methylenedioxymethamphetamine, a member of the amphetamine family. At lower doses, MDMA causes distortions of emotional perceptions.
9. A drug that distorts perception, thought, and feeling. This term is typically used to refer to drugs with hallucinogenic effects.
10. An illness whose essential feature is persistent and recurrent maladaptive gambling behavior that disrupts personal, family, or vocational pursuits.
11. A substance that binds to and activates a receptor to a lesser degree than a full agonist.

A. Pathological Gambling
B. Psychotropic
C. Functional
D. Personality Disorders
E. Reward
F. Partial Agonist
G. Anorexia Nervosa
H. Ecstasy
I. Psychedelic Drug
J. Psychoactive
K. Cerebrum

11. Find the hidden words. The words have been placed horizontally, vertically, or diagonally. When you locate a word, draw an ellipse around it.

I	Y	S	O	T	O	A	N	G	O	I	E	U	X	Y	N	M	U	B	V	U	I	O
W	S	C	B	K	T	C	E	F	D	M	D	W	O	G	Y	I	G	S	N	U	O	C
U	P	H	Z	M	H	C	U	Q	O	P	O	U	L	O	H	Y	S	J	S	Y	U	H
I	H	I	N	U	N	R	K	P	A	K	A	Y	W	P	S	V	Y	A	M	S	A	
A	T	Z	O	J	K	L	O	K	A	I	V	Z	U	P	O	P	N	O	P	H	X	L
E	M	O	B	I	G	T	B	E	M	R	O	M	T	R	E	A	T	M	E	N	T	L
J	T	P	Z	B	P	U	I	P	I	E	H	L	Z	J	Y	K	L	Y	W	R	V	U
S	V	H	W	L	K	R	O	H	N	D	Z	K	X	U	N	L	K	T	P	Z	X	C
B	Q	R	W	X	E	A	L	Z	E	H	D	O	F	Q	X	M	G	Q	J	M	N	I
I	S	E	A	Y	M	T	O	A	R	S	V	T	A	O	Q	J	K	N	W	F	V	N
X	O	N	I	N	T	E	G	R	A	T	E	D	T	R	E	A	T	M	E	N	T	O
W	O	I	I	W	C	D	Y	I	R	E	M	I	S	S	I	O	N	N	K	N	X	G
C	X	A	V	E	N	T	R	A	L	S	T	R	I	A	T	U	M	F	G	G	W	E
D	C	O	N	T	I	N	G	E	N	C	Y	M	A	N	A	G	E	M	E	N	T	N
E	V	G	M	E	N	D	Z	P	H	M	Y	J	K	O	P	Z	M	E	S	B	J	S
R	D	A	D	D	I	C	T	I	O	N	O	N	L	Y	S	E	R	V	I	C	E	S

1. Any mechanism by which treatment interventions for co-occurring disorders are combined within the context of a primary treatment relationship or service setting.
2. A broad group of drugs that cause distortions of sensory perception. The prototype hallucinogen is lysergic acid diethylamide (LSD).
3. Mentally and physically in harmony with and connected to the culture in which one lives.
4. Substance abuse treatment is an organized array of services and interventions with a primary focus on treating substance abuse disorders.
5. Hampered or held back from being able to do some mental or physical task.
6. Programs that by law or regulation, by choice, or for lack of resources cannot accommodate patients who have psychiatric illnesses that require ongoing treatment.
7. A treatment approach based on providing incentives to support positive behavior change.
8. A brain chemical, classified as a neurotransmitter, found in regions of the brain that regulate movement, emotion, motivation, and reinforcement of rewarding behavior.
9. A medical term meaning that major disease symptoms are eliminated or diminished below a pre-determined harmful level.
10. An area of the brain that is part of the basal ganglia and includes the nucleus accumbens.
11. A type of psychosis where persons are subject to hallucinations occurring in the absence of insight into their pathological nature.
12. The study of the anatomy, function, and diseases of the brain and nervous system.

A. Treatment
B. Neurobiology
C. Dopamine
D. Schizophrenia
E. Acculturated
F. Contingency Management
G. Hallucinogens
H. Impaired
I. Integrated Treatment
J. Ventral Striatum
K. Remission
L. Addiction Only Services

12. Find the hidden words. The words have been placed horizontally, vertically, or diagonally. When you locate a word, draw an ellipse around it.

H	H	P	S	Y	C	H	O	P	H	A	R	M	A	C	O	L	O	G	I	C	A	L
W	X	R	K	C	E	R	T	B	Z	Q	B	S	A	E	X	N	B	B	M	E	M	N
I	N	E	U	R	O	L	E	P	T	I	C	M	E	D	I	C	A	T	I	O	N	F
U	C	E	B	U	I	M	P	U	L	S	I	V	I	T	Y	E	D	E	W	R	F	I
A	D	D	E	R	A	L	L	E	A	D	D	I	C	T	I	O	N	E	H	H	Q	J
O	Y	P	H	A	R	M	A	C	O	D	Y	N	A	M	I	C	S	Y	T	D	N	E
W	P	C	V	D	J	J	I	E	H	B	M	S	G	V	N	W	V	J	Z	O	I	X
T	E	N	D	Z	L	I	M	B	I	C	S	Y	S	T	E	M	K	H	A	Y	R	W
X	O	A	J	T	I	V	Z	Z	W	G	V	Y	C	T	K	B	Y	U	N	P	O	S
C	U	L	T	U	R	A	L	L	Y	C	O	M	P	E	T	E	N	T	J	Q	P	G
N	O	R	E	P	I	N	E	P	H	R	I	N	E	K	Y	X	H	C	V	V	J	G
N	P	R	O	T	E	A	S	E	I	N	H	I	B	I	T	O	R	M	B	B	E	P
I	B	A	S	A	L	G	A	N	G	L	I	A	B	N	J	P	A	F	Z	F	C	E
D	G	I	W	Q	T	E	B	K	B	C	P	D	A	C	T	N	X	O	X	S	J	A
G	R	W	G	Z	F	C	O	N	S	T	R	I	C	T	E	D	P	U	P	I	L	S
F	Y	R	E	Y	T	R	E	A	T	M	E	N	T	R	E	T	E	N	T	I	O	N

1. A drug used to treat psychosis, especially schizophrenia.
2. Pertaining to medications used to treat mental illnesses.
3. The area of the brain that plays an important role in positive forms of motivation, including the pleasurable effects of healthy activities like eating, socializing, and sex.
4. Keeping clients involved in treatment activities and receiving required services.
5. Medications used to treat HIV; they interfere with the action of this enzyme, thus interfering with viral reproduction.
6. A chronic, relapsing disorder characterized by compulsive (or difficult to control) drug seeking and use despite harmful consequences, as well as long-lasting changes in the brain.
7. Interconnected brain structures that process feelings, emotions, and motivations. It is also important for learning and memory.
8. Biopsychosocial or other treatment that is adapted to suit the special cultural beliefs, practices, and needs of a client.
9. A brand name amphetamine for treating ADHD.
10. The way a drug acts on the body.
11. A neurotransmitter that affects heart rate, blood pressure, stress, and attention.
12. A tendency to act without foresight or regard for consequences and to prioritize immediate rewards over long-term goals.
13. Pupils that are temporarily narrowed or closed. This is usually a sign of opioid abuse.

A. Constricted Pupils
B. Adderall
C. Addiction
D. Psychopharmacological
E. Basal Ganglia
F. Treatment Retention
G. Pharmacodynamics
H. Protease Inhibitor
I. Limbic System
J. Culturally Competent
K. Impulsivity
L. Norepinephrine
M. Neuroleptic Medication

13. Find the hidden words. The words have been placed horizontally, vertically, or diagonally. When you locate a word, draw an ellipse around it.

T	H	E	R	A	P	E	U	T	I	C	A	L	L	I	A	N	C	E	R	O	A	K
W	T	X	Z	T	N	G	L	K	J	M	H	R	E	C	O	V	E	R	Y	S	C	R
F	C	O	N	C	O	M	I	T	A	N	T	T	R	E	A	T	M	E	N	T	L	T
A	G	C	E	U	N	E	V	E	S	U	I	C	I	D	A	L	I	T	Y	C	K	K
B	E	I	O	T	C	A	V	Z	T	Q	N	Z	F	M	W	M	T	R	E	M	O	R
S	Y	N	W	A	Q	U	A	D	R	A	N	T	S	O	F	C	A	R	E	Z	M	X
T	I	X	F	B	F	S	D	O	L	V	B	F	B	Y	N	P	B	V	F	S	D	T
I	D	Z	I	R	I	N	F	E	C	T	I	O	U	S	S	X	R	G	K	L	S	L
N	G	W	W	Y	Q	H	B	A	S	A	L	G	A	N	G	L	I	A	Q	B	B	D
E	E	H	V	O	K	X	U	E	U	T	T	P	T	G	T	N	Z	G	X	E	L	Q
N	M	P	R	R	T	D	F	X	C	C	R	Z	U	A	W	E	M	T	M	F	R	Y
C	R	R	A	G	I	T	A	T	I	O	N	C	Q	F	C	H	K	D	W	R	O	U
E	F	W	T	E	R	Z	W	R	Q	X	U	L	S	R	V	T	D	S	G	Z	N	X
A	P	C	O	N	T	I	N	G	E	N	C	Y	M	A	N	A	G	E	M	E	N	T
D	C	U	L	T	U	R	A	L	P	R	O	F	I	C	I	E	N	C	Y	X	C	P
S	Y	U	I	G	G	R	H	T	P	U	G	U	G	B	T	H	E	M	L	M	Q	A

1. A process of change through which people with substance use disorders improve their health and wellness, live self-directed lives, and strive to reach their full potential.
2. Treatment of two or more mental or physical disorders at the same time.
3. Able to spread by an agent such as a virus or bacterium.
4. The area of the brain that plays an important role in positive forms of motivation, including the pleasurable effects of healthy activities like eating, socializing, and sex.
5. A conceptual framework that classifies clients in four basic groups based on relative symptom severity, rather than by diagnosis.
6. An approach to treatment that maintains that the form or frequency of behavior can be altered through a planned and organized system of consequences.
7. A restless inability to keep still.
8. A type of relationship between client and clinician in which both are working cooperatively toward the same goals, with mutual respect and understanding.
9. A measure or estimate of a person's likelihood of committing suicide. A high-risk behavior associated with cod, especially (although not limited to) serious mood disorders.
10. Not using drugs or alcohol.
11. An involuntary and rhythmic movement in the muscles, most often in the hands, feet, jaw, tongue, or head.
12. The highest level of cultural capacity, which implies an ability to perceive the nuances of a culture in depth and a willingness to work to advance in proficiency through leadership.

A. Basal Ganglia
D. Contingency Management
G. Quadrants of Care
J. Therapeutic Alliance
B. Suicidality
E. Agitation
H. Infectious
K. Recovery
C. Cultural Proficiency
F. Abstinence
I. Concomitant Treatment
L. Tremor

14. Find the hidden words. The words have been placed horizontally, vertically, or diagonally. When you locate a word, draw an ellipse around it.

E	L	O	H	T	R	E	A	T	M	E	N	T	R	E	T	E	N	T	I	O	N	H
V	D	B	S	E	R	V	I	C	E	I	N	T	E	G	R	A	T	I	O	N	T	W
G	Z	R	E	D	M	E	M	Z	O	A	N	X	A	E	G	R	E	L	A	P	S	E
W	G	H	L	Y	L	R	D	B	Y	Q	W	S	Y	H	K	L	P	O	B	T	J	O
G	J	Q	F	V	S	E	R	O	T	O	N	I	N	I	Z	Z	L	X	P	R	M	G
L	K	A	M	K	P	V	C	H	F	C	Y	T	N	P	P	M	N	P	C	A	K	Z
W	Q	Q	E	Z	N	Q	L	Y	L	F	F	M	M	P	J	L	H	Y	Z	U	W	T
M	U	E	D	L	I	Q	C	G	N	M	W	V	E	O	N	K	U	T	A	M	X	Y
J	D	W	I	Z	X	L	H	D	D	E	O	P	G	C	Q	M	B	L	F	A	Q	W
N	F	L	C	N	O	D	D	I	N	G	O	U	T	A	Z	J	K	H	Y	Z	R	N
Y	C	X	A	K	I	Y	F	O	W	J	Z	C	I	M	X	G	P	O	A	I	I	O
J	A	L	T	E	R	W	Q	M	E	I	D	M	R	P	Q	N	I	G	D	D	G	Q
U	N	O	I	C	D	C	D	V	T	X	R	I	Y	U	P	B	M	F	R	B	O	B
S	A	V	O	Q	Q	G	S	H	X	E	C	X	S	P	N	X	B	O	U	N	R
L	L	M	N	C	U	L	T	U	R	A	L	S	E	N	S	I	T	I	V	I	T	Y
P	E	R	S	O	N	A	L	I	T	Y	D	I	S	O	R	D	E	R	S	E	S	B

1. An area of the brain crucial for learning and memory.
2. The use of a substance to lessen the negative effects of stress, anxiety, or other mental disorders without the guidance of a health care provider.
3. A breakdown or setback in a person's attempt to change or modify any particular behavior.
4. No one set of treatment interventions constitutes integrated treatment.
5. Keeping clients involved in treatment activities and receiving required services.
6. Slang term for the early stages of depressant-induced sleep.
7. Rigid, inflexible, and maladaptive behavior patterns of sufficient severity to cause internal distress or significant impairment in functioning.
8. A neurotransmitter involved in a broad range of effects on perception, movement, and emotions. Serotonin and its receptors are the targets of most hallucinogens.
9. Violent mental or physical harm to a person, damage to an organ, etc.
10. The capacity and willingness of a clinician or other service provider to be open to working with issues of culture and diversity.

A. Trauma
B. Service Integration
C. Hippocampus
D. Serotonin
E. Relapse
F. Cultural Sensitivity
G. Personality Disorders
H. Self Medication
I. Treatment Retention
J. Nodding Out

15. Find the hidden words. The words have been placed horizontally, vertically, or diagonally. When you locate a word, draw an ellipse around it.

L	V	E	N	T	R	A	L	S	T	R	I	A	T	U	M	W	B	M	C	R	P	B
I	M	S	M	M	V	K	O	L	A	N	F	A	Z	N	P	D	C	G	B	J	G	P
N	T	H	E	R	A	P	E	U	T	I	C	C	O	M	M	U	N	I	T	Y	J	L
T	Y	B	E	N	Z	O	D	I	A	Z	E	P	I	N	E	F	T	G	K	F	K	B
R	K	I	N	B	E	P	B	Z	C	D	Z	K	Z	Y	R	B	H	Y	G	X	J	V
A	P	F	V	W	J	A	N	Q	D	D	F	P	L	V	S	M	C	M	K	O	A	H
N	Z	G	G	E	J	N	G	D	I	D	I	A	G	U	D	R	E	U	O	O	I	Z
A	Z	T	V	O	D	M	U	T	U	A	L	S	E	L	F	H	E	L	P	Z	P	L
S	V	C	O	N	T	I	N	G	E	N	C	Y	M	A	N	A	G	E	M	E	N	T
A	J	J	N	Q	I	C	E	Z	P	R	E	M	I	S	S	I	O	N	R	Z	N	H
L	M	U	Z	X	O	F	A	P	U	H	P	Z	M	Y	A	G	M	J	V	J	H	O
X	H	Z	R	S	E	D	C	N	V	B	P	S	Y	C	H	O	S	O	C	I	A	L
G	W	E	A	W	G	I	D	J	P	S	Y	C	H	O	S	I	S	U	D	G	J	W
O	S	U	B	S	T	A	N	C	E	U	S	E	D	I	S	O	R	D	E	R	S	Q
S	C	I	C	O	G	N	I	T	I	V	E	E	D	Z	X	X	R	Y	W	M	V	L
R	U	U	X	F	C	W	G	Q	C	M	G	X	U	T	B	P	V	D	O	L	A	F

1. A type of CNS depressant sometimes prescribed to relieve anxiety, panic, or acute stress reactions. Some benzodiazepines are prescribed short-term to promote sleep.
2. Pertaining to the mind's capacity to understand concepts and ideas.
3. An approach to recovery from substance use disorders that emphasizes personal responsibility, self-management, and clients' helping one another.
4. Slang term for Smoke able methamphetamine.
5. Involving a person's psychological well-being, as well as housing, employment, family, and other social aspects of life circumstances.
6. A class of substance-related disorders that includes both substance abuse and substance dependence.
7. An area of the brain that is part of the basal ganglia and includes the nucleus accumbens.
8. A state in which a mental or physical disorder has been overcome or a disease process halted.
9. A consciously designed social environment or residential treatment setting in which the social and group process is harnessed with therapeutic intent.
10. Delta-9-tetrahydrocannabinol; the main mind-altering ingredient in marijuana.
11. Taken through the nose.
12. A mental disorder that is characterized by distinct distortions of a person's mental capacity, ability to recognize reality, and relationships to others.
13. An approach to treatment that maintains that the form or frequency of behavior can be altered through a planned and organized system of consequences.

A. Contingency Management
B. Ice
C. Remission
D. Mutual Self Help
E. Therapeutic Community
F. Psychosocial
G. THC
H. Ventral Striatum
I. Intranasal
J. Benzodiazepine
K. Substance Use Disorders
L. Psychosis
M. Cognitive

16. Find the hidden words. The words have been placed horizontally, vertically, or diagonally. When you locate a word, draw an ellipse around it.

Q	Y	H	Y	G	I	Y	B	R	A	I	N	S	T	E	M	J	V	P	H	Y	C	J
L	L	Q	M	U	M	M	F	R	X	B	D	E	P	I	B	J	H	A	A	R	P	D
P	E	R	S	O	N	A	L	I	T	Y	D	I	S	O	R	D	E	R	S	Z	Y	E
P	X	I	N	F	E	C	T	I	O	U	S	S	S	R	Y	Z	R	T	K	Q	D	E
M	E	T	H	A	D	O	N	E	R	T	Y	O	Z	Z	B	F	U	I	C	S	P	I
M	A	D	R	U	G	G	E	D	D	R	I	V	I	N	G	Y	K	A	T	H	M	S
H	E	C	O	L	L	A	B	O	R	A	T	I	O	N	P	U	M	L	A	Y	C	L
U	Z	E	W	S	N	B	D	P	E	Y	S	J	N	E	C	K	E	A	Y	B	H	Q
J	R	M	J	O	J	U	N	Z	C	D	J	H	T	L	L	T	M	G	W	H	E	C
O	A	Y	R	K	R	C	V	Z	B	E	E	P	M	K	J	Y	S	O	J	C	F	V
O	Z	F	K	Q	I	N	T	E	G	R	A	T	I	O	N	Y	K	N	M	F	Z	L
G	P	S	Y	C	H	O	P	H	A	R	M	A	C	O	L	O	G	I	C	A	L	C
L	K	X	Y	C	L	D	D	C	F	D	D	Y	B	K	N	D	Y	S	C	X	T	L
Y	L	Z	B	D	K	N	W	E	S	J	K	Z	Y	B	U	G	Q	T	B	R	M	U
C	H	C	O	N	T	I	N	G	E	N	C	Y	M	A	N	A	G	E	M	E	N	T
R	X	A	Y	B	F	L	A	S	H	B	A	C	K	B	J	J	J	Z	L	M	Y	A

1. A substance that binds to and activates a receptor to a lesser degree than a full agonist.
2. Rigid, inflexible, and maladaptive behavior patterns of sufficient severity to cause internal distress or significant impairment in functioning.
3. A treatment approach based on providing incentives to support positive behavior change.
4. Pertaining to medications used to treat mental illnesses.
5. A sudden but temporary recurrence of aspects of a drug experience that may occur days, weeks, or even more than a year after using drugs that cause hallucinations.
6. A group of brain structures that process sensory information and control basic functions needed for survival such as breathing, heart rate, blood pressure, and arousal.
7. Able to spread by an agent such as a virus or bacterium.
8. The action of working with someone to produce or create something.
9. Relationships among mental health and substance abuse providers in which both fields are moved into a single treatment setting and treatment regimen.
10. Driving a vehicle while impaired due to the intoxicating effects of recent drug use.
11. A long-acting opioid agonist medication used for the treatment of opioid addiction and pain.

A. Partial Agonist
B. Integration
C. Methadone
D. Flashback
E. Personality Disorders
F. Psychopharmacological
G. Contingency Management
H. Collaboration
I. Brainstem
J. Drugged Driving
K. Infectious

17. Find the hidden words. The words have been placed horizontally, vertically, or diagonally. When you locate a word, draw an ellipse around it.

H	C	O	N	C	O	M	I	T	A	N	T	T	R	E	A	T	M	E	N	T	T	M
P	G	A	L	U	O	C	M	M	J	S	K	I	N	A	B	S	C	E	S	S	R	E
S	L	U	R	R	E	D	S	P	E	E	C	H	L	V	B	Z	D	J	S	J	G	N
K	O	A	D	D	I	C	T	I	O	N	U	D	I	A	A	Z	M	O	V	F	I	T
I	C	F	I	N	T	E	G	R	A	T	E	D	T	R	E	A	T	M	E	N	T	A
F	U	U	Q	N	D	V	O	M	S	J	Y	N	H	Z	H	D	G	Q	B	I	A	L
L	X	N	D	T	N	C	Z	X	N	L	C	N	Z	U	J	S	F	G	K	W	C	D
C	T	C	W	I	T	H	D	R	A	W	A	L	H	E	P	A	T	I	T	I	S	I
K	N	T	T	Z	E	L	P	P	G	Z	B	T	X	N	T	P	S	O	O	E	Y	S
V	A	I	I	F	Y	K	A	K	R	M	Y	J	D	S	G	U	C	U	M	Y	W	O
W	N	O	X	A	M	F	M	R	R	H	N	Y	V	P	M	K	T	G	B	O	E	R
P	N	N	D	K	T	U	M	U	P	T	C	F	B	Y	N	L	F	M	E	O	S	D
Z	E	A	L	L	H	D	U	K	J	O	L	K	R	H	Z	U	Q	S	L	A	X	E
B	N	L	L	S	U	Q	Z	Y	O	U	W	Z	M	P	I	R	Y	L	Q	S	J	R
G	F	Q	V	J	R	N	R	O	U	S	O	V	X	Q	A	S	N	N	U	L	U	U
O	K	F	R	R	C	P	R	E	F	R	O	N	T	A	L	C	O	R	T	E	X	R

1. A sign of depressant intoxication. When people consume significant amounts of sedative-hypnotics and opioids, their speech may become garbled, mumbled, and slow.
2. A collection of pus formed as a result of bacterial infection.
3. An inflammation of the liver, with accompanying liver cell damage and risk of death.
4. Any mechanism by which treatment interventions for co-occurring disorders are combined within the context of a primary treatment relationship or service setting.
5. Physical dependence on a substance of abuse. Inability to cease use of a substance without experiencing withdrawal symptoms.
6. Treatment of two or more mental or physical disorders at the same time.
7. The front part of the brain responsible for reasoning, planning, problem solving, and other higher cognitive functions.
8. Pertaining to a person's ability to carry out tasks.
9. A mental condition marked primarily by disorganization of personality, mind, and emotions that seriously impairs the psychological or behavioral functioning of the individual.
10. Symptoms that can occur after long-term use of a drug is reduced or stopped.

A. Concomitant Treatment
B. Hepatitis
C. Prefrontal Cortex
D. Slurred Speech
E. Integrated Treatment
F. Functional
G. Mental Disorder
H. Withdrawal
I. Skin Abscess
J. Addiction

18. Find the hidden words. The words have been placed horizontally, vertically, or diagonally. When you locate a word, draw an ellipse around it.

G	V	I	N	U	I	U	X	K	P	D	E	P	E	N	D	E	N	C	E	Y	M	H
Z	A	E	L	Q	C	R	R	R	A	F	Y	D	X	Y	M	L	C	K	E	A	W	O
X	N	X	G	I	R	A	N	O	R	E	X	I	A	N	E	R	V	O	S	A	C	I
F	V	D	O	I	O	D	U	U	A	K	Y	B	O	Z	Z	K	L	I	R	K	O	I
X	S	M	G	Y	S	Q	T	C	P	M	G	A	F	I	I	L	L	I	C	I	T	O
J	L	K	V	P	S	P	U	S	H	R	R	S	L	P	A	W	D	L	F	F	V	T
U	K	N	I	W	T	P	R	K	E	R	H	I	D	T	F	K	P	Z	B	N	C	U
T	P	F	B	B	R	P	H	A	R	M	A	C	O	K	I	N	E	T	I	C	S	Q
X	T	P	R	G	A	B	J	O	N	U	Y	P	Y	C	Y	Z	X	K	B	J	N	S
J	Q	H	E	J	I	S	D	B	A	C	E	R	E	B	E	L	L	U	M	Z	E	F
M	H	G	S	Y	N	U	Z	B	L	C	K	O	I	Q	Q	Q	A	Z	O	C	W	J
O	W	N	I	G	I	H	L	L	I	I	O	G	C	Y	I	P	P	T	M	U	R	H
Z	P	B	I	K	N	I	T	Z	A	Q	E	R	E	K	D	A	E	Q	Q	I	Y	Y
Z	K	M	J	R	G	N	E	B	R	E	W	A	R	D	S	Y	S	T	E	M	B	B
X	O	E	W	V	X	T	N	N	D	A	N	M	H	V	H	Y	K	Y	D	Z	Y	K
N	W	S	W	N	G	K	V	F	G	R	Y	T	P	F	G	E	H	W	D	V	V	Y

1. A treatment program with the capacity to provide treatment for one disorder, but that also screens for other disorders and is able to access necessary consultations.
2. The simultaneous provision of material and training to persons from more than one discipline.
3. A brain circuit that includes the ventral tegmental area, the nucleus accumbens, and the prefrontal cortex.
4. A broad term that describes objects used during the chemical preparation or use of drugs. These include syringes, syringe needles, roach clips, and marijuana or crack pipes.
5. Illegal or forbidden by law.
6. A condition that can occur with the regular use of illicit or some prescription drugs, even if taken as prescribed.
7. A disorder in which the individual refuses to maintain a normal body weight, is afraid of gaining weight, and exhibits a significant disturbance in the perception of body shape.
8. A part of the brain that helps regulate posture, balance, and coordination. It is also involved in the processes of emotion, motivation, memory, and thought.
9. What the body does to a drug after it has been taken, including how rapidly the drug is absorbed, broken down, and processed by the body.
10. Slang term for Smoke able methamphetamine.

A. Anorexia Nervosa
B. Basic Program
C. Paraphernalia
D. Reward System
E. Ice
F. Dependence
G. Illicit
H. Pharmacokinetics
I. Cerebellum
J. Cross Training

19. Find the hidden words. The words have been placed horizontally, vertically, or diagonally. When you locate a word, draw an ellipse around it.

I	V	A	D	D	I	C	T	I	O	N	O	N	L	Y	S	E	R	V	I	C	E	S
J	Z	O	N	V	T	O	R	L	F	N	C	I	H	V	D	Z	X	G	D	S	B	W
D	D	Z	A	V	E	N	T	R	A	L	S	T	R	I	A	T	U	M	D	A	T	I
M	Z	A	D	M	S	S	I	N	D	W	H	M	V	Y	A	I	A	R	I	Q	R	A
P	E	D	H	A	L	L	U	C	I	N	A	T	I	O	N	S	C	I	D	P	A	K
J	W	O	S	L	R	C	S	N	C	C	O	G	N	I	T	I	O	N	E	S	N	U
C	K	P	S	L	U	R	R	E	D	S	P	E	E	C	H	R	K	D	G	Y	S	L
D	U	A	L	L	Y	D	I	S	O	R	D	E	R	E	D	O	A	F	D	C	F	Q
A	L	M	R	R	N	A	L	O	X	O	N	E	M	J	V	A	D	P	I	H	E	Y
R	K	I	K	P	K	D	K	X	D	F	O	X	Z	Q	M	X	R	U	C	O	R	F
G	F	N	S	A	A	K	G	D	H	E	Q	N	C	T	S	S	W	V	D	T	E	X
U	F	E	N	U	W	T	S	V	X	X	J	J	M	C	R	M	S	J	P	R	N	A
W	G	P	Z	O	B	U	F	Y	T	B	V	Q	E	L	A	S	X	E	G	O	C	R
K	G	K	V	H	B	A	B	G	N	A	L	T	R	E	X	O	N	E	A	P	E	M
G	D	A	N	Q	N	F	H	Y	P	O	T	H	A	L	A	M	U	S	V	I	Y	M
X	T	R	E	A	T	M	E	N	T	R	E	T	E	N	T	I	O	N	D	C	V	N

1. A brain chemical, classified as a neurotransmitter, found in regions of the brain that regulate movement, emotion, motivation, and reinforcement of rewarding behavior.
2. A sign of depressant intoxication. When people consume significant amounts of sedative-hypnotics and opioids, their speech may become garbled, mumbled, and slow.
3. Mind-altering.
4. An opioid antagonist medication approved by the FDA to reverse an opioid overdose.
5. Sensations, sounds and
6. An area of the brain that is part of the basal ganglia and includes the nucleus accumbens.
7. A long-acting opioid antagonist medication that prevents receptors from being activated by other opioids. Naltrexone is used to treat alcohol and opioid use disorders.
8. A part of the brain that controls many bodily functions, including eating, drinking, body temperature regulation, and the release of many hormones.
9. Having been diagnosed with two disorders, for example a substance use disorder and a mental health disorder.
10. Programs that by law or regulation, by choice, or for lack of resources cannot accommodate patients who have psychiatric illnesses that require ongoing treatment.
11. The feelings, reactions, biases, and images from the past that the client with cod may project onto the clinician.
12. Relating to the act or process of thinking, understanding, learning, and remembering.
13. Keeping clients involved in treatment activities and receiving required services.

A. Cognition
B. Addiction Only Services
C. Psychotropic
D. Slurred Speech
E. Hallucinations
F. Naloxone
G. Transference
H. Dopamine
I. Treatment Retention
J. Dually Disordered
K. Naltrexone
L. Ventral Striatum
M. Hypothalamus

20. Find the hidden words. The words have been placed horizontally, vertically, or diagonally. When you locate a word, draw an ellipse around it.

Y	A	G	W	L	X	B	N	E	Q	E	D	X	M	M	N	W	U	E	U	H	D	S
C	N	F	R	D	K	F	I	M	D	J	G	M	R	K	D	X	U	H	B	Y	R	F
A	O	J	C	B	D	V	K	I	Z	T	T	G	E	R	T	U	Q	H	W	E	A	T
R	R	A	V	P	S	Y	C	H	O	S	I	S	C	S	X	J	T	H	C	N	F	E
B	E	H	Y	P	O	T	H	A	L	A	M	U	S	W	F	I	B	J	B	N	C	V
K	X	N	S	K	G	M	D	A	Q	U	C	M	E	H	S	D	E	F	I	C	I	T
B	I	C	R	A	V	I	N	G	A	G	I	T	A	T	I	O	N	F	B	D	M	Y
M	A	N	P	E	S	T	I	G	M	A	H	L	L	T	H	G	I	C	F	I	E	H
K	N	W	D	I	S	O	R	D	E	R	F	T	J	W	L	B	O	R	Y	Q	Z	D
A	E	K	P	X	Y	Z	D	G	Y	A	S	H	J	O	T	J	Z	Y	N	T	V	F
X	R	S	C	A	G	E	Q	U	E	S	T	I	O	N	N	A	I	R	E	O	P	C
N	V	A	N	A	L	G	E	S	I	C	S	X	A	N	A	X	P	P	N	V	T	E
G	O	Y	N	H	K	E	E	E	X	F	B	C	N	X	I	C	E	H	F	S	Z	C
F	S	I	U	N	W	I	I	X	P	Q	I	N	X	N	F	I	V	W	R	O	J	P
Q	A	B	L	A	C	K	O	U	T	H	S	R	M	C	E	F	K	X	O	T	O	V
W	I	T	H	D	R	A	W	A	L	L	L	Q	Z	B	H	O	O	O	R	D	O	I

1. A negative association attached to some activity or condition. A cause of shame or embarrassment.
2. A brief alcoholism screening tool.
3. In the context of substance abuse treatment, disability, or inability to function fully.
4. A disorder in which the individual refuses to maintain a normal body weight, is afraid of gaining weight, and exhibits a significant disturbance in the perception of body shape.
5. A restless inability to keep still.
6. Slang term for Smoke able methamphetamine.
7. Symptoms that can occur after long-term use of a drug is reduced or stopped.
8. A part of the brain that controls many bodily functions, including eating, drinking, body temperature regulation, and the release of many hormones.
9. A powerful, often overwhelming desire to use drugs.
10. Delta-9-tetrahydrocannabinol; the main mind-altering ingredient in marijuana.
11. A period of amnesia or memory loss, typically caused by chronic, high-dose substance abuse.
12. An illness or a disruption of some mental or physical process.
13. Delusional or disordered thinking detached from reality; symptoms often include hallucinations.
14. Brand name for benzodiazepine alprazolam.
15. A group of medications that reduce pain.

A. THC
B. Hypothalamus
C. Psychosis
D. Anorexia Nervosa
E. Cage Questionnaire
F. Deficit
G. Agitation
H. Analgesics
I. Ice
J. Stigma
K. Withdrawal
L. Disorder
M. Xanax
N. Craving
O. Blackout

1. Find the hidden words. The words have been placed horizontally, vertically, or diagonally. When you locate a word, draw an ellipse around it.

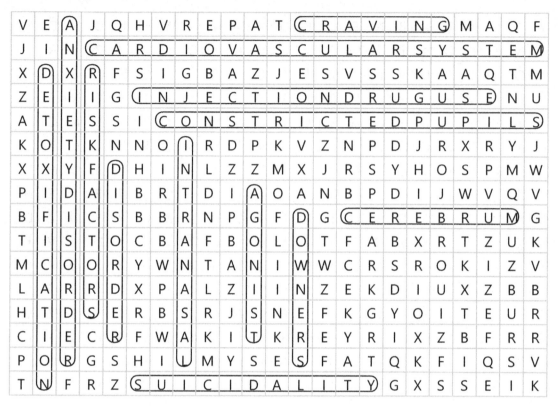

1. Slang term for drugs that exert a depressant effect on the central nervous system. In general, downers are sedative-hypnotic drugs, such as benzodiazepines and barbiturates.
2. Pupils that are temporarily narrowed or closed. This is usually a sign of opioid abuse.
3. Taken through the nose.
4. An illness or a disruption of some mental or physical process.
5. A powerful, often overwhelming desire to use drugs.
6. An illness whose essential feature is excessive anxiety and worry.
7. The act of administering drugs by injection. Blood-borne viruses, like HIV and hepatitis, can be transmitted via shared needles or other drug injection equipment.
8. The system consisting of the heart and blood vessels. It delivers nutrients and oxygen to all cells in the body.
9. A process in which the body rids itself of a drug, or its metabolites.
10. The upper part of the brain consisting of the left and right hemispheres.
11. A chemical substance that binds to and activates certain receptors on cells, causing a biological response.
12. A measure or estimate of a person's likelihood of committing suicide. A high-risk behavior associated with cod, especially (although not limited to) serious mood disorders.
13. Factors that increase the likelihood of beginning substance use, of regular and harmful use, and of other behavioral health problems associated with use.

A. Cerebrum
B. Cardiovascular System
C. Suicidality
D. Anxiety Disorder
E. Craving
F. Agonist
G. Disorder
H. Injection Drug Use
I. Constricted Pupils
J. Intranasal
K. Detoxification
L. Downers
M. Risk Factors

2. Find the hidden words. The words have been placed horizontally, vertically, or diagonally. When you locate a word, draw an ellipse around it.

O	C	A	H	R	O	P	B	J	F	J	Q	S	D	L	Q	P	U	D	D	W	D	J
W	E	I	M	E	N	T	A	L	D	I	S	O	R	D	E	R	B	Q	M	A	U	L
I	R	E	S	I	U	Q	Y	Z	K	K	H	D	X	Q	D	B	H	R	B	V	A	N
T	E	R	D	R	U	G	A	B	U	S	E	R	A	L	N	A	B	P	F	W	L	G
H	B	Y	Q	O	V	E	R	D	O	S	E	F	O	E	X	S	R	W	P	A	L	T
D	R	E	A	G	H	Q	G	N	T	C	Q	A	U	Z	I	A	T	D	G	V	Y	S
R	A	A	T	C	A	N	E	S	T	H	E	T	I	C	E	L	L	Q	Y	J	D	L
A	L	F	P	V	M	M	A	R	I	J	U	A	N	A	V	G	T	N	R	T	I	D
W	C	W	V	C	M	E	U	H	A	L	L	U	C	I	N	A	T	I	O	N	S	P
A	O	X	V	F	F	T	N	A	L	O	X	O	N	E	L	N	T	L	B	W	O	Z
U	R	A	C	W	V	H	Q	S	W	B	N	N	V	O	Z	G	G	V	C	K	R	C
Z	T	W	Y	H	H	A	O	N	V	T	E	A	M	D	T	L	P	V	T	K	D	V
Y	E	M	D	Z	A	D	Z	H	U	J	W	Z	J	I	J	I	I	B	Z	B	E	T
U	X	H	I	V	Y	O	S	A	A	J	B	Z	D	M	K	A	H	M	Q	V	R	X
X	I	A	U	D	Y	N	U	U	S	D	V	S	P	U	A	Q	N	Q	R	E	E	G
A	Y	Y	S	K	T	E	M	Z	B	F	L	A	S	H	B	A	C	K	W	S	D	F

1. The gray matter that covers the surface of the cerebral hemispheres, whose functions include sensory processing and motor control along with language, reasoning, and decision-making.
2. The area of the brain that plays an important role in positive forms of motivation, including the pleasurable effects of healthy activities like eating, socializing, and sex.
3. An overdose occurs when a person uses enough of a drug to produce a life-threatening reaction or death.
4. A mental condition marked primarily by disorganization of personality, mind, and emotions that seriously impairs the psychological or behavioral functioning of the individual.
5. An older diagnostic term that defined use that is unsafe, use that leads a person to fail to fulfill responsibilities or gets them in legal trouble.
6. The Indian hemp plant cannabis sativa; also called "pot" and "weed."
7. A drug that causes insensitivity to pain and is used for surgeries and other medical procedures.
8. A long-acting opioid agonist medication used for the treatment of opioid addiction and pain.
9. Having been diagnosed with two disorders, for example a substance use disorder and a mental health disorder.
10. A sudden but temporary recurrence of aspects of a drug experience that may occur days, weeks, or even more than a year after using drugs that cause hallucinations.
11. Sensations, sounds and
12. Symptoms that can occur after long-term use of a drug is reduced or stopped.
13. An opioid antagonist medication approved by the FDA to reverse an opioid overdose.

A. Withdrawal
B. Drug Abuse
C. Hallucinations
D. Flashback
E. Marijuana
F. Naloxone
G. Dually Disordered
H. Anesthetic
I. Mental Disorder
J. Overdose
K. Basal Ganglia
L. Methadone
M. Cerebral Cortex

3. Find the hidden words. The words have been placed horizontally, vertically, or diagonally. When you locate a word, draw an ellipse around it.

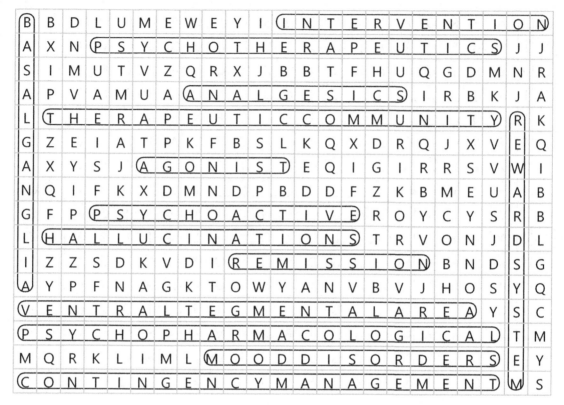

1. Sensations, sounds and
2. Having a specific effect on the brain.
3. A brain circuit that includes the ventral tegmental area, the nucleus accumbens, and the prefrontal cortex.
4. The area of the brain that plays an important role in positive forms of motivation, including the pleasurable effects of healthy activities like eating, socializing, and sex.
5. A medical term meaning that major disease symptoms are eliminated or diminished below a pre-determined harmful level.
6. Encompasses the specific treatment strategies, therapies, or techniques that are used to treat one or more disorders.
7. A consciously designed social environment or residential treatment setting in which the social and group process is harnessed with therapeutic intent.
8. A chemical substance that binds to and activates certain receptors on cells, causing a biological response.
9. A psychological disorder characterized by the elevation or lowering of a person's mood, such as depression or bipolar disorder.
10. An area in the brainstem that contains dopamine neurons that make up a key part of the brain reward system, which also includes the nucleus accumbens and prefrontal cortex.
11. Pertaining to medications used to treat mental illnesses.
12. A group of medications that reduce pain.
13. Drugs that have an effect on the function of the brain and that are often used to treat psychiatric disorders.
14. A treatment approach based on providing incentives to support positive behavior change.

A. Mood Disorders
B. Therapeutic Community
C. Basal Ganglia
D. Contingency Management
E. Psychopharmacological
F. Reward System
G. Psychoactive
H. Hallucinations
I. Remission
J. Analgesics
K. Agonist
L. Ventral Tegmental Area
M. Psychotherapeutics
N. Intervention

4. Find the hidden words. The words have been placed horizontally, vertically, or diagonally. When you locate a word, draw an ellipse around it.

P	R	O	T	E	A	S	E	I	N	H	I	B	I	T	O	R	C	U	L	P	O	D
C	A	N	N	A	B	I	N	O	I	D	S	E	D	U	I	C	O	Q	W	R	C	U
B	R	Q	P	T	H	Y	U	Z	K	Q	Z	C	N	S	B	K	N	O	Z	O	H	A
F	J	O	N	B	V	A	Q	H	F	M	F	S	P	Z	C	Z	T	L	U	G	Z	L
C	C	R	Q	E	K	S	L	O	B	U	X	T	V	C	K	T	I	C	I	N	R	L
S	R	G	N	A	P	U	O	D	A	S	H	A	T	V	Q	X	N	O	H	O	H	Y
K	A	A	M	M	J	D	V	R	B	N	U	S	G	S	L	D	U	C	M	S	M	D
Q	C	N	K	P	G	X	E	F	O	M	D	Y	R	K	S	S	I	K	W	I	J	I
O	K	I	V	H	Z	H	I	N	T	R	A	N	A	S	A	L	N	T	F	S	V	S
B	M	Z	C	E	E	M	P	I	R	I	C	A	L	A	H	L	G	O	P	F	H	O
I	A	A	M	T	H	R	E	C	E	P	T	O	R	K	C	F	C	Y	W	Z	D	R
G	J	T	U	A	P	S	Y	C	H	O	A	C	T	I	V	E	A	J	J	I	X	D
I	D	I	F	M	T	L	P	F	L	C	E	G	B	O	C	F	R	L	K	K	K	E
C	E	O	S	I	T	J	W	G	R	U	C	H	R	Y	C	R	E	G	C	C	P	R
P	X	W	B	N	Y	A	B	R	U	K	B	B	Y	K	Y	Z	F	T	P	J	V	E
W	E	Y	L	E	I	V	A	D	D	I	C	T	I	O	N	M	I	Y	X	V	C	D

1. Care that supports a client's progress, monitors his or her condition, and can respond to a return to substance use or a return of symptoms of mental disorder.
2. Slang term for methylenedioxymethamphetamine, a member of the amphetamine family. At lower doses, MDMA causes distortions of emotional perceptions.
3. Relying on observation or experience rather than theoretical principles or theory.
4. Chemicals that bind to cannabinoid receptors in the brain.
5. Having been diagnosed with two disorders, for example a substance use disorder and a mental health disorder.
6. A stimulant drug that acts on the central nervous system (CNS).
7. Cocaine that has been chemically modified so that it will become a gas vapor when heated at relatively low temperatures.
8. Physical dependence on a substance of abuse. Inability to cease use of a substance without experiencing withdrawal symptoms.
9. An entity that provides mental health services in two or three service settings and is not classified as a psychiatric or general hospital or as a residential treatment center.
10. Having a specific effect on the brain.
11. Taken through the nose.
12. Medications used to treat HIV; they interfere with the action of this enzyme, thus interfering with viral reproduction.
13. A molecule located on the surface of a cell that recognizes specific chemicals and transmits the chemical message into the cell.
14. A clinician's judgment or estimate of how well a disorder will respond to treatment.

A. Intranasal
B. Receptor
C. Dually Disordered
D. Amphetamine
E. Continuing Care
F. Prognosis
G. Psychoactive
H. Cannabinoids
I. Crack
J. Organization
K. Addiction
L. Protease Inhibitor
M. Ecstasy
N. Empirical

5. Find the hidden words. The words have been placed horizontally, vertically, or diagonally. When you locate a word, draw an ellipse around it.

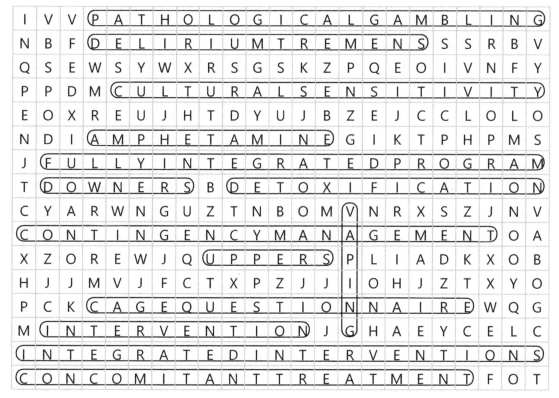

1. A treatment program that actively combines substance abuse and mental health interventions to treat disorders, related problems, and the whole person more effectively.
2. A clearing of toxins from the body.
3. An illness whose essential feature is persistent and recurrent maladaptive gambling behavior that disrupts personal, family, or vocational pursuits.
4. The capacity and willingness of a clinician or other service provider to be open to working with issues of culture and diversity.
5. Specific treatment strategies in which interventions for two or more disorders are combined in a single session or interaction, or in a series of interactions or multiple sessions.
6. Inhaling the aerosol or vapor from an electronic cigarette, e-vaporizer, or other device.
7. A stimulant drug that acts on the central nervous system (CNS).
8. Encompasses the specific treatment strategies, therapies, or techniques that are used to treat one or more disorders.
9. Slang term used to describe drugs that have a stimulating effect on the central nervous system. Examples include cocaine, caffeine, and amphetamines.
10. A brief alcoholism screening tool.
11. A treatment approach based on providing incentives to support positive behavior change.
12. A state of confusion accompanied by trembling and vivid hallucinations.
13. Treatment of two or more mental or physical disorders at the same time.
14. Slang term for drugs that exert a depressant effect on the central nervous system. In general, downers are sedative-hypnotic drugs, such as benzodiazepines and barbiturates.

A. Concomitant Treatment
B. Amphetamine
C. Delirium Tremens
D. Downers
E. Integrated Interventions
F. Fully Integrated Program
G. Cultural Sensitivity
H. Contingency Management
I. Vaping
J. Intervention
K. Pathological Gambling
L. Uppers
M. Detoxification
N. Cage Questionnaire

6. Find the hidden words. The words have been placed horizontally, vertically, or diagonally. When you locate a word, draw an ellipse around it.

A	M	P	H	E	T	A	M	I	N	E	E	T	R	C	K	U	Q	M	H	V	P	F
V	U	S	D	F	I	X	O	P	C	H	K	O	E	E	A	Z	T	N	G	H	T	J
W	E	D	J	W	T	K	T	M	Z	G	I	E	Y	P	T	Z	W	C	O	C	M	H
D	E	T	O	X	I	F	I	C	A	T	I	O	N	O	G	Q	Q	N	O	H	I	X
C	L	W	E	L	E	C	T	R	O	N	I	C	C	I	G	A	R	E	T	T	E	Y
C	Z	A	V	F	I	U	K	C	I	W	Z	C	J	Z	N	K	F	F	G	J	X	P
C	G	C	X	F	F	R	I	O	G	T	B	R	R	E	C	O	V	E	R	Y	R	A
C	E	N	T	R	A	L	N	E	R	V	O	U	S	S	Y	S	T	E	M	V	H	I
U	R	W	G	K	Q	O	E	R	O	T	Y	S	X	F	M	B	M	W	U	S	I	D
O	V	E	R	D	O	S	E	C	P	T	Z	P	G	A	S	I	N	O	Y	W	M	R
A	J	S	P	N	S	R	L	E	S	P	J	O	P	P	F	D	A	O	A	Q	C	D
G	U	J	O	L	G	F	J	D	U	S	U	I	C	I	D	A	L	I	T	Y	A	S
U	A	D	D	A	D	D	E	R	A	L	L	E	E	P	M	E	A	J	G	S	L	C
D	C	A	R	D	I	O	V	A	S	C	U	L	A	R	S	Y	S	T	E	M	K	N
P	S	Y	C	H	O	T	R	O	P	I	C	M	E	D	I	C	A	T	I	O	N	J
P	S	Y	C	H	O	P	H	A	R	M	A	C	O	L	O	G	I	C	A	L	V	V

1. A process of change through which people with substance use disorders improve their health and wellness, live self-directed lives, and strive to reach their full potential.
2. Legally forced or compelled.
3. A battery-operated device that people use to inhale an aerosol, which typically contains nicotine, flavorings, and other chemicals.
4. A brand name amphetamine for treating ADHD.
5. A drug that has an effect on the mind and sometimes affects behavior as well.
6. An overdose occurs when a person uses enough of a drug to produce a life-threatening reaction or death.
7. A process in which the body rids itself of a drug, or its metabolites.
8. The system consisting of the nerves in the brain and spinal cord.
9. Pertaining to medications used to treat mental illnesses.
10. The system consisting of the heart and blood vessels. It delivers nutrients and oxygen to all cells in the body.
11. A measure or estimate of a person's likelihood of committing suicide. A high-risk behavior associated with cod, especially (although not limited to) serious mood disorders.
12. A stimulant drug that acts on the central nervous system (CNS).

A. Overdose
D. Adderall
G. Psychotropic Medication
J. Suicidality

B. Detoxification
E. Electronic Cigarette
H. Central Nervous System
K. Psychopharmacological

C. Recovery
F. Coerced
I. Cardiovascular System
L. Amphetamine

7. Find the hidden words. The words have been placed horizontally, vertically, or diagonally. When you locate a word, draw an ellipse around it.

P	X	C	Y	G	Z	C	A	G	E	Q	U	E	S	T	I	O	N	N	A	I	R	E
H	K	F	J	D	E	T	O	X	I	F	I	C	A	T	I	O	N	V	I	V	U	O
B	Z	W	J	L	E	Y	C	X	N	R	B	A	S	I	C	P	R	O	G	R	A	M
D	J	C	O	N	T	I	N	G	E	N	C	Y	M	A	N	A	G	E	M	E	N	T
C	S	U	B	S	T	A	N	C	E	U	S	E	D	I	S	O	R	D	E	R	V	V
K	F	I	X	F	D	B	F	T	O	L	E	R	A	N	C	E	Y	F	I	B	Y	R
N	Y	M	M	X	Q	N	B	L	R	Z	J	R	R	U	E	L	O	W	X	I	J	N
L	C	P	E	Y	O	L	A	T	X	E	D	C	Z	L	J	O	U	M	V	B	K	D
K	W	U	T	F	O	J	W	U	J	R	E	W	A	R	D	I	K	T	O	D	C	W
Z	C	L	H	C	B	R	T	V	G	O	I	N	T	E	R	V	E	N	T	I	O	N
R	I	S	A	V	W	U	K	B	G	Z	J	A	G	S	A	B	D	Z	O	W	T	J
K	I	I	D	G	S	V	J	T	Z	T	K	P	Q	Q	W	B	A	X	P	Y	I	M
P	T	V	O	C	Q	G	C	A	X	R	F	Z	M	F	G	Z	P	E	Z	A	I	G
F	Z	I	N	K	Q	C	A	N	N	A	B	I	N	O	I	D	S	C	D	A	D	B
Z	X	T	E	K	W	V	O	D	B	O	H	S	C	B	E	Q	D	K	P	B	L	T
P	X	Y	Z	G	J	T	S	Z	E	Z	A	U	Q	G	B	C	J	L	K	L	C	K

1. A treatment approach based on providing incentives to support positive behavior change.
2. A long-acting opioid agonist medication used for the treatment of opioid addiction and pain.
3. A clearing of toxins from the body.
4. A treatment program with the capacity to provide treatment for one disorder, but that also screens for other disorders and is able to access necessary consultations.
5. Pleasurable feelings that reinforce behavior and encourage repetition.
6. Encompasses the specific treatment strategies, therapies, or techniques that are used to treat one or more disorders.
7. Chemicals that bind to cannabinoid receptors in the brain.
8. A brief alcoholism screening tool.
9. A condition in which higher doses of a drug are required to achieve the desired effect.
10. A medical illness caused by disordered use of a substance or substances.
11. A tendency to act without foresight or regard for consequences and to prioritize immediate rewards over long-term goals.

A. Reward
B. Contingency Management
C. Basic Program
D. Intervention
E. Methadone
F. Detoxification
G. Impulsivity
H. Cannabinoids
I. Tolerance
J. Cage Questionnaire
K. Substance Use Disorder

8. Find the hidden words. The words have been placed horizontally, vertically, or diagonally. When you locate a word, draw an ellipse around it.

P	T	Q	E	D	V	C	O	G	N	I	T	I	O	N	T	N	R	N	Y	R	I	J
S	A	K	Q	A	B	S	T	I	N	E	N	T	L	U	K	C	K	I	R	H	L	C
Y	X	P	B	B	E	Q	Z	R	E	E	J	B	F	Y	Y	M	M	L	C	C	H	O
C	W	A	R	T	A	P	B	A	Z	K	Y	W	S	X	D	M	Q	J	H	S	P	M
H	Q	E	W	Q	U	A	D	R	A	N	T	S	O	F	C	A	R	E	B	O	S	P
O	F	D	E	L	I	R	I	U	M	T	R	E	M	E	N	S	W	L	P	Y	Y	E
S	W	P	F	D	B	O	J	H	D	A	Y	Q	E	T	K	F	N	B	V	A	C	T
I	W	C	U	J	R	S	E	Q	E	U	T	P	K	B	O	J	R	O	W	P	H	E
S	C	I	F	H	U	A	A	C	Q	J	R	U	Q	O	C	T	V	V	M	I	O	N
J	T	D	I	L	A	T	E	D	P	U	P	I	L	S	C	J	H	J	G	D	S	C
E	B	N	Z	F	F	Y	N	X	M	P	R	S	C	Z	V	C	Z	Y	V	Z	I	Y
U	N	W	X	B	N	F	I	F	W	A	L	T	W	X	O	V	S	O	L	Q	S	O
W	I	F	A	V	Q	P	A	R	T	I	A	L	A	G	O	N	I	S	T	H	T	H
G	H	L	N	K	I	M	P	U	L	S	I	V	I	T	Y	D	K	N	R	X	S	A
P	H	B	A	I	N	T	E	G	R	A	T	E	D	T	R	E	A	T	M	E	N	T
M	E	X	X	V	E	N	T	R	A	L	S	T	R	I	A	T	U	M	V	E	L	A

1. Any mechanism by which treatment interventions for co-occurring disorders are combined within the context of a primary treatment relationship or service setting.
2. Relating to the act or process of thinking, understanding, learning, and remembering.
3. Pupils that have become temporarily enlarged.
4. Brand name for benzodiazepine alprazolam.
5. A state of confusion accompanied by trembling and vivid hallucinations.
6. A tendency to act without foresight or regard for consequences and to prioritize immediate rewards over long-term goals.
7. A substance that binds to and activates a receptor to a lesser degree than a full agonist.
8. Not using substances of abuse at any time.
9. An area of the brain that is part of the basal ganglia and includes the nucleus accumbens.
10. Delusional or disordered thinking detached from reality; symptoms often include hallucinations.
11. A mental disorder that is characterized by distinct distortions of a person's mental capacity, ability to recognize reality, and relationships to others.
12. A conceptual framework that classifies clients in four basic groups based on relative symptom severity, rather than by diagnosis.
13. An ability, capacity, skill, or set of skills.

A. Delirium Tremens
B. Ventral Striatum
C. Xanax
D. Partial Agonist
E. Psychosis
F. Dilated Pupils
G. Competency
H. Quadrants of Care
I. Cognition
J. Abstinent
K. Psychosis
L. Integrated Treatment
M. Impulsivity

9. Find the hidden words. The words have been placed horizontally, vertically, or diagonally. When you locate a word, draw an ellipse around it.

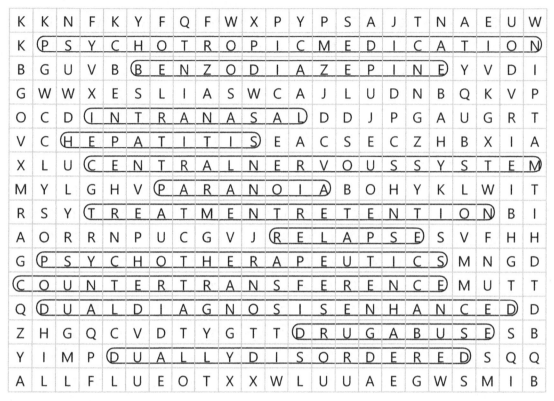

1. A drug that has an effect on the mind and sometimes affects behavior as well.
2. Drugs that have an effect on the function of the brain and that are often used to treat psychiatric disorders.
3. Having been diagnosed with two disorders, for example a substance use disorder and a mental health disorder.
4. Taken through the nose.
5. A type of CNS depressant sometimes prescribed to relieve anxiety, panic, or acute stress reactions. Some benzodiazepines are prescribed short-term to promote sleep.
6. A type of delusion, or false idea, that is unchanged by reasoned argument or proof to the contrary.
7. An older diagnostic term that defined use that is unsafe, use that leads a person to fail to fulfill responsibilities or gets them in legal trouble.
8. Keeping clients involved in treatment activities and receiving required services.
9. In drug addiction, relapse is the return to drug use after an attempt to stop.
10. An inflammation of the liver, with accompanying liver cell damage and risk of death.
11. The feelings, reactions, biases, and images from the past that the clinician may project onto the client with cod.
12. Of or pertaining to programs that have a higher than average level of integration of substance abuse and mental health treatment services.
13. The system consisting of the nerves in the brain and spinal cord.

A. Treatment Retention
B. Drug Abuse
C. Relapse
D. Psychotropic Medication
E. Paranoia
F. Psychotherapeutics
G. Benzodiazepine
H. Dual Diagnosis Enhanced
I. Countertransference
J. Dually Disordered
K. Intranasal
L. Hepatitis
M. Central Nervous System

10. Find the hidden words. The words have been placed horizontally, vertically, or diagonally. When you locate a word, draw an ellipse around it.

M	A	T	U	F	E	D	H	E	B	A	N	Y	C	E	R	E	B	R	U	M	W	U
L	N	R	B	F	U	N	C	T	I	O	N	A	L	Y	E	E	I	W	W	H	G	E
I	O	I	I	W	Y	D	S	K	Y	L	Q	O	A	L	M	T	W	W	Y	R	W	Y
F	R	T	P	U	T	I	D	S	P	Q	X	N	Z	A	V	Z	W	F	B	E	J	G
L	E	V	Z	A	M	Y	T	S	S	P	A	Z	I	K	F	C	P	S	B	W	E	V
O	X	R	I	O	C	P	Z	Q	Y	M	X	Q	U	P	P	M	J	T	P	A	I	V
P	I	P	S	Y	C	H	O	A	C	T	I	V	E	L	C	Q	X	E	P	R	U	S
K	A	D	E	X	N	R	T	N	H	L	Y	X	E	C	S	T	A	S	Y	D	Y	D
F	N	S	P	A	T	H	O	L	O	G	I	C	A	L	G	A	M	B	L	I	N	G
J	E	E	T	U	T	T	V	D	T	S	J	G	D	O	S	Q	Z	F	X	C	T	
M	R	X	B	X	S	W	H	R	R	L	W	L	F	K	G	T	L	V	B	Z	O	A
L	V	N	H	O	E	U	V	A	O	X	S	F	D	Y	W	H	S	W	A	W	O	M
H	O	M	U	Y	E	L	X	M	P	E	E	Y	O	T	B	J	T	J	N	C	M	Q
N	S	D	G	B	P	A	R	T	I	A	L	A	G	O	N	I	S	T	M	K	M	S
Y	A	A	C	A	N	P	S	Y	C	H	E	D	E	L	I	C	D	R	U	G	D	B
M	P	E	R	S	O	N	A	L	I	T	Y	D	I	S	O	R	D	E	R	S	Q	A

1. The upper part of the brain consisting of the left and right hemispheres.
2. A disorder in which the individual refuses to maintain a normal body weight, is afraid of gaining weight, and exhibits a significant disturbance in the perception of body shape.
3. Mind-altering.
4. Pleasurable feelings that reinforce behavior and encourage repetition.
5. Rigid, inflexible, and maladaptive behavior patterns of sufficient severity to cause internal distress or significant impairment in functioning.
6. Pertaining to a person's ability to carry out tasks.
7. Having a specific effect on the brain.
8. Slang term for methylenedioxymethamphetamine, a member of the amphetamine family. At lower doses, MDMA causes distortions of emotional perceptions.
9. A drug that distorts perception, thought, and feeling. This term is typically used to refer to drugs with hallucinogenic effects.
10. An illness whose essential feature is persistent and recurrent maladaptive gambling behavior that disrupts personal, family, or vocational pursuits.
11. A substance that binds to and activates a receptor to a lesser degree than a full agonist.

A. Pathological Gambling
B. Psychotropic
C. Functional
D. Personality Disorders
E. Reward
F. Partial Agonist
G. Anorexia Nervosa
H. Ecstasy
I. Psychedelic Drug
J. Psychoactive
K. Cerebrum

11. Find the hidden words. The words have been placed horizontally, vertically, or diagonally. When you locate a word, draw an ellipse around it.

I	Y	S	O	T	O	A	N	G	O	I	E	U	X	Y	N	M	U	B	V	U	I	O
W	S	C	B	K	T	C	E	F	D	M	D	W	O	G	Y	I	G	S	N	U	O	C
U	P	H	Z	M	H	C	U	Q	O	P	O	U	L	O	H	Y	S	J	S	Y	U	H
I	H	I	N	U	N	U	R	K	P	A	K	A	Y	W	P	S	V	Y	A	M	S	A
A	T	Z	O	J	K	L	O	K	A	I	V	Z	U	P	O	P	N	O	P	H	X	L
E	M	O	B	I	G	T	B	E	M	R	O	M	T	R	E	A	T	M	E	N	T	L
J	T	P	Z	B	P	U	I	P	I	E	H	L	Z	J	Y	K	L	Y	W	R	V	U
S	V	H	W	L	K	R	O	H	N	D	Z	K	X	U	N	L	K	T	P	Z	X	C
B	Q	R	W	X	E	A	L	Z	E	H	D	O	F	Q	X	M	G	Q	J	M	N	I
I	S	E	A	Y	M	T	O	A	R	S	V	T	A	O	Q	J	K	N	W	F	V	N
X	O	N	I	N	T	E	G	R	A	T	E	D	T	R	E	A	T	M	E	N	T	O
W	O	I	I	W	C	D	V	I	R	E	M	I	S	S	I	O	N	N	K	N	X	G
C	X	A	V	E	N	T	R	A	L	S	T	R	I	A	T	U	M	F	G	G	W	E
D	C	O	N	T	I	N	G	E	N	C	Y	M	A	N	A	G	E	M	E	N	T	N
E	V	G	M	E	N	D	Z	P	H	M	Y	J	K	O	P	Z	M	E	S	B	J	S
R	D	A	D	D	I	C	T	I	O	N	O	N	L	Y	S	E	R	V	I	C	E	S

1. Any mechanism by which treatment interventions for co-occurring disorders are combined within the context of a primary treatment relationship or service setting.
2. A broad group of drugs that cause distortions of sensory perception. The prototype hallucinogen is lysergic acid diethylamide (LSD).
3. Mentally and physically in harmony with and connected to the culture in which one lives.
4. Substance abuse treatment is an organized array of services and interventions with a primary focus on treating substance abuse disorders.
5. Hampered or held back from being able to do some mental or physical task.
6. Programs that by law or regulation, by choice, or for lack of resources cannot accommodate patients who have psychiatric illnesses that require ongoing treatment.
7. A treatment approach based on providing incentives to support positive behavior change.
8. A brain chemical, classified as a neurotransmitter, found in regions of the brain that regulate movement, emotion, motivation, and reinforcement of rewarding behavior.
9. A medical term meaning that major disease symptoms are eliminated or diminished below a pre-determined harmful level.
10. An area of the brain that is part of the basal ganglia and includes the nucleus accumbens.
11. A type of psychosis where persons are subject to hallucinations occurring in the absence of insight into their pathological nature.
12. The study of the anatomy, function, and diseases of the brain and nervous system.

A. Treatment
D. Schizophrenia
G. Hallucinogens
J. Ventral Striatum
B. Neurobiology
E. Acculturated
H. Impaired
K. Remission
C. Dopamine
F. Contingency Management
I. Integrated Treatment
L. Addiction Only Services

12. Find the hidden words. The words have been placed horizontally, vertically, or diagonally. When you locate a word, draw an ellipse around it.

H	H	P	S	Y	C	H	O	P	H	A	R	M	A	C	O	L	O	G	I	C	A	L
W	X	R	K	C	E	R	T	B	Z	Q	B	S	A	E	X	N	B	B	M	E	M	N
I	N	E	U	R	O	L	E	P	T	I	C	M	E	D	I	C	A	T	I	O	N	F
U	C	E	B	U	I	M	P	U	L	S	I	V	I	T	Y	E	D	E	W	R	F	I
A	D	D	E	R	A	L	L	E	A	D	D	I	C	T	I	O	N	E	H	H	Q	J
O	Y	P	H	A	R	M	A	C	O	D	Y	N	A	M	I	C	S	Y	T	D	N	E
W	P	C	V	D	J	J	I	E	H	B	M	S	G	V	N	W	V	J	Z	O	I	X
T	E	N	D	Z	L	I	M	B	I	C	S	Y	S	T	E	M	K	H	A	Y	R	W
X	O	A	J	T	I	V	Z	Z	W	G	V	Y	C	T	K	B	Y	U	N	P	O	S
C	U	L	T	U	R	A	L	L	Y	C	O	M	P	E	T	E	N	T	J	Q	P	G
N	O	R	E	P	I	N	E	P	H	R	I	N	E	K	Y	X	H	C	V	V	J	G
N	P	R	O	T	E	A	S	E	I	N	H	I	B	I	T	O	R	M	B	B	E	P
I	B	A	S	A	L	G	A	N	G	L	I	A	B	N	J	P	A	F	Z	F	C	E
D	G	I	W	Q	T	E	B	K	B	C	P	D	A	C	T	N	X	O	X	S	J	A
G	R	W	G	Z	F	C	O	N	S	T	R	I	C	T	E	D	P	U	P	I	L	S
F	Y	R	E	Y	T	R	E	A	T	M	E	N	T	R	E	T	E	N	T	I	O	N

1. A drug used to treat psychosis, especially schizophrenia.
2. Pertaining to medications used to treat mental illnesses.
3. The area of the brain that plays an important role in positive forms of motivation, including the pleasurable effects of healthy activities like eating, socializing, and sex.
4. Keeping clients involved in treatment activities and receiving required services.
5. Medications used to treat HIV; they interfere with the action of this enzyme, thus interfering with viral reproduction.
6. A chronic, relapsing disorder characterized by compulsive (or difficult to control) drug seeking and use despite harmful consequences, as well as long-lasting changes in the brain.
7. Interconnected brain structures that process feelings, emotions, and motivations. It is also important for learning and memory.
8. Biopsychosocial or other treatment that is adapted to suit the special cultural beliefs, practices, and needs of a client.
9. A brand name amphetamine for treating ADHD.
10. The way a drug acts on the body.
11. A neurotransmitter that affects heart rate, blood pressure, stress, and attention.
12. A tendency to act without foresight or regard for consequences and to prioritize immediate rewards over long-term goals.
13. Pupils that are temporarily narrowed or closed. This is usually a sign of opioid abuse.

A. Constricted Pupils
B. Adderall
C. Addiction
D. Psychopharmacological
E. Basal Ganglia
F. Treatment Retention
G. Pharmacodynamics
H. Protease Inhibitor
I. Limbic System
J. Culturally Competent
K. Impulsivity
L. Norepinephrine
M. Neuroleptic Medication

13. Find the hidden words. The words have been placed horizontally, vertically, or diagonally. When you locate a word, draw an ellipse around it.

T	H	E	R	A	P	E	U	T	I	C	A	L	L	I	A	N	C	E	R	O	A	K
W	T	X	Z	T	N	G	L	K	J	M	H	R	E	C	O	V	E	R	Y	S	C	R
F	C	O	N	C	O	M	I	T	A	N	T	T	R	E	A	T	M	E	N	T	L	T
A	G	C	E	U	N	E	V	E	S	U	I	C	I	D	A	L	I	T	Y	C	K	K
B	E	I	O	T	C	A	V	Z	T	Q	N	Z	F	M	W	M	T	R	E	M	O	R
S	Y	N	W	A	Q	U	A	D	R	A	N	T	S	O	F	C	A	R	E	Z	M	X
T	I	X	F	B	F	S	D	O	L	V	B	F	B	Y	N	P	B	V	F	S	D	T
I	D	Z	I	R	I	N	F	E	C	T	I	O	U	S	S	X	R	G	K	L	S	L
N	G	W	W	Y	Q	H	B	A	S	A	L	G	A	N	G	L	I	A	Q	B	B	D
E	E	H	V	O	K	X	U	E	U	T	T	P	T	G	T	N	Z	G	X	E	L	Q
N	M	P	R	R	T	D	F	X	C	C	R	Z	U	A	W	E	M	T	M	F	R	Y
C	R	R	A	G	I	T	A	T	I	O	N	C	Q	F	C	H	K	D	W	R	O	U
E	F	W	T	E	R	Z	W	R	Q	X	U	L	S	R	V	T	D	S	G	Z	N	X
A	P	C	O	N	T	I	N	G	E	N	C	Y	M	A	N	A	G	E	M	E	N	T
D	C	U	L	T	U	R	A	L	P	R	O	F	I	C	I	E	N	C	Y	X	C	P
S	Y	U	I	G	G	R	H	T	P	U	G	U	G	B	T	H	E	M	L	M	Q	A

1. A process of change through which people with substance use disorders improve their health and wellness, live self-directed lives, and strive to reach their full potential.
2. Treatment of two or more mental or physical disorders at the same time.
3. Able to spread by an agent such as a virus or bacterium.
4. The area of the brain that plays an important role in positive forms of motivation, including the pleasurable effects of healthy activities like eating, socializing, and sex.
5. A conceptual framework that classifies clients in four basic groups based on relative symptom severity, rather than by diagnosis.
6. An approach to treatment that maintains that the form or frequency of behavior can be altered through a planned and organized system of consequences.
7. A restless inability to keep still.
8. A type of relationship between client and clinician in which both are working cooperatively toward the same goals, with mutual respect and understanding.
9. A measure or estimate of a person's likelihood of committing suicide. A high-risk behavior associated with cod, especially (although not limited to) serious mood disorders.
10. Not using drugs or alcohol.
11. An involuntary and rhythmic movement in the muscles, most often in the hands, feet, jaw, tongue, or head.
12. The highest level of cultural capacity, which implies an ability to perceive the nuances of a culture in depth and a willingness to work to advance in proficiency through leadership.

A. Basal Ganglia
D. Contingency Management
G. Quadrants of Care
J. Therapeutic Alliance

B. Suicidality
E. Agitation
H. Infectious
K. Recovery

C. Cultural Proficiency
F. Abstinence
I. Concomitant Treatment
L. Tremor

14. Find the hidden words. The words have been placed horizontally, vertically, or diagonally. When you locate a word, draw an ellipse around it.

E	L	O	H	T	R	E	A	T	M	E	N	T	R	E	T	E	N	T	I	O	N	H
V	D	B	S	E	R	V	I	C	E	I	N	T	E	G	R	A	T	I	O	N	T	W
G	Z	R	E	D	M	E	M	Z	O	A	N	X	A	E	G	R	E	L	A	P	S	E
W	G	H	L	Y	L	R	D	B	Y	Q	W	S	Y	H	K	L	P	O	B	T	J	O
G	J	Q	F	V	S	E	R	O	T	O	N	I	N	I	Z	Z	L	X	P	R	M	G
L	K	A	M	K	P	V	C	H	F	C	Y	T	N	P	P	M	N	P	C	A	K	Z
W	Q	Q	E	Z	N	Q	L	Y	L	F	F	M	M	P	J	L	H	Y	Z	U	W	T
M	U	E	D	L	I	Q	C	G	N	M	W	V	E	O	N	K	U	T	A	M	X	Y
J	D	W	I	Z	X	L	H	D	D	E	O	P	G	C	Q	M	B	L	F	A	Q	W
N	F	L	C	N	O	D	D	I	N	G	O	U	T	A	Z	J	K	H	Y	Z	R	N
Y	C	X	A	K	I	Y	F	O	W	J	Z	C	I	M	X	G	P	O	A	I	I	O
J	A	L	T	E	R	W	Q	M	E	I	D	M	R	P	Q	N	I	G	D	D	G	Q
U	N	O	I	C	D	C	D	V	T	X	R	I	Y	U	P	B	M	F	R	B	O	B
S	A	V	O	Q	Q	G	S	G	H	X	E	C	X	S	P	N	X	B	O	U	N	R
L	L	M	N	C	U	L	T	U	R	A	L	S	E	N	S	I	T	I	V	I	T	Y
P	E	R	S	O	N	A	L	I	T	Y	D	I	S	O	R	D	E	R	S	E	S	B

1. An area of the brain crucial for learning and memory.
2. The use of a substance to lessen the negative effects of stress, anxiety, or other mental disorders without the guidance of a health care provider.
3. A breakdown or setback in a person's attempt to change or modify any particular behavior.
4. No one set of treatment interventions constitutes integrated treatment.
5. Keeping clients involved in treatment activities and receiving required services.
6. Slang term for the early stages of depressant-induced sleep.
7. Rigid, inflexible, and maladaptive behavior patterns of sufficient severity to cause internal distress or significant impairment in functioning.
8. A neurotransmitter involved in a broad range of effects on perception, movement, and emotions. Serotonin and its receptors are the targets of most hallucinogens.
9. Violent mental or physical harm to a person, damage to an organ, etc.
10. The capacity and willingness of a clinician or other service provider to be open to working with issues of culture and diversity.

A. Trauma
B. Service Integration
C. Hippocampus
D. Serotonin
E. Relapse
F. Cultural Sensitivity
G. Personality Disorders
H. Self Medication
I. Treatment Retention
J. Nodding Out

15. Find the hidden words. The words have been placed horizontally, vertically, or diagonally. When you locate a word, draw an ellipse around it.

L	V	E	N	T	R	A	L	S	T	R	I	A	T	U	M	W	B	M	C	R	P	B
I	M	S	M	M	V	K	O	L	A	N	F	A	Z	N	P	D	C	G	B	J	G	P
N	T	H	E	R	A	P	E	U	T	I	C	C	O	M	M	U	N	I	T	Y	J	L
T	Y	B	E	N	Z	O	D	I	A	Z	E	P	I	N	E	F	T	G	K	F	K	B
R	K	I	N	B	E	P	B	Z	C	D	Z	K	Z	Y	R	B	H	Y	G	X	J	V
A	P	F	V	W	J	A	N	Q	D	D	F	P	L	V	S	M	C	M	K	O	A	H
N	Z	G	G	E	J	N	G	D	I	D	I	A	G	U	D	R	E	U	O	O	I	Z
A	Z	T	V	O	D	M	U	T	U	A	L	S	E	L	F	H	E	L	P	Z	P	L
S	V	C	O	N	T	I	N	G	E	N	C	Y	M	A	N	A	G	E	M	E	N	T
A	J	J	N	Q	I	C	E	Z	P	R	E	M	I	S	S	I	O	N	R	Z	N	H
U	M	U	Z	X	O	F	A	P	U	H	P	Z	M	Y	A	G	M	J	V	J	H	O
X	H	Z	R	S	E	D	C	N	V	B	P	S	Y	C	H	O	S	O	C	I	A	L
G	W	E	A	W	G	I	D	J	P	S	Y	C	H	O	S	I	S	U	D	G	J	W
O	S	U	B	S	T	A	N	C	E	U	S	E	D	I	S	O	R	D	E	R	S	Q
S	C	I	C	O	G	N	I	T	I	V	E	E	D	Z	X	X	R	Y	W	M	V	L
R	U	U	X	F	C	W	G	Q	C	M	G	X	U	T	B	P	V	D	O	L	A	F

1. A type of CNS depressant sometimes prescribed to relieve anxiety, panic, or acute stress reactions. Some benzodiazepines are prescribed short-term to promote sleep.
2. Pertaining to the mind's capacity to understand concepts and ideas.
3. An approach to recovery from substance use disorders that emphasizes personal responsibility, self-management, and clients' helping one another.
4. Slang term for Smoke able methamphetamine.
5. Involving a person's psychological well-being, as well as housing, employment, family, and other social aspects of life circumstances.
6. A class of substance-related disorders that includes both substance abuse and substance dependence.
7. An area of the brain that is part of the basal ganglia and includes the nucleus accumbens.
8. A state in which a mental or physical disorder has been overcome or a disease process halted.
9. A consciously designed social environment or residential treatment setting in which the social and group process is harnessed with therapeutic intent.
10. Delta-9-tetrahydrocannabinol; the main mind-altering ingredient in marijuana.
11. Taken through the nose.
12. A mental disorder that is characterized by distinct distortions of a person's mental capacity, ability to recognize reality, and relationships to others.
13. An approach to treatment that maintains that the form or frequency of behavior can be altered through a planned and organized system of consequences.

A. Contingency Management
B. Ice
C. Remission
D. Mutual Self Help
E. Therapeutic Community
F. Psychosocial
G. THC
H. Ventral Striatum
I. Intranasal
J. Benzodiazepine
K. Substance Use Disorders
L. Psychosis
M. Cognitive

16. Find the hidden words. The words have been placed horizontally, vertically, or diagonally. When you locate a word, draw an ellipse around it.

Q	Y	H	Y	G	I	Y	B	R	A	I	N	S	T	E	M	J	V	P	H	Y	C	J
L	L	Q	M	U	M	M	F	R	X	B	D	E	P	I	B	J	H	A	A	R	P	D
P	E	R	S	O	N	A	L	I	T	Y	D	I	S	O	R	D	E	R	S	Z	Y	E
P	X	I	N	F	E	C	T	I	O	U	S	S	S	R	Y	Z	R	T	K	Q	D	E
M	E	T	H	A	D	O	N	E	R	T	Y	O	Z	Z	B	F	U	I	C	S	P	I
M	A	D	R	U	G	G	E	D	D	R	I	V	I	N	G	Y	K	A	T	H	M	S
H	E	C	O	L	L	A	B	O	R	A	T	I	O	N	P	U	M	L	A	Y	C	L
U	Z	E	W	S	N	B	D	P	E	Y	S	J	N	E	C	K	E	A	Y	B	H	Q
J	R	M	J	O	J	U	N	Z	C	D	J	H	T	L	L	T	M	G	W	H	E	C
O	A	Y	R	K	R	C	V	Z	B	E	E	P	M	K	J	Y	S	O	J	C	F	V
O	Z	F	K	Q	I	N	T	E	G	R	A	T	I	O	N	Y	K	N	M	F	Z	L
G	P	S	Y	C	H	O	P	H	A	R	M	A	C	O	L	O	G	I	C	A	L	C
L	K	X	Y	C	L	D	D	C	F	D	D	Y	B	K	N	D	Y	S	C	X	T	L
Y	L	Z	B	D	K	N	W	E	S	J	K	Z	Y	B	U	G	Q	U	B	R	M	U
C	H	C	O	N	T	I	N	G	E	N	C	Y	M	A	N	A	G	E	M	E	N	T
R	X	A	Y	B	F	L	A	S	H	B	A	C	K	B	J	J	J	Z	L	M	Y	A

1. A substance that binds to and activates a receptor to a lesser degree than a full agonist.
2. Rigid, inflexible, and maladaptive behavior patterns of sufficient severity to cause internal distress or significant impairment in functioning.
3. A treatment approach based on providing incentives to support positive behavior change.
4. Pertaining to medications used to treat mental illnesses.
5. A sudden but temporary recurrence of aspects of a drug experience that may occur days, weeks, or even more than a year after using drugs that cause hallucinations.
6. A group of brain structures that process sensory information and control basic functions needed for survival such as breathing, heart rate, blood pressure, and arousal.
7. Able to spread by an agent such as a virus or bacterium.
8. The action of working with someone to produce or create something.
9. Relationships among mental health and substance abuse providers in which both fields are moved into a single treatment setting and treatment regimen.
10. Driving a vehicle while impaired due to the intoxicating effects of recent drug use.
11. A long-acting opioid agonist medication used for the treatment of opioid addiction and pain.

A. Partial Agonist
B. Integration
C. Methadone
D. Flashback
E. Personality Disorders
F. Psychopharmacological
G. Contingency Management
H. Collaboration
I. Brainstem
J. Drugged Driving
K. Infectious

17. Find the hidden words. The words have been placed horizontally, vertically, or diagonally. When you locate a word, draw an ellipse around it.

	H	C	O	N	C	O	M	I	T	A	N	T	T	R	E	A	T	M	E	N	T	T	M
	P	G	A	L	U	O	C	M	M	J	S	K	I	N	A	B	S	C	E	S	S	R	E
	S	L	U	R	R	E	D	S	P	E	E	C	H	L	V	B	Z	D	J	S	J	G	N
	K	O	A	D	D	I	C	T	I	O	N	U	D	I	A	A	Z	M	O	V	F	I	T
	I	C	F	I	N	T	E	G	R	A	T	E	D	T	R	E	A	T	M	E	N	T	A
	F	U	U	Q	N	D	V	O	M	S	J	Y	N	H	Z	H	D	G	Q	B	I	A	L
	L	X	N	D	T	N	C	Z	X	N	L	C	N	Z	U	J	S	F	G	K	W	C	D
	C	T	C	W	I	T	H	D	R	A	W	A	L	H	E	P	A	T	I	T	I	S	I
	K	N	T	T	Z	E	L	P	P	G	Z	B	T	X	N	T	P	S	O	O	E	Y	S
	V	A	I	I	F	Y	K	A	K	R	M	Y	J	D	S	G	U	C	U	M	Y	W	O
	W	N	O	X	A	M	F	M	R	R	H	N	Y	V	P	M	K	T	G	B	O	E	R
	P	N	N	D	K	T	U	M	U	P	T	C	F	B	Y	N	L	F	M	E	O	S	D
	Z	E	A	L	L	H	D	U	K	J	O	L	K	R	H	Z	U	Q	S	L	A	X	E
	B	N	U	L	S	U	Q	Z	Y	O	U	W	Z	M	P	I	R	Y	L	Q	S	J	R
	G	F	Q	V	J	R	N	R	O	U	S	O	V	X	Q	A	S	N	N	U	L	U	U
	O	K	F	R	R	C	P	R	E	F	R	O	N	T	A	L	C	O	R	T	E	X	R

1. A sign of depressant intoxication. When people consume significant amounts of sedative-hypnotics and opioids, their speech may become garbled, mumbled, and slow.
2. A collection of pus formed as a result of bacterial infection.
3. An inflammation of the liver, with accompanying liver cell damage and risk of death.
4. Any mechanism by which treatment interventions for co-occurring disorders are combined within the context of a primary treatment relationship or service setting.
5. Physical dependence on a substance of abuse. Inability to cease use of a substance without experiencing withdrawal symptoms.
6. Treatment of two or more mental or physical disorders at the same time.
7. The front part of the brain responsible for reasoning, planning, problem solving, and other higher cognitive functions.
8. Pertaining to a person's ability to carry out tasks.
9. A mental condition marked primarily by disorganization of personality, mind, and emotions that seriously impairs the psychological or behavioral functioning of the individual.
10. Symptoms that can occur after long-term use of a drug is reduced or stopped.

A. Concomitant Treatment
B. Hepatitis
C. Prefrontal Cortex
D. Slurred Speech
E. Integrated Treatment
F. Functional
G. Mental Disorder
H. Withdrawal
I. Skin Abscess
J. Addiction

18. Find the hidden words. The words have been placed horizontally, vertically, or diagonally. When you locate a word, draw an ellipse around it.

G	V	I	N	U	I	U	X	K	P	D	E	P	E	N	D	E	N	C	E	Y	M	H
Z	A	E	L	Q	C	R	R	R	A	F	Y	D	X	Y	M	L	C	K	E	A	W	O
X	N	X	G	I	R	A	N	O	R	E	X	I	A	N	E	R	V	O	S	A	C	I
F	V	D	O	I	O	D	U	U	A	K	Y	B	O	Z	Z	K	L	I	R	K	O	I
X	S	M	G	Y	S	Q	T	C	P	M	G	A	F	I	L	L	I	C	I	T	O	
J	L	K	V	P	S	P	U	S	H	R	R	S	L	P	A	W	D	L	F	F	V	T
U	K	N	I	W	T	P	R	K	E	R	H	I	D	T	F	K	P	Z	B	N	C	U
T	P	F	B	B	R	P	H	A	R	M	A	C	O	K	I	N	E	T	I	C	S	Q
X	T	P	R	G	A	B	J	O	N	U	Y	P	Y	C	Y	Z	X	K	B	J	N	S
J	Q	H	E	J	I	S	D	B	A	C	E	R	E	B	E	L	L	U	M	Z	E	F
M	H	G	S	Y	N	U	Z	B	L	C	K	O	I	Q	Q	Q	A	Z	O	C	W	J
O	W	N	I	G	I	H	L	L	I	I	O	G	C	Y	I	P	P	T	M	U	R	H
Z	P	B	I	K	N	I	T	Z	A	Q	E	R	E	K	D	A	E	Q	Q	I	Y	Y
Z	K	M	J	R	G	N	E	B	R	E	W	A	R	D	S	Y	S	T	E	M	B	B
X	O	E	W	V	X	T	N	N	D	A	N	W	H	V	H	Y	K	Y	D	Z	Y	K
N	W	S	W	N	G	K	V	F	G	R	Y	T	P	F	G	E	H	W	D	V	V	Y

1. A treatment program with the capacity to provide treatment for one disorder, but that also screens for other disorders and is able to access necessary consultations.
2. The simultaneous provision of material and training to persons from more than one discipline.
3. A brain circuit that includes the ventral tegmental area, the nucleus accumbens, and the prefrontal cortex.
4. A broad term that describes objects used during the chemical preparation or use of drugs. These include syringes, syringe needles, roach clips, and marijuana or crack pipes.
5. Illegal or forbidden by law.
6. A condition that can occur with the regular use of illicit or some prescription drugs, even if taken as prescribed.
7. A disorder in which the individual refuses to maintain a normal body weight, is afraid of gaining weight, and exhibits a significant disturbance in the perception of body shape.
8. A part of the brain that helps regulate posture, balance, and coordination. It is also involved in the processes of emotion, motivation, memory, and thought.
9. What the body does to a drug after it has been taken, including how rapidly the drug is absorbed, broken down, and processed by the body.
10. Slang term for Smoke able methamphetamine.

A. Anorexia Nervosa
B. Basic Program
C. Paraphernalia
D. Reward System
E. Ice
F. Dependence
G. Illicit
H. Pharmacokinetics
I. Cerebellum
J. Cross Training

19. Find the hidden words. The words have been placed horizontally, vertically, or diagonally. When you locate a word, draw an ellipse around it.

I	V	A	D	D	I	C	T	I	O	N	O	N	L	Y	S	E	R	V	I	C	E	S
J	Z	O	N	V	T	O	R	L	F	N	C	I	H	V	D	Z	X	G	D	S	B	W
D	D	Z	A	V	E	N	T	R	A	L	S	T	R	I	A	T	U	M	D	A	T	I
M	Z	A	D	M	S	S	I	N	D	W	H	M	V	Y	A	I	A	R	I	Q	R	A
P	E	D	H	A	L	L	U	C	I	N	A	T	I	O	N	S	C	I	D	P	A	K
J	W	O	S	L	R	C	S	N	C	C	O	G	N	I	T	I	O	N	E	S	N	U
C	K	P	S	L	U	R	R	E	D	S	P	E	E	C	H	R	K	D	G	Y	S	L
D	U	A	L	L	Y	D	I	S	O	R	D	E	R	E	D	O	A	F	D	C	F	Q
A	L	M	R	R	N	A	L	O	X	O	N	E	M	J	V	A	D	P	I	H	E	Y
R	K	I	K	P	K	D	K	X	D	F	O	X	Z	Q	M	X	R	U	C	O	R	F
G	F	N	S	A	A	K	G	D	H	E	Q	N	C	T	S	S	W	V	D	T	E	X
U	F	E	N	U	W	T	S	V	X	X	J	J	M	C	R	M	S	J	P	R	N	A
W	G	P	Z	O	B	U	F	Y	T	B	V	Q	E	L	A	S	X	E	G	O	C	R
K	G	K	V	H	B	A	B	G	N	A	L	T	R	E	X	O	N	E	A	P	E	M
G	D	A	N	Q	N	F	H	Y	P	O	T	H	A	L	A	M	U	S	V	I	Y	M
X	T	R	E	A	T	M	E	N	T	R	E	T	E	N	T	I	O	N	D	C	V	N

1. A brain chemical, classified as a neurotransmitter, found in regions of the brain that regulate movement, emotion, motivation, and reinforcement of rewarding behavior.
2. A sign of depressant intoxication. When people consume significant amounts of sedative-hypnotics and opioids, their speech may become garbled, mumbled, and slow.
3. Mind-altering.
4. An opioid antagonist medication approved by the FDA to reverse an opioid overdose.
5. Sensations, sounds and
6. An area of the brain that is part of the basal ganglia and includes the nucleus accumbens.
7. A long-acting opioid antagonist medication that prevents receptors from being activated by other opioids. Naltrexone is used to treat alcohol and opioid use disorders.
8. A part of the brain that controls many bodily functions, including eating, drinking, body temperature regulation, and the release of many hormones.
9. Having been diagnosed with two disorders, for example a substance use disorder and a mental health disorder.
10. Programs that by law or regulation, by choice, or for lack of resources cannot accommodate patients who have psychiatric illnesses that require ongoing treatment.
11. The feelings, reactions, biases, and images from the past that the client with cod may project onto the clinician.
12. Relating to the act or process of thinking, understanding, learning, and remembering.
13. Keeping clients involved in treatment activities and receiving required services.

A. Cognition
B. Addiction Only Services
C. Psychotropic
D. Slurred Speech
E. Hallucinations
F. Naloxone
G. Transference
H. Dopamine
I. Treatment Retention
J. Dually Disordered
K. Naltrexone
L. Ventral Striatum
M. Hypothalamus

20. Find the hidden words. The words have been placed horizontally, vertically, or diagonally. When you locate a word, draw an ellipse around it.

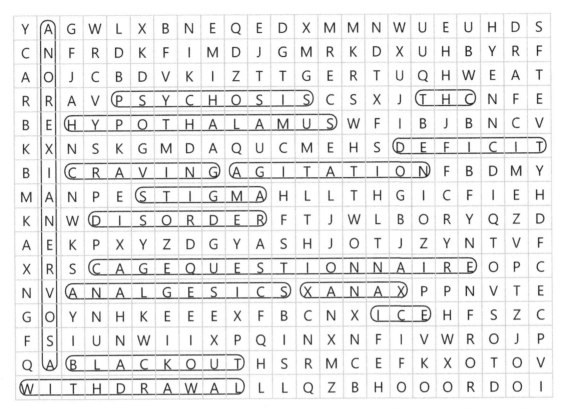

1. A negative association attached to some activity or condition. A cause of shame or embarrassment.
2. A brief alcoholism screening tool.
3. In the context of substance abuse treatment, disability, or inability to function fully.
4. A disorder in which the individual refuses to maintain a normal body weight, is afraid of gaining weight, and exhibits a significant disturbance in the perception of body shape.
5. A restless inability to keep still.
6. Slang term for Smoke able methamphetamine.
7. Symptoms that can occur after long-term use of a drug is reduced or stopped.
8. A part of the brain that controls many bodily functions, including eating, drinking, body temperature regulation, and the release of many hormones.
9. A powerful, often overwhelming desire to use drugs.
10. Delta-9-tetrahydrocannabinol; the main mind-altering ingredient in marijuana.
11. A period of amnesia or memory loss, typically caused by chronic, high-dose substance abuse.
12. An illness or a disruption of some mental or physical process.
13. Delusional or disordered thinking detached from reality; symptoms often include hallucinations.
14. Brand name for benzodiazepine alprazolam.
15. A group of medications that reduce pain.

A. THC
E. Cage Questionnaire
I. Ice
M. Xanax
B. Hypothalamus
F. Deficit
J. Stigma
N. Craving
C. Psychosis
G. Agitation
K. Withdrawal
O. Blackout
D. Anorexia Nervosa
H. Analgesics
L. Disorder

Made in the USA
Las Vegas, NV
10 November 2023